Pricing Guidelines for Arts & Crafts

Linda & Dean -
Thank you for your
valuable contribution
to this book.
Best to you both as
you grow your business!
Sylvia

Pricing Guidelines for Arts & Crafts

Successful, Professional Crafters Share Their
Pricing Strategies to Help YOU Set
Profitable Prices for Your Arts & Crafts

Sylvia Landman

Writers Club Press
San Jose New York Lincoln Shanghai

Pricing Guidelines for Arts & Crafts
Successful, Professional Crafters Share Their Pricing Strategies to
Help YOU Set Profitable Prices for Your Arts & Crafts

Writers Club Press
an imprint of iUniverse.com, Inc.

For information address:
iUniverse.com, Inc.
620 North 48th Street, Suite 201
Lincoln, NE 68504-3467
www.iuniverse.com

ISBN: 0-595-1018-0

Printed in the United States of America

Introduction

"What should I charge for my handmade goods?" "Should I ever lower my prices?" "Will customers object if I raise my price?" "If I sell too low, consumers may assume my work is of low quality and workmanship but if I set prices too high, I lose sales." "How do others in my field price their work?"

"Published designers who receive phone calls from editors interested in buying their work stutter when asked, 'What do you want for your design?'" Creative people responding to calls from publishers, shops, manufacturers or consumers often feel unprepared and insecure about establishing a fair yet profitable price for their goods.

As a professional craft designer and small business teacher/writer since the mid 60's I hear these questions repeatedly. Attending professional conferences and listening to my students, I find that the topic that bedevils every artisan is: *Pricing*!

Craft magazines that target consumers who craft from home also find readers asking pricing questions. Trade journals, relied upon by craft professionals, deal constantly with questions and suggestions surrounding pricing issues. "Letters to the Editor" in these publications feature not only questions from readers about making money from their artistic skills but ask what they should charge for their products. Online mailing lists for professional crafters of all types continue to proliferate on the Internet and though these groups deal with many topics, none appear so frequently as pricing.

Crafters with years of experience and those just beginning to sell their work always need information about pricing structures and what price range the market will bear for particular items. Listening to them at national craft shows and conferences each year, I find this paradox: Each artisan wants to know what others earn from publishers, wholesalers, catalogers and even retail customers but this is the very information they hold back themselves while networking.

Heard at craft conferences for professionals is: "What did this magazine pay you to publish your design?" Answers vary from, "The usual," "Between $50 and $200," "I can't remember," and other vague replies. Why is this so?

X   Do we fear we will appear underpaid when compared to others?

X   Do we fear that if we earn more than others, they will rush to crowd our markets?

X   Do we want to know where to stop negotiation with a publisher, manufacturer or each other if we only knew the limits?

X   How we all wish to know more about pricing strategies without revealing our own!

More than one hundred, professional artisans from across the United States in many craft disciplines, responded to my questions filling my fourth book dealing with the craft industry, ***Pricing Guidelines for Arts & Crafts***. From goldsmiths to quilters, from sculptors to knitters, each chapter begins with what I call a "Pricing Template" provided by an artisan in each craft arena. Generously and openly, each person provided price sheets, formulae, schedules and answered my many questions about how they arrived at their prices. Many shared snippets of their ideas, tips and comments about their pricing strategies. These comments appear in simple, direct quotes sprinkled throughout the book.

Many crafters provided so much in-depth information about their price setting experiences that I chose one to end each chapter. Each person explains how and where they buy their raw materials, how they find the best prices, where and how they find buyers, the process of producing their craft and close by sharing their pricing secrets with you the reader.

Few craft business books provide advice about setting prices let alone offer it in all media. As you read about pricing techniques from many talented artisans in varied fields, you will learn invaluable information to help you find the perfect pricing strategy for you, your business, your media and the geographical area in which you live. Learn to price for publishers, craft shows, the Internet, gallery and consignment shops and of course, on commission.

Following each chapter, you will find a list of each contributor with full contact information enabling you to write, call or visit their business on the World Wide Web. In a few instances, the same person appears in more than one chapter affirming a fact many of us who craft professionally already know—the frequent crossover from one craft to another.

The *Appendix* will provide you with many resources including books, magazines, catalogs and an ever-growing list of individual and group craft websites exploding on the World Wide Web. If you doubt that it's possible to make a living in the craft industry, I offer the following data from the largest craft organization in the world. "The *Hobby Industry Association,*" (HIA) reported that the January 2000 HIA trade show held at the Anaheim Convention Center in California exceeded 20,150 crafters and exhibitors. Non-U.S. participants from 64 countries made up 17% of total buyer attendance. The show featured 1,118 craft exhibitors in 2,927 booths. In 1998, HIA research found that the arts & crafts industry generated eleven billion dollars which will surely rise by the end of 2000 when the next surveys appear. Is there any doubt that the industry has room for you?

Forward

Sylvia's first books, "*Crafting for Dollars*", "*Make Your Quilting Pay for Itself,*" and "*Quilting for Fun & Profit*" opened a whole new world not only for me but others as well. These books teach us how to make our "hobbies" into paying propositions. Later, I was privileged to meet Sylvia, as she began writing a regular column for the National Quilting Association's "Quilting Quarterly." I always find her writing succinct, thoroughly researched and a pleasure to read.

Following the guidelines in this book, you may discover that beloved crafting activities can provide more than just personal and creative satisfaction—they can provide a comfortable income as well. It is a privilege and honor to write the Foreword for this book, as I am a great admirer of Sylvia Landman both personally and professionally as one of her many editors. I trust it will be as enjoyable and profitable for you, the reader, as it has been for me.

Marilyn Maddalena
Quilt Appraiser, Quilt Judge
Publications Chair, NQA, *The Quilting Quarterly*

Contents

Chapter 1

The Art of Pricing Your Crafts

To become a **profitable** craft professional, one must price handmade items with both the consumer and artisan in mind. *Pricing Guidelines for Arts & Crafts* brings you the inside story from my own experience as a professional designer plus more than one hundred artisans from many craft disciplines interviewed just for this book.

"Value" is how your customers perceive your product in relation to what they want and how much they are willing to spend. If a particular item is a welcome addition to a buyer's established collection, he may accept whatever price you set. If buyers perceive your product as poorly constructed or made of inferior materials, they may not accept the lower quality no matter how low your price may be compared to your competitors. Marketing experts say that consumers *will* spend more for a product if they clearly recognize it as one of higher quality. Products described as, "Fade-proof," "Shrink Proof," "Non-toxic," "100 % Cotton," "Contains no lead," and the all-important, "Handmade in America," are examples of products boasting increased quality for which consumers will pay."

Pricing Basics

Pricing handmade products require you to evaluate what you have created compared to the labor and materials used to manufacture it. Setting prices fair to both maker and buyer bedevils nearly every artisan in every creative endeavor, from quilters to wood-workers and jewelers to decorative painters. The *right* price must be high enough to cover all costs, make a profit and yet low enough to attract consumers.

Usually, artisans have years of experience in their field before they begin to sell but often have very little experience in setting prices knowledgeably for what they have made. Appropriate pricing for handmade arts and crafts is an art in itself.

The earlier an artisan entering the professional arena settles on solid pricing structures the earlier they will become profitable. Raising or lowering prices too often makes buyers wary giving the impression of an unstable business. Developing a solid price method early also prepares crafters to determine profitability which in turn prepares them to choose and purchase raw materials and wholesalers. Professional artisans in every field, seasoned or just beginning, lament the same questions:

*How Will I Know When to Raise My Prices?

*Just What Is My Time Worth, Anyway? Minimum Wage? More? How Much More?

*How Can I Compete with Others Who Make Similar Products but Charge Less?

*How Can I Increase My Profit and Keep My Costs to a Minimum?

*What Do I Say If Buyers Tell Me My Products Cost Too Much?

*A Common Dilemma: What Should You Do When a Price You Quoted to a Customer Doesn't Cover Your Costs after You've Begun or Completed the Project?

*   *   *

Before answering these questions, I'd like to take the time to define the elements one must consider in pricing anything.

Labor costs should include not only how long it takes *you* to make a single item but must also consider what you would have to pay an employee to duplicate it when you need help. You may be happy to charge $4 per hour to craft your item because you work from home eliminating childcare expenses. But what will you do if you become ill or need to pay someone to help if you receive an order too large to fill by yourself? Will you find others willing to work for this amount? Consider this question when you build labor costs into your price structure as it is critical in today's market.

Raw Materials include all the supplies required to manufacture your product. Fabric, thread, wood, metal and beads seem obvious. But don't overlook the small items such as glue, nails, pins and paint.

Overhead refers to the non-productive, incidental expenses too small to calculate individually. Examples: rent, utilities, postage, insurance, wear and tear on your equipment, travel, repairs and maintenance, telephone, packaging and shipping supplies, delivery and freight charges, cleaning, insurance, office supplies, office or craft studio employees, show fees, and postage.

Wholesale prices are those at which you sell your products to someone else who, in turn, will resell them to the ultimate consumer.

Retail refers to the price paid by the person who buys the product and takes it home—the "ultimate consumer." People who buy handmade items rarely concern themselves with how much time it took to make them. This is why the final price you choose for each item you sell must conform to what the market will bear

Wages refer to the sum you pay someone else who works for you. This is expense is often confused with "Owner's Draw" which means when you, the owner of your business write yourself a check from your account to pay yourself.

Profit refers to money which remains after you sell merchandise for more than it cost you to manufacture it. Profit is why we work. New business owners often fail to add profit into their price structure. They merely consider both wholesale and retail prices based on the cost of materials, labor, and overhead —an expensive mistake. Now, to answer the previous list of questions:

How Will I Know When To Raise My Prices?

Learn if a price you are considering is acceptable to your target consumers. Some shoppers consider price first when choosing to buy. Others consider quality, variety, service or convenience first. You must know about your customers' desires in relation to your products when setting prices. What matters most to *your* customers?

Next, find out what your competitors charge. How does your product differ from theirs? Attend craft shows and study the craft trade journals to learn this information. Visit craft malls and shops in your area. Listen as customers chat about an object they are thinking of buying.

Consider a marketing technique called "penetration strategy" when you offer a product for the first time. This means you will keep price to a minimum during an introduction phase in order to gain market share or presence as you jump into the competition. For example, your preliminary advertising may say "Special Introductory Price", or "For a limited time only."

Take care not to continue your introductory prices for too long. Once you have credibility and market share you can begin to raise prices with careful timing.

Residents of large cities may be willing to pay more for an object than those in small, rural towns where more people craft themselves. People will also pay more for an item when they recognize an element of increased value. (Cotton over blends, for example, or glass over plastic). However, it makes no difference *how* you arrive at your asking price if it is too high or too low for your market. The market itself, not your costs, labor or overhead determines the price at which you can sell your goods.

*   *   *

Karen Serna, of *Morning Star Creations* makes dream-catchers, beadwork, moccasins, and Native American crafts. Karen's method of determining whether or not to raise the price for her products is to price her products low at first to see if they sell. If they sell too fast, she raises the price slightly to see if selling continues. For example, after vending at a State Fair, she found she could not keep up with the demand for her 3" Mini Dream-catchers priced at $6.00 each. She suspected she had under-priced them after selling fifty of them immediately after the show opened. She raised the price to $7.00 for the next fair, not too much of an increase, but one that raised her profits.

Karen recognized she had arrived at a fair price when she set a price that compensated her for her investment of time, energy and expense to create products which also considered what customers wanted to spend. Rather than seeking the "right" price, Karen used an acceptable price range to avoid under-pricing her work.

*   *   *

If you convey the attitude that, "This is just a little something I do in my spare time" or, "Anyone could do this", or "I keep my prices low because I work from home," your pricing structure will probably be too low.

One of my students told me she had been selling beaded jewelry for two years and wanted to expand her activities into full-time work. She said she priced her pieces by doubling what the raw materials cost. Beading does not require expensive raw materials but is very labor intensive. When I asked her how much she charged for a pair of Bedouin earrings she was wearing, she explained the supplies cost about $6. She had been selling these for $12 though making one pair took her 4-6 hours. Surprise came over her when I pointed out that at this price, she had been paying herself about $2 per hour for her labor—less than half of our state's minimum wage!

Women working from home, sad to say, often under value their labor until they gain more experience in the market as sellers.

Ignorance about current market trends and checking out competition may also cause you to charge too much. Do not let personal friends and family tell you what you should charge. Remember, they may not be thinking objectively, but subjectively based upon their relationship with you. You must learn all you can about the market and how your product fits into it objectively.

What Is My Time Worth, Anyway? Minimum Wage? More? How Much More?

Many crafters, especially when starting out, find these questions perplexing. They wonder if they should charge by the hour or the piece. Some feel that if they work from home they should not charge what the identical item would cost in a shop. Others feel that minimum wage is enough when setting an hourly wage. Watch out, for this can create problems later when you hire someone else to help you make your product and your price structure is based on minimum wage. You may not find anyone else willing to work for as little per hour as you do.

How Can I Compete with Others Who Make Similar Products but Charge Less?

Another student told me she was unhappy with the profit she was earning for her hand-made doll outfits. She explained that the only other person selling similar outfits at craft shows she attended, sold them for $30 while my student sold hers for $10. She boasted about how many more outfits she sold than her competitor. Unfortunately, she did not recognize that the other person not only charged more per outfit while selling fewer items, but she earned more which covered all her expenses plus profit. My student sold more units but did not earn enough to cover booth expenses at this particular show. She learned too late that cheaper is not always better.

                    *   *   *

John Dunney, co-owner of *Garden Folk Art & Rustic Country* comments about setting prices too high or too low, "If buyers come to know you for quality and service, if you stand behind your work and are willing to take an occasional loss on an item in order to serve your customer, you will command a higher price in spite of others who charge less. By serving your customers, your name and reputation will become synonymous with lasting value, and people will feel they are making an investment when they purchase one of your items."

John vends at a Folk Art show held in the same city three times a year. He says that if each time he attends, he were to show an item at an increasingly higher price, customers would receive a negative impression about his business. Says John, "I do not change my prices regardless of the venue. Prices remain the same whether I sell in the poorest part of town or in the San Francisco Bay Area. Lots of my customers follow me around so I try to remain consistent." John continues, "You may find it necessary to change prices periodically—usually upward. While prior notification isn't required, and most price lists have a disclaimer stating that prices are subject to change without notice, you will find that customers appreciate it if you do let them know in advance. This is also a good opportunity to gain sales, at the old price which is to your benefit as well as the customer's. The time to evaluate and change prices in the crafts industry is just prior to the two main show seasons in January and June. Try to only raise prices on items that are specifically out-of-line due to some previously hidden or increased cost and you will find that price stability creates loyal customers."

[end John Dunney]

How Can I Increase My Profit and Keep My Costs to a Minimum?

There are only two ways to increase your profits while competing in the marketplace. One is to lower your expenses, the other is to raise your prices. If you have a good product and your customers correctly perceive its benefits, make sure your advertising and literature describes why they may pay more, (Handmade rather than machine-made, all-natural materials, etc.,) some will consider it.

What Do I Say if Buyers Say My Item Costs Too Much?

When you set prices higher that your competitors, consider justifying the difference to your customers when you speak to them and in your brochures, sales letters, website, etc. For example, if they state that your price is "too high," consider explaining how you choose higher quality materials, or have better or faster service, or explain your unconditional guarantee.

When customers say your price is "too low," you can explain that your company has acquired more production methods or has lower overhead and thus can pass the savings on to the customer. "Not likely", you ask? Consider quilters. For many years people who quilted for others had no option other than to do the work by hand. Technology has provided more options with the advent of long-armed quilting machines which can do the same work in less than a tenth of the time it took for hand-quilting. Thus, machine quilters generally charge less than their counterparts who quilt by hand.

Consider demand-oriented pricing when trying to decide if you are charging too much making customers hesitant to buy. Demand-oriented pricing means answering the question, "What is your consumer willing to pay?" Study your competitors and the market in general. Evaluate your pricing structure continually as material costs increase or inflation rises.

Large, labor-intensive products make it easier to arrive at a per-item cost. For smaller items produced in volume, consider obtaining a per item cost by dividing the material cost of a batch of items by the number you can reasonably produce.

Let us suppose you make Christmas tree ornaments and want to decide what to charge for each one to sell at a craft show. Total all raw materials you will use to make 100 as your first step. Determine the price for Styrofoam balls, plus ribbons, fabric, sequins, pins, glitter, beads, and glue.

Let's say the total comes to $300 including freight charges to ship all the raw materials to your studio. Selling each ornament for $12, you will break-even after you sell the 25th ornament. ($12x25). Selling the remaining 75 would be all profit which includes your labor for all 100 ornaments.

Now, consider the amount of time (labor) you spent making all the ornaments. Would the resulting $900 (75 @ $12 ea.) compensate you fairly for your time and talent? If the compensation falls below minimum wage, you may want to reconsider. Think about how you can reduce costs and speed up production.

A Common Dilemma: What Should You Do When a Price You Quoted to a Customer Doesn't Cover Your Costs after You've Begun or Completed the Project?

At times communication between crafter and customer can create a common dilemma. You talk with the customer and listen as they relate what they want made and how they want the finished product to look. But half-way into the project, you realize that the project will take longer, consume more materials than expected or require unexpected and additional labor you could not foresee. Always uncomfortable and embarrassing to deal with after the fact, new crafters are likely to accept the loss and work harder for less. Here is a real example.

A crafter belonging to a professional organization approached the membership with a pricing problem that posed this dilemma for her. The crafter, a seamstress had quoted a fixed price to a customer for making draperies. As the work progressed, the seamstress realized she had not anticipated the length of time it would take to accommodate small changes requested by the customer. By the time she completed the job, the original price was no longer profitable for her but she was hesitant to raise the price when the customer picked up the goods feeling she would portray herself as unprofessional to be listing "add-on" prices.

The crafter asked, "Do I charge her more AFTER I've already given her a bid now that I recognize the increased complexity of my work? The customer continued to add requests after we had agreed upon the price. Some of these added much more in labor than I had planned when giving original quote. Should I explain to her that all the extras she requested went over my estimate or will that make me sound unprofessional? Should I just accept the difference and consider it a lesson? I don't want to give my work away but don't want to anger my first customer. Please advise."

Another crafter responded to the seamstress explaining that she had owned a retail interior design store for ten years. She said that 75% percent of her business was custom orders for window treatments and furniture.

She advised, "Unfortunately, I believe you must take a loss on this since you committed to your price too early, but look at what you've learned! In the beginning, I felt lucky if I broke even on a job because I hadn't learned enough about how to quote a job properly. All you can do now is to start writing down all the little details that will help you price your next job. For example, charge extra for piping, ruffles and decking. Details like these must be clear BEFORE you quote a price for a job. Make sure all such details appear in your dated contract which include your client's signature. When clients change their mind or want to add something after you have quoted a price, consider saying, 'I can do this for you but it will cost you extra, (quote the exact dollar amount) in addition to the original quoted price."

Diane O'Neil, owner of *Our Beary Best Crafts, Candleskirt & Friendship Angels*, addresses the same problem. "I too am a seamstress and faced a similar situation when I agreed to make ruffled curtains. The customer provided basic width and lengths and the type of fabric she wanted and I based all my pricing on this information. When the customer gave me the exact measurements they differed from 1/16 of an inch to 1/8. No two curtains measured exactly the same because her rods hung at different heights. My customer already knew that purchased curtains would never work yet she expected me to observe all these different sizes depriving me of the opportunity to cut all the fabric at once. Today, I charge $10-$12 per hour depending on complexity and provide my customer with an approximate time frame. I tell customers that if they add more details or make changes, it will cost them more. Make a checklist of all the variables that could happen. Include this information on your order form. Below, I've listed a few possibilities to think about. Each of these should be assigned a separate price per hour for your time:

X   Sewing on the bias.

X   If customer supplies fabric, will they supply extra for errors or miscalculations? If not, how will you handle this?

X   Buttons, cording and other embellishments requiring hand sewing or basting.

X   Hand Quilting

X   Hand washing, ironing and preparing fabric beforehand

X   Fabric with special patterns, such as stripes, checks, plaids.

X   Patterns supplied by customers that need altering due to their inconsistencies. (Let the customer know that the patterns will be reviewed and if any problems arise or alterations are needed this is billed at a separate cost.)

"Try listing these add-ons on the back of a laser printed Order Form with your basic prices added on the front. Have the customer sign it," Diane adds. "Make sure they read it and know what they're signing. This way you have it handy and can add to it when needed and you won't forget to ask them any questions if you feel apprehensive.

CONTRIBUTORS TO THIS CHAPTER:

Karen Serna
Morning Star Creations
1769 Pine St.
Silverton, OR 97381
Phone: 503-873-9076
E:mail: K1Serna@aol.com

John & Lorraine Dunney,
Garden Folk Art & Rustic Country
Address 295 Main Street,
Yuba City, CA 95991
Phone/Fax 530 755-3424
E-Mail jdunney@jps.net
Website: http://www.jps.net/jdunney

Diane O'Neil
Our Beary Best Crafts, Candleskirt & Friendship Angels
prefers not to list address

Chapter 2

A Choice of Pricing Methods

X   Pricing by the Project
X   Pricing by the Square Inch/Foot/Yard
X   Pricing Based on Spools of Thread
X   Pricing Based on Balls of Yarn
X   Pricing Based on Yardage or Materials Consumed
X   Pricing by the Hour
X   Establishing a Pricing Template
X   Devising a Pricing Range
X   When to Adjust Your Prices
X   Two Tiered Pricing Levels to Sell at Retail & Wholesale
X   Underpricing Your Crafts and Labor

Pricing by the Project

A perfect formula to set prices for all craft products and services for every crafter does not exist. You must assess the popularity and trends in your particular field, the geographical area in which you live and whether or not your products are high ticket items. When you have researched all of this, you will be happy to know that you may choose from several methods to set a price for a specific project whether you sell only one or dozens.

1   Total the figures for labor, raw materials, overhead and profit. Double the sum to determine the wholesale cost. Triple it to arrive at the retail cost of a specific project.

2   Consider the direct labor method which focuses on labor particularly for crafts that are labor-intensive but require very few or no raw materials. Supposing you make

beaded earrings. Seed beads and earring findings are inexpensive but what if it takes three hours to make a pair? You might charge $8 per hour, ($24) and add $4 to the total to cover supplies for each pair. The final price would be $28 per pair using this method.

3   Finding the break-even point is an excellent pricing method to arrive at a set price per project if you make similar or identical items. The break-even point comes when income equals expenses for a specific quantity of similar products you make. Suppose you have made 100 machine-knitted infant sweaters to sell at a local craft show. Total all raw materials you will use to make all of them. Let's say the total comes to $200 including freight charges to ship raw materials directly to your studio. Selling each sweater for $20, you will break-even after you sell the 10th. Selling the remaining 90 would be all profit which covers your expenses and your labor for making all 100 sweaters.

4   Thank building contractors who generally use a simple profit system when pricing a single job. They add up the actual costs: Labor, raw materials and overhead. To this they add 15% for profit. Crafters, especially fine jewelers who make objects requiring costly materials can make this system work to their advantage too. Simply tack on 15% more to the total of your labor, raw materials and overhead to arrive at your final selling price.

5   Mark up pricing works well when the cost to manufacture a product is fairly consistent. For example, if a single item cost $6.50 to buy and consumers will pay $10.00 for it after you artistically alter it, the dollar markup is $3.50 ($10.00-$6.50) or 35% percent. Ask yourself whether a general mark up of 35% would be consistently profitable to you for other objects you produce even when larger or smaller. Wholesale price of goods is the basis for mark up pricing.

Let us take an example of a fine artist who buys plain china dinnerware and hand-paints each piece. If the painter pays $6.50 for the plain coffee mug and sells it for $10 after painting, the mark up price is 35% as shown in the example above. Now, our painter can expand this system and buy large platters or dainty cups and saucers and merely price the completed, hand-painted item for 35% above the wholesale cost. Keep in mind that mark up is always a percent of the actual retail price of any item.

6   A crafter who makes many small, miscellaneous craft objects to sell exclusively at craft fairs, explains that he uses one of the following two methods to price each item he makes even though they vary in size, intricacy of workmanship and price. He adjusts them based on the local market where he is vending at craft shows.

     1   Establish a minimum wage, add the cost of raw materials, then add 10% to 25% to offset the costs of booth space, price tags, advertising, business cards and distance traveled to the show. Earrings, his top-selling items, provide an example. If it takes him one hour (at $6.00 per hour labor) and $4.00 in raw materials to make one pair of earrings, method #1 looks like this: Labor: $6.00 + Raw Materials, $4.00 = $10.00. Covering show expenses @25% ($2.50) his final price to the customer is $12.50.

     2   Multiply the cost of raw materials by 3. When painting simple faces on flat stones, raw materials cost $3.00 including 20 minutes labor. He arrives at his selling price of $9.00. When our crafter's material costs remain low but the painted project is detailed and labor-intensive he multiplies by 4 or 5 to arrive at his selling price.

Pricing by the Square Inch/Foot/Yard

Bakers often charge a given price for a single donut or cookie rather than by a dozen. Why not crafters? You may find it easier and practical to charge by each specific element consumed in producing your product or service. Here are a few examples:

• Wood-workers often charge by the square inch, foot or yard of wood consumed in manufacturing a single item. The more raw material they consume, in precise measurements, the higher price a customer pays.

• Needlepointers and cross-stitchers often base their fee on covering a single square inch of fabric. When they set a fee per square inch, they merely determine the total number of square inches in an individual and multiply by their square inch price.

• A quilter I know determines the square foot measurement of quilts she makes and multiplies it by $20 for easy design/work, $25 for medium design work and $30 for complex designs. I compared her method to the price of a quilt I had sold to a craft magazine months before. I used her method to compare the amount I received from the magazine where neither the publisher nor I itemized how we determined the price.

My quilt measured 36"x42" or 1,512 square inches. I divided this by 144 inches, the equivalent of 1 square foot = 10.5 ft. Since my quilt featured intricate appliqué and hand-quilting, I multiplied $30 by 10½ feet and charged $315 to do the work, plus raw materials. The design featured fabric painting, piecing and quilting all by hand. The publisher of the craft magazine paid me $310 for my work. Since publishers customarily return quilts and other projects after photography, I had the option of keeping or reselling my quilt. Though I had not heard of the system presented by the quilter above, using her formula proved that my publisher had paid me a fair price and that her system was valid.

Pricing Based on Spools of Thread

Quilters often charge by the spool of quilting thread. Thus, when a client wants a quilt-top hand-quilted, the price depends on the amount of thread consumed. Large quilts with sparse hand-quilting may cost the same as small wall hangings bearing profuse, close quilting. The concept is simple. It takes the same amount of time to make so many stitches, widely spaced or close together. More about this in chapter 4.

Pricing Based on Balls of Yarn Consumed

See chapter 8 for variations on basing your fees by the amount of yarn consumed in a project. Weavers, knitters, crocheters and others who work with yarn can even have an adjustable rate such as:

Price per Ball of Yarn:	Simple	Intermediate	Complex
	$8	$9	$10

Using this system, if a customer asks you to make something which consumes 6 balls of yarn, you would charge: $48 $54 $60

Pricing Based on Yardage Consumed

Think about charging by the yardage consumed in your labor. For example, if draperies you make for a customer consume 8 total yards of fabric, and you charge $35 per yard representing your labor, you would charge a total of $360. Of course, the customer buys the fabric, thread and other notions such as drapery hooks, rods, etc.

Pricing by the Hour

Setting a price based on an hour's labor, this method works well when you set a fee primarily based upon performing a service rather than selling a product. Suppose you offer to restring necklaces for your customers. You need no raw materials other than stringing cord. Time yourself to determine an hourly rate which compensates you fairly for your labor then multiply by total hours spent.

Establishing a Pricing Template

A "Pricing Template" means a system that you can use repeatedly to determine the selling price of a particular item(s). Once you calculate labor, raw materials, overhead and the profit you wish to earn each time you make a specific item, you no longer have to calculate each item individually. Simply apply your "Pricing Template" to a group of items even if they are somewhat dissimilar.

I devised my system as a solution to a pricing problem I encountered early in my career doing custom sewing, knitting, crocheting and embroidery for customers. Having such a system in place benefits all artisans as they struggle to price in a way that is fair to both crafter and customer.

Interviewing the many artisans for this book, I asked them to present their pricing ideas using the Pricing Template below. Thus, each chapter begins with the Pricing Template of a particular crafter in that specific chapter. Each used my model to devise their own system. You will find variations in Pricing Templates but they all have one element in common. Each person applies a predetermined system to price different items in their line as I did more than thirty years ago.

I base my Pricing Template on knitting a single skein of worsted-weight yarn, any fiber:

Simple Patterns:	Intermediate Patterns	Advanced Patterns
3½-4 oz Skeins	$12	$14	$16

For a woman's simple sweater requiring 8 skeins, I charge $96 ($12 x 8 skeins = $96.) If the customer requests a sweater made up of intermediate patterns such as easy cables, small repeat laces, easy textured patterns, etc., I charge at the $14 rate as this technique requires more time and skill. (8 x $14 = $112), an increase of $16 for more intricate work.

What about the customer who wants a complex sweater in knitted lace or dozens of colors which require a high skill level and takes more time? A garment like this would consume more yarn so I move to 9 skeins x $16 and charge $144 for the labor alone.

Many years ago, a new client came to see me after seeing three sweaters I had made for a friend who wore size 12 garments. She already knew the price I had charged my friend and expected the same. However, the new customer weighed 300 pounds and wore a size #24! She felt that a sweater was, well, a sweater. Fortunately, I had my chart ready, (My future Pricing Template). I showed her that knitting the identical garment for her would take not 7 skeins but 11 or 12. She could see this would take more time, involve more stitches and effort. My price chart helped her understand that it was fair to raise my price based upon the materials consumed in making the project. Everyone came away satisfied. My Pricing Template idea was born!

Devising a Pricing Range

Making quilts for sale is the sole occupation of a quilter I spoke to recently. She sets her prices based on finished size. Each price bracket includes a range based on whether the design is simple, medium or intricate. Here is her system based on size for labor only. Customers purchase all materials and notions.

Miniatures up to 2 feet: $125-$150 (Simple: $125, Medium: $135, Intricate: $150)

Wall quilts up to 4 feet: $100-$175 see above

Full size bed quilts up to King size: $350-$500

When to Adjust Your Prices

Learn what the market will bear which requires research and time. Visit galleries, craft shops, shows, malls, boutiques and even online craft catalogs to help you set your prices competitively in the area in which you plan to sell them. Consider cutting your total retail prices by 5%-10% when selling in a rural or low-income geographical area and raising them by the same amount from the original price when selling in a top-selling market in an urban area.

*   *   *

Kathy Crofoot, of Kathy's Cache, describes what caused her to adjust prices. "I multiply my total costs by three and consider the resulting price," says Kathy. "If it's too high for my market, I find a less expensive way to make it or don't make it all. If the price seems too low to enter a current market, I raise prices to remain competitive," she adds. Kathy shares an experience illustrating the value of keeping up with fads and trends in the craft marketplace. She explains, "I introduced a design featuring cats and the product took off like wildfire! I couldn't keep my cats on the table for more than the first hour of the first two shows. I took this as a sign to raise my price to $2.50 and to watch what would happen. Once again, I could not keep them in stock. I raised the price again. The show season ended before I could settle on a final price, but I did not have a single cat motif left to carry over into the new year's inventory. This year, I plan to make more and see if the price will go a little higher to guide me as to what the market will bear," she concluded.

Two Tiered Pricing Levels to Sell at Both Retail and Wholesale

Selling at wholesale means a retailer will sell your item at the same price you do but expects to buy your merchandise for less, usually 50% less. Many seasoned crafters decide to sell their products not only to consumers at full retail prices but also sell to shop owners, distributors, and catalogers at wholesale who in turn, sell their products for them. When intermediaries like these sell your products *for* you, they expect to buy *from* you at wholesale prices. This of course, is how they make a profit.

*   *   *

Karen Murphy, former owner of a ceramic store adds a shop-owner's views about wholesale pricing. "You must add both a profit and commission amount (15%-20%) to your price before doubling total costs for retail. I owned a store so my overhead was much higher than working from home. I calculated 10%-15% to allow for commission and 10-20% allowed for profit. Suppose you received so many orders, and you had to hire labor? Your pricing formula would mean nothing unless you performed the work yourself! Usually my wholesale price is about 30-40% off of retail though some products don't make good wholesale items because they are too labor intensive. I did not wholesale every product I made."

Karen makes an excellent point when she says, "When selling at wholesale, the retail store becomes the customer and you want repeat business. Thus, don't wholesale items that you feel the retail store can't double. The biggest advantage of wholesaling is the guaranteed sale. Attending a craft shows today, I may take $10,000 in merchandise in the hopes I can sell $5,000. Selling wholesale eliminates guessing. You sell $5,000 and earn $5,000. Since wholesale buyers buy from samples or catalogs, no time is lost making the items that don't sell. Hiring employees means their wages must be covered by a guaranteed sale."

Karen's store enabled her to receive daily feedback from customers to keep her in touch with what they like. Says Karen, "My retail store helped pay the overhead for my wholesale business. My sales amounted to 20% retail and 80% wholesale. I could never earn the retail dollars I still earn selling at wholesale but I am assured of a monthly income. Whether you wholesale or retail, buy your supplies for the lowest possible prices. Keep your product line more competitive and keep your profit margin high! When I begin creating an item, I may buy at retail until I know for sure the supplies required. Once I develop my line I hunt for the best deals in purchasing the supplies. Doing this I get the best price possible plus the assurance that I will have all the raw materials needed for the upcoming season. Ordering in bulk (unpackaged) can be a great savings. Why pay for packaging and then pay employees to unpackage? Every penny saved helps you become a more profitable business and gives you an edge over your competition by selling lower prices." Of course, I like making a higher profit but depend on the guaranteed income wholesale selling provides. "Why not enjoy the best of both?"

*　　　　　　*　　　　　　*

Crafters often feel confused as they set up two different pricing schedules, one price when selling an item to sell at retail, another to sell it at wholesale. Some, in fact, choose to sell only at retail just to avoid this dilemma but, it need not be so daunting. The fundamental process when preparing to sell a craft product at both retail and wholesale, is to create a basic price that can be at least doubled or tripled.

When you plan to sell at wholesale to shop owners, you must at least double the total costs of your product so you can still make a profit and triple it when you sell directly to the consumer. Sharing in your profit allows stores to pay for rent, salaries and advertising. Catalogers who add your product to their pages will incur expenses such as photography, advertising, color separations and postage. They too must earn a small profit from selling your product for you. Selling the work of others keeps retailers such as these in business themselves.

Deciding whether or not to sell at both retail and wholesale requires research but note the advantage of wholesale selling. Retail customers do not necessarily become frequent, repeat customers. Wholesale customers, when happy with your product, generally order frequently and will usually increase their orders from you if your items sell well.

A doll-maker in the Midwest devised an interesting way to price her dolls for both retail and wholesale selling. Doll-makers often find that their labor costs outweigh materials costs. In our example, the doll-maker totals the cost of goods plus labor and triples the total to arrive at a retail price. When selling wholesale, she simply takes off 25-30% but requires the shop to buy a minimum of four dolls to receive the discount.

*　　　　　　*　　　　　　*

Beverly Johnson, owner of *Dolls & Craft Designs by Bev*, presents her view of selling both at retail and wholesale. "When I sold at wholesale, I presented a price list with MY retail price on it and state that my wholesale cost will be 50% of that. I guarantee not to sell for less in the same town as the shop buying my goods and agree not to sell to any other shop in that town. This policy brought me many repeat buyers so I am happy with the arrangement. I believe as long as a shop who buys wholesale from you; knows what your retail price is, they can do what they want and you are under no obligation to raise your prices to meet their price. They have a right to get that price or they would not be asking it in my opinion. I do suggest crafters research on prices for similar items in a single area."

Speaking of doll makers, **Lee J. Maltenfort and his wife, Judy,** make life-size dolls as owners of, *The Upstairs Maids, Inc.* Explaining the concept of selling at both retail and wholesale very well, Lee says, "Selling wholesale traditionally means a retailer sells your item at the same price you do, but buys merchandise from you at 50% off. The 100% markup, also known as key-stoning, covers the retailer's costs of operation and contributes to their profit." Lee offers several questions a crafter should consider before undertaking to sell at both retail and wholesale.

1   Can you make money selling your work for half of what you sell it for at retail shows? If so, wholesaling is an option. If not, selling at wholesale may not be for you, unless of course, your work still sells at a higher price than you've been getting for it at craft shows.

2   Does the person who wants to sell for you, let's say at a home-party for example, sell in the same marketplace as you? If so, you have a problem. If not, you can sell to her at a price lower than your retail, but still high enough so she can make a profit too.

3   Wholesaling means you do not have to bear the expense, time, money and energy of attending shows yourself or opening your own shop. It means you should review your costs of operation in view of selling at 50% of your retail to determine if it can become profitable for you."

More about wholesaling in Chapter 7, from the Maltenfort's dolls.

    *   *   *

Underpricing Your Crafts and Labor

Denise Schultz expresses disappointment about low prices paid to quilt makers. Says Denise, "Two years ago, I entered several quilts in an auction to raise money for a local woman's shelter and for the artists (50/50). I was shocked by the very low prices the quilts brought. I recorded the prices for all quilts sold and figured the number of square feet in each quilt. Then, I estimated cost of materials of top, batting, and backing, with a little extra for thread and incidentals. I deducted cost of materials from the price paid for each quilt, with the balance being allocated to labor. I divided the cost for labor by the federal minimum hourly wage. If the artist received minimum wages (not for the skilled labor) they would only receive enough to pay them for thirty hours to make a queen size quilt! Quilters know it takes at least five or six times that long to make such a large quilt!"

"This should become an eye-opener, to harden artists' resolve not to underprice their work, and to make the buyers understand why current pricing structures are inadequate. I see this as a necessary part of the maturing of the quilt industry. It shouldn't be only superstar quilt-makers who command a living wage for their work. Not only is our work undervalued in the marketplace, we are actually paying someone to take our quilts from us!"

"There are many aspects of this situation to explore. For example, much of what people buy today is designed to wear out, break, or become obsolete, whereas part of the monetary value of quilts that we construct them to last for generations. We should not see ourselves as low-paid workers, earning less than the U.S. sweatshop workers of an earlier era or foreign sweatshops today.

"Unfortunately, the oppressor (in terms of the pricing set-up of economic exploitation) is not just the purchaser, but the quiltmaker as well for setting prices too low. We cannot possibly expect the marketplace to change voluntarily. We have to work on our side of the equation.

People do not do us a favor by buying our quilts. Instead, they need to know we can sell them something of high intrinsic value in terms of materials + labor + durability, not to mention the artistic value which the marketplace does not recognize."

"Many quiltmakers with whom I talk, particularly older quilters, say they do not consider themselves artists, (even though the content of their work clearly disproves this) and hold the view that people do them a favor when they buy their work. They only see the small amount of money that can either help meet their immediate financial needs or be recycled into buying materials for the next quilt. My background includes technical writing and editing, and financial analysis so I know enough to explore these interacting factors that perhaps others don't have the experience to look for. I don't mean to criticize quilt-makers for not thinking of it. I want them to value themselves and their work...more highly in the future." and my voice continues, "To end this chapter..."

To end this chapter, let me reiterate what I said on the opening pages. The market, not your costs, labor or overhead determines the price at which you can sell your goods. No other factor matters as much as your knowledge of your market. "What the market will bear," must always be your bottom line!

CONTRIBUTORS TO THIS CHAPTER:

Kathy Crofoot,
Kathy's Cache,
P. O. Box 157
Platteville, WI 53818
Phone: (608) 348-2872
Fax: 608-348-2860
Website: http://www.kathyscache.com

Karen Murphy
sold her profitable business

Beverly Johnson,
Doll & Fabric Designs By Bev
2608 TW Miller Lane
Westville, FL 32464
Phone: 850-548-9413
Fax: 850-548-5073
E-mail: ralphina@unforgettable.com
Website: http://www.4cdm.com/dbb

Judy and Lee J. Maltenfort,
The Upstairs Maids, Inc. (Life-size dolls)
308 West Saint Julian Street
Savannah GA 31401
Phone: 912-234-3884; 800-503-3913
E-Mail: Eljayem@earthlink.net
Website: http://www.avillageontheriver.com/upstairs-maids

Denise Schultz
Box 28
Petaluma, CA 94904
Phone: 707-789-0931
E-mail: Spiral11@aol.com

Chapter 3

Quilting

Pricing template: Barbara Siedlecki
In-depth interview: Jill Reicks

Quilting has become such a large segment of the craft industry, that it has become an industry in itself. Its annual Houston, TX event, International Quilt Market, (for quilt professionals) and International Quilt Festival (for the general public) is larger and better attended than any other specific craft event in the U.S. In the October issue of *Craftrends Magazine*, a trade journal for the entire craft industry, Kevin Menken states that quilting generates $1.2 billion per year in the U.S.

Shop-owners, teachers, designers, manufacturers and quilt lovers come from all over the world to attend the Houston event. Recently it has spilled over into providing three other huge quilt markets in different parts of the country too. Quilting has grown so much that several "spin-off" industries have evolved in response to demand from quilters.

Today, we see manufacturers who do little else but produce specialty tools for quilters. National book publishers publish quilting books, exclusively. In the next chapter, read about people who make a living supporting and offering services to the quilting industry. I unearthed so many designers dedicated exclusively to producing quilting patterns that I could not include them all.

I attended a three-hour pledge drive by a Public Broadcasting Station in Redding California, to raise money for its programs in August 1999. Quilters, speakers and teachers kept the telephone ringing and pledges coming to such an extent that management acknowledged that only "The Three Tenors" and "River-Dance" produced more revenue. A best-selling book published after many years of research, *The 100 Best Quilts in the Twentieth Century*, reduced from 1,720 entries and you can see them all on the Web.

There are so many types, styles, sizes and ages of quilts, it is impossible to derive a single way to price making, buying, finishing or quilting them all but the professional quilters in this chapter share their pricing ideas freely.

*   *   *

Barbara Siedlecki, of *Cabin Fever Crafts*, says, "When pricing my quilted tote bags, I considered several factors," begins Barbara. "I accounted exactly for the amount of fabric and labor I put into a single bag. I based my pricing schedule on a very plain, basic style and made a chart for possible add-ons customers might request such as pockets, decorations and finishing touches. I add these factors together before quoting a price for one of my quilted tote bags":

1 I figure fabric cost at retail price. If I can purchase it for less, I may lower the price if I do a similar bag on commission. However, if the customer buys the fabric, I begin with retail price as a reference point.

2 Labor costs challenge me when what I earn differs from what the market will bear. Because the time and effort I put into my tote bags reflects upon me as a designer, I use high quality fabric and expect anyone who commissions a piece from me to do the same.

3 I base my pricing system on a simple design. The amount shown in parentheses reflects what the market will bear in my geographical area. I offer these as guidelines and suggest you investigate your own particular market and adjust as needed. My pattern, *A Bag for All Reasons,* is for a quilted tote bag with a loose lining. It is fast and easy to make and lends itself to adding special embellishments.

Small Quilted Tote:

Fabric cost:	3/4 yard x retail cost ($8.95 per yd) =	$6.75
Batting cost: $3.75	Total Material cost:	$10.50
Labor: 1-1/2 hours at $7.50 per hour =		$11.25
Cost of goods + labor = $21.75 rounded to		$22.00 ($15)

Medium Quilted Tote:

Fabric cost:	1 yard x $8.95 per yard =	$8.95
Batting cost: $4.00	Total Material cost:	$12.95
Labor cost: 1-1/2 hours	at $7.50 =	$11.25

(It takes me the same time to make both sizes.)

Total cost: $24.20 rounded to $24.00. ($20)

Large Quilted Tote

Fabric cost: 1-1/3 yard x retail cost   ($8.95) = $12.00
Batting cost: $5.00
Total Materials Cost: $17.00
Labor: 2 hours at $7.50   = $15.00
Total cost: $32.00 ($25)

Consider consignment fees if you sell this way. Shop owners who consign to sell your goods deserve a portion of the selling price. I buy my equipment which includes rotary cutters, rulers and cutting boards. Thread may not sound like a big item for each bag but becomes an expense since I do heavy quilting. Sewing machines have become a necessity but not an inconsequential expense paid over time and added to the cost of the finished product.

When possible, I make more than one bag at a time as two bags do not take twice the time. The more I make and sew in sections, e.g., all the seams at one time, all the quilting, handles etc., the less time it takes. Fabric purchased on sale also reduces costs while increasing profit. Below, you will find my chart outlining extra charges I may incur for:

A plain pocket: add $3.00 plus fabric

A pieced or machine appliqué pocket: add $5.00 plus fabric

A complicated pocket with Seminole Patchwork, zipper, button or snaps, add $7.00 plus findings and fabric. Extra or fancy quilting: add $5.00-$10.00 depending on intricacy.

*   *   *

Karen Bush, of Birdsong Quilts says, "I sell quilted wall-hangings and I charge what the fabric costs multiplied by three to find my direct cost. I arrive at my selling price by allowing 1/3 of the price for actual fabric costs, 1/3 for labor and 1/3 for profit. When hand-quilting a piece made by someone else, I charge by the square foot depending on the design but marking and basting are always separate charges. A set price for the overall quilt doesn't work as some quilts have intricate hand-quilting while others are not heavily quilted."

*   *   *

Merry May, of School House Enterprises says, "I had been crafting many years before I started my quilting business, in 1998. I treat my quilting business as if it's a full-time job. I devote about 5%-10% of my time to producing work to sell but quilting on commission is only a part of my business. I teach classes, own and operate a small mail order business, and manufacture paper foundation sheets for mass-producing quilting patterns," says Merry. Though she prefers selling directly to consumers, galleries attract a wider audience, so she sells there too. "When I sell through a gallery, I cut my price a little so that after the gallery adds its commission to my price, the work will still sell."

Merry buys raw materials from local shops, because she wants to support those who provide moral support to her. She explains, "I like buying locally so I can examine the quality of the goods I buy, and frequently receive a teacher's discount applied to my purchases. If I can't find what I need locally, I order through catalogs," she adds.

Lowering prices for selling her quilted items has come up for Merry. "Surprisingly, I find that lowering my price doesn't always sell the item," Merry explains. "Often, it's a matter of finding the right customer for the piece. However, I have raised prices as my skill level increased."

Merry prices her items by the square foot and adjusts dollar amounts based on the project's intricacy. "I give people a rough estimate but if they request a maximum price I should not exceed, I calculate a higher price per square foot. This way, the final price is within a range we both agreed upon but I price my time at $10 per hour."

Merry found the Internet creates sales made through her online catalog. "But" she adds, "you must continually promote your business by linking with other busier sites and offering people a reason to visit yours. For example, I've been offering a free mystery quilt series through someone else's website for a year with a direct link from the mystery quilt site to mine. This generated a lot of catalog requests and orders directly from my site."

Says Merry, "I determine a quilt's square footage then multiply by $20 for a simple quilt or $25 if I find it more complex and detailed. This gives me a starting place and here' how it works:

To calculate the price on making a wall quilt which measures 44 inches square, I determine the total square inches by multiplying 40 x 40 which equals 1,600 sq. inches. Divide this by 144 (the equivalent of a square foot) and you have 11.11. Multiplying by $20, this comes to $222.20 which I may round to $220 or $225 to make the quilt. If you use the $25 factor, the asking price of the quilt would be $277.75. After all of this, I check market prices to be sure my labor as a quiltmaker can compete. If necessary, I raise or lower the price so it fits within market demand."

*   *   *

Judy Sims shares her system for pricing her quick Log Cabin quilts. Says Judy, "First. I examined each step in the process. I divided my work segments into eight hour days. Next, I spent one whole day cutting fabric pieces, allowing myself a 15 minute break in the morning and afternoon. At the end of the day, I recorded the number of quilts I actually had cut out."

Judy continues, "The next day, I repeated the process but this time I began to sew the blocks, assembly line-style until I had a stack of blocks. At day's end, I recorded the number of blocks I had and how many quilts I could assemble from those blocks. On the third day, I assembled the blocks and finished each quilt before going on to the next. At the end of the day, I recorded the number of quilts and portions of quilts I had completed."

No one could doubt the efficiency of calculating the value of one's time using Judy's plan. Based on her schedule, she knew exactly how much hands-on-time went into each quilt. Judy continues, "Cutting took one quarter of my time. Piecing each block took half the time. Assembling took the last quarter of my time," Judy explains. I finished two quilts plus two blocks for more quilts or 1½ quilts. I divided my three 24 hour days by 1½ and came up with the actual time involved."

Judy spells out her system's results: "At 6.86 hours per quilt multiplied by $5.00 per hour, I found I had $34.30 in labor alone. Next, I added up the total for all my materials and came up with my basic cost per quilt. If materials cost $20, I add my labor, $34.30 to total $54.30."

Judy continues, "If the quilt market approximates $150 per quilt and you sell at wholesale, you need to divide that figure by 50%. At $75 per quilt, your profit is $20.70, a 28% profit margin. If you can keep that figure above 10%, you are doing well," says Judy. Did I mention that Judy uses speed methous to make her quilts then does the quilting by machine?

*　　　　　　　　*　　　　　　　　*

Cathy Hooley runs a home-based quilting business selling small to medium sized quilts used as wall hangings, baby quilts, table runners, table mats, place mats, pillows and holiday items like tree skirts, stockings and ornaments. She sells directly to consumers at retail prices. Cathy works alone, using only 100% cotton fabric and thread in her products, a preference of many buyers today. She also uses only cotton batting between quilt layers to accentuate traditional style and look as cotton batts produce a flatter finish.

Pricing her products fairly and attentive to the available market, Cathy uses the actual cost system described in chapter two of this book: Labor, Overhead, Raw Materials.

"Until recently, I didn't have a pricing system," said Cathy. "I set my prices to what I felt people would pay, without considering how much work went into making the items. Many people told me my prices were too low, but I didn't believe customers would pay more so I continued to sell what I could. Finally, I realized that I was losing money even when I was selling many items so I decided to get serious and develop a pricing system," Cathy explains.

"Each time I make an item for the first time, I calculate raw material costs and my labor based at $10 per hour." Working 40 hours per week, she earned $400 and realized that paying taxes would be partially offset by her expenses. Cathy presents her system:

Labor: $10 per hour for everything made by machine and $6 per hour for hand sewing. Cathy explains that she does not value hand sewing less but it consumes more hours. Charging $10 per hour for slower handwork would price her out of the market.

Overhead: Cathy determined her overhead expenses were approximately, $2,000. Referring back to 40 hours per week, 2,000 hours per year equals $1 per hour in overhead. She added this amount to her labor rate. Below are Cathy's overhead expenses:

$200 per year: Website fee

$400 per year: Bank charges

$350 per year: Car and gasoline expenses

$200 per year: Notions, thread, needles, rotary cutters, tools, etc.

$50 per year: Required Subscriptions to keep Cathy up to date on the quilting industry.

$500 per year: Craft show fees

$200 per year: Tent display miscellaneous costs at craft shows.

Raw Materials: This includes fabric, thread and batting which varies from one item to another.

Profit: To this subtotal, Cathy adds 25% for profit which provides her a margin for negotiation when considering consignment fees and quantity discounts. Below, prices for Cathy's products using her pricing system.

Wall hangings:	from $65 for 18 x18 inch square, to $450 for quilts 45 inches square, both machine and hand quilted.
Pillows:	from $20 to $40.depending on size, complexity, i.e., ruffles, etc.
Place Mats:	from $8 each for simple mats, sold in sets of 4 to $18 each if complex and sold in pairs
Table Runners :	from $32 to $48, depending on the size, complexity.
Table Mats:	from $20 to $65, depending on the size and pattern.

Cathy prefers not to make bed size quilts as buyers expect to pay the same prices as they do for imports and discount chain-stores. Those prices make customers reluctant to pay a fair price for handmade goods. Cathy has devised a contingency plan to test her pricing strategy. She explains: "On larger items I also consider a square foot test. To be competitive, the price per square foot for my quilts should fall into the $15-$30 range. If my formula yields a price that is outside this range, I adjust it accordingly. If prices are too high, I determine whether I can make the item using fewer costly materials or speed up my process. If I cannot, I don't make the item. If my price is lower than the square foot calculation compared to similar items on the market, I raise my price," she explains.

"I use this system for everything I make but I'm always looking for ways to make things less expensively. I like this system because I can see easily out how much flexibility I have in my pricing. I know that I'm asking a fair price and receive a fair return. I know how I arrived at my prices and can work on cost elements that seem too high. I know instantly how much I can afford to mark something down. For consignment sales, I don't have to mark up the cost to cover the entire consignment fee if I don't want to."

*   *   *

Darla Moore, of *The Sweet Pea Patch*, has made quilts and dolls since 1991. Darla buys her raw materials in interesting, innovating ways. Says Darla, "Though I may buy from catalogs and craft stores, my favorite method is to attend auctions and tag sales for vintage fabrics and decorative items. Darla says, "I rarely buy anything at retail. Instead, I get as many different catalog sources for a particular product as possible then I chart prices on the items they carry that I use. Doing this allows me to compare prices quickly and recognize sale items at local stores that actually sell for below wholesale."

Darla describes her pricing structure. "To set retail prices, I take material costs, labor, wages paid to others plus 10% for overhead costs. I total this and double it. Determining wholesale costs comes easy. I simply cut the retail price in half. She translates this as she prices her bed quilts: For my Quilts I charge: (materials + labor + 10%)x2 = retail price. Half of that equals my wholesale price.

*   *   *

Another valuable contribution on the subject of pricing quilts comes from expert, Elsie Vredenburg, owner of *Quilts by Elsie,* founded in 1978. Elsie works full-time in her home-based business spending 75% of her time in quilt-related tasks, reserving 25% for clerical tasks.

She sells quilts and quilt patterns at retail, directly to consumers. Says Elsie, "I purchase supplies from local shops, quilt shows and wherever I find what I want. I buy on sale when possible. While vending at craft shows and making quilts in larger volume, I bought more at wholesale. Today, I still buy unbleached muslin for quilt backs and batting at wholesale. I quilted off and on for nearly 20 years before hanging out my shingle in my front yard, which is still there."

As to lowering prices, she replies, "When vending at craft shows, many buyers have a 'flea market' mentality and want to dicker. Quickly, I learned I wanted to control my prices—not customers. I decided not to lower prices just to avoid packing up my products to cart them home. After all, I had more upcoming shows. I only lower prices I want to move a particular item because it did not sell."

What about raising prices? Elsie explains, "For more than 20 years that I have quilted for others, my prices risen about 400%. I'm still on the low end, but must try to keep pace with inflation."

Elsie describes her pricing system. "My business essentially has three arms and I deal with each one separately:

Quilting for others: I began quilting twenty years ago for customers who had completed their quilt-top and wanted me to quilt it. I charge by the spool of thread, currently $100 per spool for hand-quilting. I add $6.00 per hour for marking, binding, ironing and anything else I do to prepare the quilt for hand-quilting. I charge the customer for any materials I provide."

Sale of quilts and quilted items: "On smaller items, I charge $10-$11 per hour, which includes materials," she says. Elsie continues, "Several years ago, an article in *The Crafts Report* suggested the following formula for pricing crafts. Expenses were totaled up including materials and overhead. Next you enter the figure you'd like to earn in a year and divide the total by the number of hours you wanted to work. The result would be your hourly rate which you then multiplied by the number of hours it took to make the item. When I make quilts, I use a combination of both these systems, figuring an hourly rate for everything except hand-quilting which I price the same way as I do for custom quilting."

Patterns. See next chapter for information about Elsie's patterns. Elise continues. "A quilter in my local quilting chapter uses a very simple approach in pricing her quilts. For pieced or appliqué quilts alike, she charges five cents per square inch. Exceptions to this system occur when a customer chooses a very simple, quick technique such as working pre-stamped, cross-stitch quilts where quilting is sparse. These charges are for hand quilting only. If the hand-quilting will be perfuse such as in stipple quilting, (stitching lines no further apart than ¼ inch) she charges seven or eight cents per square inch. Pricing for this quilter is indeed a simple matter," Elsie concludes.

In-depth-interview: Jill Reicks

Jill Reicks expanded her business by opening her own shop just after being interviewed for this book. Jill's new shop, Lydia's Sisters is located in Cresco, Iowa but she began her original quilting business in 1988.

How much time do you devote to your quilting business?

I spend more than 40 hours a week

Do you sell both retail and wholesale or just directly to the ultimate consumer?

I sell mostly at retail but do sell some products at wholesale.

Do you ever buy raw materials at retail prices, "on-sale?"

No, I buy at wholesale only.

How long had you been quilting before you began to sell what you made?

I began to quilt the same year I started the business. I began making pillows and bags using cross-stitch inserts as the prime design feature. I took them to craft shows and found they sold very well. Next, I combined quilting with cross-stitch for wall quilts then I specialized in quilting as it grew more popular.

Have you ever lowered prices because you found they were too high?

Yes, I lowered them in relation to demographics. I haven't done this often but when I find that a specific area won't tolerate my prices, I look for a new marketing strategy perhaps moving to a different geographical area to vent or create a different product.

Have you ever raised your prices? Why?

Yes. I evaluated the actual cost of marketing and creating a product and learned a great deal about my pricing structure. Now I pay more attention to overhead expenses which caused me to raise my prices.

Please describe your system for pricing your items.

My pricing structure has grown with my knowledge. Presently, I calculate 30% of my price for advertising. I calculate the raw materials and labor costs into the product. I work these figures into a spreadsheet that adjusts when the price of fabric goes up or the price of labor increases. I frequently evaluate the structure to make sure I have considered all variables. This is important because I get many calls from companies wanting me to try their marketing strategy, advertising in their publications or using their Website. I need to know how much product I would have to sell to justify the expense that a salesperson may suggest.

Do you consider labor when you set your prices?

Yes. People who work for me all run their own businesses. They bid on jobs for me and we agree upon a price for a certain quantity and time. I then add these calculations into my pricing spreadsheet. Complete records are essential to making decisions for your business. I use a full-accounting software package that gives me the opportunity to calculate all expenses and to evaluate all different areas of sales. Many software programs exist for this analysis.

Do you consider raw materials when you set your prices?

Yes, I calculate their cost into my spreadsheet. When I went to market recently, I changed my price per yard on fabric to the average of the highest-priced fabrics that I purchased.

How do you determine overhead?

Overhead is more history than science. I look at my expenses from previous years. Using even the simplest accounting program, one can evaluate figures over the past three years. From those numbers I come up with a percentage that represents my overhead. This is the part of my business that isn't numerically accurate because if I purchase a new computer that has all the bells and whistles, in large part I am purchasing it for my convenience. Therefore, I wouldn't calculate the whole of that expense into my overhead. Overhead is not precise for me since I work out of my home.

How do you determine profit?

My next goal is to determine profit by calculating a percentage as I did with advertising and overhead percentages. Some say we should write ourselves a monthly check. Failing to do this, I am prone to expand my inventory when I notice a surplus of money in my account.

Do you sell at: Craft shows?

I have in the past. My goal is NOT to in the future.

Retail shops including boutiques and specialty stores?

Yes, some.

On consignment? If so, how do you determine what to charge in view of the shop owner's percentage?

The two businesses I work with have calculated a percentage. One of these, a nonprofit organization, donates all of its income to a shelter for women and children. Their percentage is 30%. That percentage is equal to the percentage I have calculated in my price for advertising. Therefore, I consider my tradeoff to be on pricing. Another business charges me 15%. The market in that area is not as strong, yet I keep that market because the people who run the consignment are efficient and honest in all our dealings. Theft is very low at that shop but consignment is my least favorite sales technique. The benefits are very few so I must have specific reasons to sell on consignment. I receive requests every week to sell at consignment somewhere but prefer not to.

Do you sell via the Internet or from a Website? If yes, did this increase the business you were doing before?

I advertise my e-mail address but it generates very few sales. I followed surveys done by magalogs about Internet access. Market shares exist for Internet sales but I do not feel sure this is lucrative enough for me to hire someone to create a Website for me. I plan to learn HTML and create a site of my own.

QUICK REVIEW OF PRICING METHODS IN THIS CHAPTER:

X   Use Pricing Templates based upon raw material costs and adjust on a sliding scale for small, medium and large projects.

X   Multiply fabric costs by three to = direct cost. Final selling price: 1/3 of the price for actual fabric costs, 1/3 for labor and 1/3 for profit.

X   Charge by the square foot when quilting for others but marking and basting are separate charges.

X   Price quilted items by the square foot, in dollar amounts based on intricacy of the project.

X   Try pricing your time at $10 per hour and see if this works for you.

X   Charge by the hour if you can use fast, assembly-line piecing techniques.

X   Calculate raw material costs, labor, overhead and profit, based on per hour rate.

X   Check catalog prices on items use frequently. This way, you can compare to see if "on-sale" prices are genuine.

X   Consider this Pricing Template: materials + labor wages + 10%)x2 = retail price. Half of that equals the wholesale price.

X   Charge $100 per spool for hand-quilting. Add $6.00 per hour for marking, binding, ironing and all tasks to prepare the quilt for hand-quilting. Customers should pay for all materials. Charges $10-$11 per hour, which includes materials for smaller items.

X   Charge five cents per square inch for or pieced or appliqué quilts.

X   Compute the break-even point (the number of items sold to recoup initial investment.) Anything over that becomes profit.

X   Calculate 30% of price for advertising plus total costs of all raw materials and labor. Use a spreadsheet to adjust when the price of fabric or labor increases.

CONTRIBUTORS IN THIS CHAPTER:

Barbara Seidlecki
Cabin Fever Crafts
P.O. Box 7604
Kalispell, MT 59904-0604
Voice/Fax (406) 257-0434
E-mail: cbnfvr@digisys.net

Karen S. Bush
Birdsong Quilts
409 Morningside Drive
Richmond, MO
Phone: 816-470-8976
Fax: 816-470-6189
E-mail: Birdsong@worldnet.att.net
http://www.idahoquilt.com

Merry May
Box 305
Tuckahoe, NJ 08250-0305
Phone: 609-628-2231
Fax 609-628-3048
E-mail cluesew@jerseycape.com

Judy Sims
4514 4th St. N.W.
Albuquerque, NM 87107
Phone: 505-344-8086
Fax: 505-344-1740
E-mail: CNGCCC@aol.com
http://www.angelfire.com/biz2/craftsnetworkguild/index.html

Cathy Hooley
Goose Tracks Quilts
PO Box 265
Broadalbin, NY 12025
Phone: 518-842-8700
FAX: 815-364-0456 (yes, 815 vs. 518 is correct for my fax number-it's e-fax!)
E-mail: Cathy@goosetracks.com
http://www.goosetracks.com

Darla Moore
2885 CR 25 N
Bellefontaine, Ohio, 43311
Phone: 937-468-2848
E-mail: darla@bright.net
http://www.bright.net/~darla/sppatch.htm

Elsie Vredenburg
Address: Box 301
Tustin, MI 49688
Phone: (616) 825-2572
E-mail: E-mail: elf@netonecom.net
http://www.netonecom.net/~elf

Jill Reicks
Lydia's Sisters
Pine Needles Quilt Shop, Cresco, IA
Street Address: 1605 Quinlan Ave.
City, State, Zip: Lawler, IA 52154
Phone: 515-394-3448
E-mail: Lydias@sbt.net

Chapter 4

Quilting Products & Services

Pricing Template: Cliff and Patsy Monk
In-depth Interview: Linda & Dean Moran

Quilting is such a big industry that it has created several spin-off industries. One of these involves people who provide not only gadgets and tools but services to busy quilters by designing, binding, repairing, appraising, quilting and even finishing quilts for them. Supply breeds demand and now that quilt addicts can have others finish their work for them they cannot wait to make more quilts and see them completed even faster.

∗   ∗   ∗

Cliff and Patsy Monk began their joint quilting venture in the reverse order from many other working couples in the quilting industry. Cliff's quilting activities began when he was only seven years old but Patsy didn't begin to quilt until she married Cliff in 1987, which inspired her to take it seriously!

Cliff and Patsy Monk machine quilt for customers who prefer not to hand-quilt their completed quilt-top. They put their Gammill Long-Arm Quilting Machine to work in 1989, with Cliff using it 40 hours per week, working from home. Patsy teaches quilting and is herself, a quiltmaker. She puts in fewer hours than her husband as she still has an outside job. The Monks work primarily for the individual maker of a quilt-top though Patsy also makes liturgical garments for ministers as well.

Cliff recently raised his prices due to the growing demand for his work. He begins estimating his price by measuring the square yardage of a quilt then considering the intricacy of the pattern the customer chooses. Patsy says she looks at the intricacy first and begins pricing at $20.00 per square foot increasing accordingly.

Professional Machine Quilters charge for their services in different ways. Some charge by the hour, yard, inch or by the overall quilt size. Some even charge by the bobbin of thread they consume. Each method has merits and drawbacks. "We determine the square yardage of a quilt and divide this into 1,296 square inches to charge for pantograph patterns, the easiest to do with long-arm quilting machines."

Small pattern	Medium Patterns	Large Patterns
$15.00 sq. yd	$13.00 sq. yd.	$10.00 sq. yd.

Patsy explains that pantograph patterns[1] also known as edge-to-edge quilting, begins with long sheets of paper placed under a plastic cover on the back of the machine. The pantograph traces a design using a stylus mounted on the side of the machine to create quilted patterns stitched by the long-arm quilting machine. It traces the pattern, copies it, and stitches in thread through all three layers of a quilt. Pantographs vary in complexity. Some are one-pass patterns but others require multiple passes to complete the machine quilting. Smooth, free flowing lines are easiest to follow but those with points or diamonds make a pattern more difficult. Stippling or meandering quilting is easiest of all but uses up the most time and thread. Labor becomes intensive as the quilter must maintain a constant speed of machine movement as she/he negotiates frequent curves and turns in an effort to fill up an area without crossing over previous stitches.

Patsy defines what the Monks find most difficult and labor intensive—the custom quilt. Consider a quilt-top where the owner wishes one section quilted in floating stars, then diagonal lines in the main blocks and wants one or two border patterns. "This type of a quilt is the most difficult to price yet always draws crowds at shows," says Patsy.

As machine quilters purchase or design new patterns and develop a selection, the Monks suggest that she/he work the pattern onto a sample for customers to see. This enables them to appreciate the complexity of the work and to see how the Monks price their labor. With the popularity of long-arm quilting machines, quilters can complete hundreds of quilts per year rather than one to four as in hand-quilting.

The Monks price custom quilting on a case-by-case basis. Prices start at $20.00 sq. yd.

When they began their quilting business, they advertised to quilters who had completed quilt tops but wanted someone else to hand-quilt them. They placed small ads in guild newsletters saying, "It is NOT a quilt until it is quilted—our job is to quilt them!" As their business grew, prices went up as their skill increased.

Both Cliff and Patsy consider labor, raw materials and overhead when setting prices for their work but they have a simple definition of their profit. "Gross intake minus cost = profit" says Patsy. However, the Monks value their time quite differently. Cliff considers his experience, and past performance when setting prices for his time. Patsy says that if she loves the work she is creating, cost is not as important to her.

"Cliff works on all sizes of quilts but I prefer clothing," admits Patsy. "I love doing tote bags, liturgical work, especially stoles and banners. If I leave my nursing job, we could do more but I have grown accustomed to nursing. I also believe God prepares us to do what we should be doing, and doesn't give us more than we can handle. But I also keep Mother Theresa's quote, in mind, "I wish He didn't trust me so much!""

Monica Novini began her quilting business in 1996 working from home so she could care for her small children. Nonetheless, she works a staggering 60 to 100 hours per week producing The *Perfect Square,* a reusable iron-on transfer used to make and cut perfect half-square triangles which challenge most quilters.

Monica remembers the first time she learned the grid method for making half-square triangles but found the drawing and measuring time consuming and tedious. "Fabric moves when you draw on it" explains Monica, "so first I tried using a fine sand paper beneath it. This prevented the fabric from shifting and eliminated inaccurate marking but the pencil kept getting dull from the sandpaper and I had to stop and sharpen it often wasting more time." Monica found it difficult to measure accurately and to figure how much fabric she would need. She determined to find a better way. After much research and phone calls she found a printer who thought he could produce her idea on paper. "Printing the lines as fine as I wanted them turned out to be much harder than he thought," says Monica. "I felt disheartened by this and put *Perfect Square* on the back burner for several years and got a job."

When Monica left her outside job, she looked at *Perfect Square* once again. "I signed up for a small business marketing and management class and found a new printing company willing to work with me," she explains. "Small, family owned printers can be more flexible and together we have worked out the printing details so *Perfect Square* would work the way I had envisioned while not making too difficult for the printers," she said.

Monica does not actually produce her product—the printer does. She sells her completed, printed patterns at wholesale to shops and mail-order catalogs. Marketing, advertising, promotion, packaging, mailing, bookkeeping, customer service, correspondence both traditional and via E-mail along with designing her own literature consume her business hours. "Currently, I am creating quilt patterns that will make use of *Perfect Square*. Eventually, Monica wants to sell her designs in the form of note cards, posters, magnets, books and patterns but due to the success of *Perfect Square,* she now produces patterns called, *Perfect Hexagon* and *Perfect Triangles.*

Monica describes her pricing structure. "The suggested retail price of *Perfect Square* is $10 per package of five reusable sheets. When I sell retail, I also charge $10 and include postage so that neither the shop owners I sell to nor I have an unfair advantage. I didn't feel it would be fair not to sell at retail to individuals who had no other way to obtain the product, yet I didn't want to sell it at a lesser price and be unfair to the shop owner."

Because Monica does not actually create her product, she simply considers the price of printing and packaging to arrive at her price. "I just looked at my costs, multiplied them by a number that I thought would give me a profit, and looked to see if this resulted in a reasonable price. It worked so I used it."

Monica sells to quilt shops and attends quilt markets to reach her clientele but is quite pleased with her experiences selling from her Website. She offers a free sample on her site in exchange for a self-addressed, stamped envelope. Says Monica, "I get more from my site than anywhere else on the net where I advertise."

Kelly Baird, offers the quilting community a popular and innovative product. Owner of The Quiltmakers Quilt Shop, Kelly bought the two-year-old shop in May 1996. With the purchase of the shop, she purchased the rights to Quiltmaker's Photo Transfer Paper™. Says Kelly, "When I began to consider buying the shop, I knew the transfer paper had to be part of the deal."

"Studying their financial records, I realized that the principal reason this new shop had made a profit so quickly, was selling transfer paper. I stuck to my guns and refused to buy the shop until the former owners signed over their rights and claims to the paper."

Transfer paper has become enormously popular with all quilters from hobbyists to professionals as the specially treated paper enables quilters to transfer images and photographs to fabric. Quilters then embellish and quilt their project having the faces and scenes they treasure as principal elements in their quilts.

Kelly continues, "When I took over the business, I thought the price of the transfer paper was too high," says Kelly. "I cringed when telling customers the cost and can't count how many walked out because they found it too expensive. I decided to package it more efficiently and to find a more direct source to purchase it. Afterward, I lowered my prices and have been extremely pleased with my sales."

Kelly explains her product in detail: "I package a specially coated, heat transfer textile paper so quilters can transfer photos and other mementos onto fabric. Using a color Laser copier, quilters copy their items onto the transfer paper. Next, they cut the copied images apart, and iron them directly onto fabric with a household iron."

Kelly recognized the real value of the transfer paper when she offered it at consumer quilt shows. She began to sell it to wholesale customers but it wasn't until she took it to The International Quilt Market in Houston in 1996, that wholesale orders outstripped her retail orders for the paper.

A year later, due to the paper's success, Kelly introduced an Inkjet transfer paper during the Houston quilting event. Says Kelly, "This is the only paper on the market I know of that is completely permanent and washable. To relate the two products, I chose a blanket name for them, 'Creative Copy.' I call them *Creative Copy Photo Transfer Paper*, and *Creative Copy Inkjet Transfer Paper*. I sell them though popular catalogs but some, such as *Keepsake Quilting* prefer to list the paper as "'Quiltmakers Photo Transfer Paper.'"

Kelly has plans for the future of her shop and its star products. "While I plan to do more research and educate myself about break-even analysis and fixed costs, at this time I price each element from the components that make up an item such as labor, time and overhead. Then, I double or triple total costs to a price the market will bear. I have worked with many people who do not consider their own worth when figuring costs. This oversight makes profits look higher but does not truly represent the status of the business and its profits," she says.

In January 1999, Kelly added full service photo-transfer for customers who prefer not to do it themselves. "I leased a high quality Panasonic scanner and laser color printer, and purchased a professional T-shirt press. The copier paper works well in laser printers. For a per-sheet fee, we copy, adjust color and image, print the transfer, trim it and iron it onto the fabric the customer chooses. We offer this service for mail-order customers as well," adds Kelly.

Kelly closes with advice to others. "I believe the most important thing crafting entrepreneurs need to remember is that their time is valuable. If they don't account for their time, they short-change themselves and their business. Continue to make choices. Find more cost-effec-tive supplies and materials and do everything possible to provide a high-quality product."

Emma Graham established a home-based interior decorating business many years ago which frequently required her to turn narrow fabric tubes right side out. Her engineer hus-band observed her frustration and began to try to make tube turning easier for her. Before long, Emma says, her husband invented a set of tools to turn the narrowest tubes easily and quickly.

Invented in 1985, the Grahams applied for a patent for their tools completing the process two years later. In 1987 they began offering their tools to quilters, sewers and any-one who worked with fabric. Today, the Grahams manufacture not only *Fasturn,* the tools for turning tubes but other items such as *Fastube*, Universal Presser Foot and many pat-terns which make good use of their tools. The Grahams sell to distributors, wholesalers and retail shops throughout the U.S. through their mail-order catalog.

Emma says her pricing system for the tools remains simple. She totals raw materials, labor and overhead then multiplies by six to determine retail price and by five to set wholesale and distributor prices. The Grahams vended at sewing and quilting trade shows but this year, opened their own retail store featuring their own notions plus those of others such as bias tape makers, pleaters, patterns and the wonderful Ott portable lamps. Though the Grahams have not yet jumped on the web, they plan to do so. For now, this far-from-retired senior couple teach others to make children's clothes for safe houses and started a group that makes Toobie Dolls to donate to hospitals and police departments who come in contact with needy chil-dren. Toobie Dolls are constructed from fabric tubes. What else?

Margie Lee Bevis, of Marbled Fabric and Accessories began marbling fabric in 1986.

Says Margie, "Demand for marbled fabric for quilting has increased so much in the last two years that I work nine or 10 hours a day, six days per week marbling or dyeing fabric that I sell to quilt shops or at retail shows," says Margie. "My business used to be mostly retail; sell-ing fabric at various quilt shows or selling scarves, ties, and purses at craft shows. However, after showing my fabric at several wholesale shows, I have little time for retail shows as my wholesale accounts consume most of my time."

"I have only raised my prices twice in the eleven years that I have been selling marbled fabric," says Margie. "Although, the costs of goods increase yearly, I absorb a small loss because

I operate with low overhead working from a studio behind my home. But, I may have to raise my prices soon, because of the increased cost of paint, fabric, and advertising," she explains.

"Pricing my items involves a lot of thought. I total my costs but the price of the item cannot exceed what people will pay for it, she says. "Determining the value of my time challenged me most. I started with how much time I devoted to my business, and how much money I needed to make to survive and pay expenses. Once I came up with an hourly amount I felt I could live with, I determined how many pieces of fabric I could produce in an hour, divided it into the amount I needed to earn each hour, and added this amount to my other expenses. Bear in mind that the more experience you gather producing a quality product, the more money you should earn" advises Margie.

Alice Furrey, owner of *Star*Struck Quilting* began machine quilting for others in 1989. "From the beginning" says Alice, "I worked full time because I always loved sewing and quilt making. I thought that buying a quilting machine to finish a few quilts for others as well as for myself would fill in my spare time. Little did I know then that this venture would nearly consume all my time."

Continuing, Alice says, "I spend most of my time quilting other people's quilt-tops. Customers send me their quilts from across the country—from Alaska to Florida. I have shelves of quilt-tops waiting for me which accounts for about 80% of my work time."

Alice admits that designing and making her own quilts remains her first love. "I sell two of my original patterns locally and want to produce more but my focus is quilting for others. Occasionally, I make quilts on commission. Alice has raised her prices at times. She explains that she was far too conservative in the beginning and did not price her quilts high enough. She admits that after evaluating supplies and her time, she also had overlooked small expenses.

Today, Alice sets her prices differently. She adds cost of materials, (including thread and pattern) and than prorates the following: insurance, advertising, correspondence, phone calls, packaging & miscellaneous items. Alice explains, "I figure these by a yearly cost divided by the number of quilts I can reasonably expect to complete. I figure my time by how much total time, including record keeping, that it takes to complete a quilt. Then I make sure the resulting sum is one the market will bear in my area for comparable work. A more complicated design takes more time and my prices reflect that. The total is my basis for a wholesale price. I set my retail price by adding on 30% when on consignment in this area."

Alice explains how she determines overhead. "I include advertising, insurance, business phone calls, heat and lights in my workroom broken down into an average cost per quilt. I also considered the purchase of my quilting machine into total costs, depreciating it over five years. Next, I determined how many quilts I can usually and reasonably make in a year and divide it into one year's depreciation figure. I came up with a depreciation cost of $18 for a queen size quilt and add this figure when pricing customers' quilt tops as well as making my own quilts to sell."

Speaking of determining prices, Alice has a unique view of figuring in a profit to each quilt she makes. "Though others double or triple expenses to determine a selling price that includes profit, I find that the resulting price is just too high for people to pay. I add a rough 25% increase to my final price for profit."

Alice determines her labor in the same, sensible sort of way. "I determine my labor by observing the reasonable wage others in this area charge for comparable work. "Others" include those who make quilts, sew clothing or make home furnishings. Everyone would like to think they should earn a large sum per hour but you cannot price yourself out of the market. Competition awareness should bring your prices into line."

Sharing her advice with readers, Alice says. "I have come into contact with many women who wish to make a living working at home. Many have the mistaken notion that all they need do is buy a quilting machine and they will be ready for business. They do not realize the tremendous amount of practice and determination it takes to produce a quality product and the stamina it takes to work from home. Machine quilters must deal with countless interruptions, family demands, frustrations with the machine and time spent keeping records. Last, I want to mention the quality of your work. "Fast and Easy" may be a temptation as one strives for quantity above quality. Don't fall into this trap but think instead of your work as art rather than craft and give each piece the attention it deserves."

***Special Note About Alice Furrey:

As Alice and I concluded her contribution to this chapter, her husband wrote to tell me she had passed away. "Alice remained active in her quilting business until close to the end" says her husband, Harley Furrey. "I knew Alice was recognized nationally for her quilting achievements, but I did not have any idea how many lives she had touched until after her death. The National Machine Quilters showcase, held June 9 through 11, 1999 in

Springfield, IL featured her work as a tribute. The South Dakota State Quilter's Convention that year also dedicated the event to her memory."

Susan Nixon works full-time as a teacher so her machine-quilting business remains part-time. During the school year, she works three evenings each week and all day on two Saturdays per month. Summers, she quilts four days per week for others and reserves one day a week for herself.

Susan explains her business this way. "The nature of my machine quilting business is that I spend almost all my time providing quilting services for clients and almost none making things for myself or to sell," she says. Susan purchases batting directly from a manufacturer plus an occasional bolt of fabric, but buys thread from a distributor. She emphasizes that she always tries to set a fair price for her service.

While she does not offer discounts, she has at times, bartered. Says Susan, "I researched pricing before I began and set my prices at a point that seemed high to me but now are my norm. I haven't needed to raise or lower them. Machine quilters charge varying rates, depending on the type of quilting they do. I only do one type so it made sense to charge a flat rate including thread and batting. My rate takes into account the complexity of design, the time involved, and the supplies I use."

Overhead for Susan included electricity, phone, depreciation of the machine, insurance, advertising including e-mail and Website maintenance. She calculates all of this on a yearly basis. Susan's clients from Internet contacts and word-of-mouth so she does not need flyers or brochures.

Price setting began in earnest when Susan built the room which houses her machine. "I divided that total by the depreciation period, then by twelve months, decided on the number of quilts I could reasonably do in a month, and divided the monthly total expenses by the same number to arrive at the amount I needed to receive from each quilt to pay the overhead."

Susan adds, "As a teacher, I earned more hourly than I charged as a quilter. I decided to charge for my time machine quilting as I do when I teach a quilting class—$15 per hour. If I were to sell quilts I make, others might not find them affordable. If I piece and quilt a queen-sized Ohio Star Quilt, for example, I would charge $700 using my present pricing system. This includes elaborate quilting, such as feathered circles in the middle of the stars."

Quilt restoration is only a part of **Nancy and Bill Kirk's** business, *The Kirk Collection*. Nancy and Bill sell antique fabric, antique quilts and offer quality reproduction fabric and conservation and restoration supplies. Both Kirks work actively for the Quilt Heritage Foundation, the umbrella organization for the *Quilt Restoration Conference* and *The Crazy Quilt Society*. Nancy and Bill Kirk began their business in 1987. They work full-time and hire two full-time employees one part-timer who works from her home in Denver. "We think of her as our first virtual employee since our shop opened," smiles Nancy.

"Ours is a multifaceted business," Nancy explains. "I am developing a wholesale product line, based on plans to manufacture *Taking Care of Grandma's Quilt,* and packaging Grandma Kirk's Charm Squares and Grandpa Kirk's Feed-sack Charm Squares. I rarely do restoration myself any more except for very tricky ones and occasionally will repair a quilt for sale."

Nancy continues. "We sell both retail and some wholesale and for our antique fabrics we give a modest wholesale discount. We also are dealers for Light Impressions offering acid free tissue and boxes selling at wholesale to retail stores."

The Kirks buy antique quilts and fabrics from individuals, dealers, auctions and estate sales, and have "pickers" around the country who send them fabric. They buy notions through catalogs and insist on natural fiber batting such as cotton and silk.

Nancy is not herself a quilter. She began repairing quilts as soon as she and her husband started dealing in quilts. Five years later, they opened a shop and people began to bring them quilts and other textiles in need of repair. "We didn't have a lot of business in the shop in the beginning," says Nancy, "so I began doing repairs because I had the time and needed the money. Now, I no longer have time, but I teach restoration and have an employee who does restoration for others on a freelance basis. However, I supervise all restoration we do in the shop and occasionally will repair a quilt for sale," she says.

"Today, we raise prices to cover higher costs, but we generally do an across-the-board increase with every new catalog," Nancy explains. "We may repackage goods slightly so we don't have a direct package per-dollar comparison. For example, our feed-sack charm fabric used to sell at 25 squares for $10. When we repackaged them, we sold them at 30 squares for $15. We double our costs on new items when customers can reorder and triple the price on antique items we sell costing less than $200. On antique quilts priced over $200 we generally double, unless we have an immediate market and can sell it within 24 hours. In that case we may mark up to $100 and turn it quickly."

Nancy considers labor as she sets prices. If new items require preparation and restoration, she adds the cost to the final price. For restoration only, the Kirks charge for labor plus materials. They try to give a low and a high estimate on labor but if they exceed the high estimate, they prefer to absorb the loss unless they can renegotiate during the process. Nancy explains that for restoration, she determines labor as time spent. Currently, the Kirks charge $20 per hour for most work and $25 per hour for complex embroidery restoration worked on Victorian Crazy Quilts.

"Restoration labor costs," explains Nancy, "run $12.50 per hour. Most professional restorers we know charge $10 to $25 per hour but many of us quote specific prices for certain repairs so we may say to a client, 'that is a $20 hole!' Pricing patterns and kits, I look at design and production time amortized over 200 copies plus actual production costs plus marketing, then make sure it fits with what the market will bear.

Lowering restoration prices is not something the Kirks do. They prefer to turn business away if customers feel unwilling to pay. "We simply cannot afford to do unprofitable work" Nancy explains. Selling antique fabrics, however, is another matter. The Kirks continually raise prices to reflect increased costs as old fabrics become more scarce, yet more desirable.

"A wonderful business advisor we hired in the beginning taught us about raising prices says Nancy. "First, he told us to raise our prices. He checked back in three months to see if we were losing any sales because of it. We said 'no' so he suggested we raise them again. Before he started advising us, we were not making a profit from the business. Today we support ourselves and two employees."

Internet selling has been successful for The Kirk Collection. It generates both direct sales and catalog requests, increasing international business. Online quilt news groups keeps the Kirks informed about the online quilting community.

Nancy feels strongly about her pet peeve—"If you work only to support a quilting habit, that's fine. But please consider those who must earn a living before you set your prices unrealistically low. You may make it difficult for a mother to get a fair price for her work who needs to feed her children."

Marilyn Maddalena, began appraising quilts in 1997 after a lifelong love affair with sewing and quilts. Working as an appraiser, her working time requires continual research of quilt patterns and styles and older fabrics. In addition to a huge quilt library, Marilyn uses Electric Quilt 3 and BlockBase on her computer as references sources.

Certified quilt appraisers generally charge $35 per quilt, according to Marilyn's research based on competitors' prices. She bases her fee entirely on labor explaining that it takes at least thirty minutes to appraise a quilt. Marilyn prefers to do her appraisals in shops, museums, or the owner's home, though she offers her own home for those who find it more convenient.

Marilyn's long suit is her expertise at efficient networking. Quilting shows and guild meetings are a natural place for her to inform quilters of her appraisal services. She relies on word of mouth and friends, her best advertisers, whom she keeps amply supplied with business cards and brochures. She belongs to several quilt-related associations and is listed on the Internet on Quilter's Resources and Quiltwoman.com. She maintains her own website and treasures her excellent relationships with quilt shops in the area in which she lives. She frequently holds "appraisal days" at the shops where a portion of her appraisal fee goes to the shop owners, who in turn advertise her appraisal days in their newsletters. Through another contact, she works with a local museum to appraise quilts and assist at annual antique quilt shows. Marilyn volunteers her time and appraisal services for certain community service projects.

"I find that when I tell folks informally that I am a quilt appraiser, new clients come out of the woodwork," says Marilyn. "I attended a quilt show in a small mountain town, for example. While there, I went shopping and overheard ladies in the shop talking about the wonderful quilt show in town. One mentioned she had just inherited fifty quilts from her mother. After chatting with her a little, it became obvious she didn't know what treasures she had. I advised her to have them appraised and to insure them, but she replied she did not know how or where to find an appraiser. I handed her my business card and eventually appraised her entire collection. You never know where contacts will lead you," she declares.

Marilyn explains the education necessary for appraising quilts and admits it is extensive and expensive. "I studied for three days in Paducah, KY, (home of the American Quilter's Society), took several evening classes in addition to taking classes from Barbara Brackman and other historians. I read every quilt magazine and book I can find to keep up on new fabrics, techniques and older quilts. I believe the more knowledge an appraiser has of the current market in addition to antique quilts and fabrics, the better appraiser she will become."

Tapping into the Internet regularly keeps Marilyn informed on quilt values. Marilyn simply checks on current, online auction prices. She subscribes to antique newsletters and follows quilt values in antique shops and flea markets. "When I see a quilt anywhere, I make sure I get the asking price," she says.

Marilyn describes the work of a quilt appraiser. "When I appraise a quilt, I do a full and complete appraisal which includes measurement, determination of provenance where possible, and provide a complete written description of the quilt and its condition. I take a Polaroid photo which I give to the owner with the written appraisal. I keep a copy of the appraisal and a photo for my records. I take books on the care of fabrics with me and let the owner browse through them while I appraise the quilt. Sometimes I use a scribe and sometimes I do the writing myself. I have prepared a written handout on the care of quilts, which I give to all my appraisal clients. I want to become as knowledgeable about every phrase of quilting as possible, and spend time everyday reading about them and working on my own quilts."

In Depth Interview: Linda and Dean Moran

Linda and Dean Moran, owners of *Marble-T Design* perfected their marbling skills in 1990 and entered the professional market in 1995. Since the demand for marbled fabric has increased, *Marble-T Design* has become a full-time business for both Linda and her husband, Dean.

Please describe your product.

"There is something intriguing about marbling fabric. Though centuries old, it remains an art infinite in colors and patterns," says Linda. "We began marbling as a hobby trying to create a special fabric for a quilt. We were hooked when we watched the paint and colors spread across the surface of the liquid bath. Running combs through it, creating our first pattern made us realize there was no stopping us. We also learned why beautiful fabrics can be so expensive."

"Buying marbled fabric can become addicting" declares Linda. "Just ask customers who buy it monthly and fondle it in shops. Their beauty intimidates many people who just cannot bring themselves to cut it. Some buyers say they plan to save it for something special. We reply that we will make more!"

How much time do you devote to your business?

"Both of us work in the business now that demand for fabric has increased as have our outlets and clients. When we began, we lived in apartments which limited the size of fabric pieces we could marble. When we moved into a house, we had a customized tray built as well as a set tub for rinsing enabling us to work on larger sections of fabric. Both of us marble up to three days a week."

Dean works business full-time handling the fabric production, shipping orders and doing all the follow-up tasks including bookkeeping. Linda has a full-time job running a nonprofit learning center which provides scheduling flexibility to work from home three days per week. She maintains their website and creates new patterns and marbling samples. When Linda is teaching, Dean contacts clients, and prepares and wraps products. Linda works a minimum of ten hours per month maintaining their Website and squeezing in time to produce wearables, turning them into patterns plus creating quilt-tops to showcase their fabric.

Of the time you spend on your business, how much do you devote producing something to sell?

Linda replies, "We need two to three full days to produce our marbled fabric. We use the remaining time to maintain the business aspects of *Marble T Designs*."

Do you sell both retail and wholesale or just directly to the ultimate consumer?

"We began as a retail business with a few outlets but today our business is registered as a wholesale business manufacturing a fabric product."

Where do you purchase supplies?

"Dharma catalog provides dyes and basic marbling supplies. We buy fabric from shops only when we find it on sale. Our wholesaler's permit allows us to save sales taxes but we have worked with one store so long that in addition to selling our finished fabric, they offer us discounted fabrics."

Do you ever buy raw materials on-sale or wholesale?

"When we buy raw materials, such as trims for clothing samples, we try to buy on sale. Now that our company has grown, we arranged with a shop nearby to buy fabric at wholesale, one bolt at a time. We anticipate buying more fabric in bulk by the end of the year and look forward to finding a wholesale source for paint."

How long had you been crafting before you began to sell what you made?

Marbling, like quilting requires you to maintain high quality skills. We have improved over the last two years but it took us five years to reach our present level of expertise and to define our niche in the marketplace. We initially planned to sell only to quilters which limited our marbling to cotton fabric. Now, we have reached a wider audience and marble upscale fibers too."

Have you ever lowered prices because you found they were too high?

"Dealing with quilt shops we reduced our prices before learning that shop owners were not the only place to sell. Since we expanded our market to include Website customers, we have become comfortable with our prices and do not plan to lower them. We price above wholesale on our Website using a pricing structure that allows us to run sales on a regular basis."

Have you ever raised your prices? Why?

"Yes. As we refined our marketing strategies, we began to consider higher-end markets raising prices to accommodate the incredible amount of labor involved in producing marbled fabric."

Do you have a system for pricing your items? Please describe.

"First, we determined the basic cost in producing a piece of marbled fabric. This includes paint, carrageenan, alum, distilled water, trays, pretreating, heat setting and cutting. This list helped us determine a base price for the fabric itself.

Next, we set a range for marbling depending on the type of fabric used. After that, we chose a range of prices depending on our market. Framed corporate art will sell from $75 to $700 depending on its size, framing and embellishments. Fabric for clothing designers will run from $9.00 to $30.00 per yard depending on the amount needed and the pretreating we do such as serging certain fabric edges to keep them from raveling as an example. Later set prices for fabric already purchased by someone else and given to us for marbling causing us to make clear-cut decisions about actual marbling costs."

Do you consider labor when you set your prices?

"This is a difficult question since labor is the primary element of our process. We hope to move into a regular studio which may cut our labor in half because we will be able to leave all materials and equipment set up permanently. The process of marbling begins 24 hours before actually marbling the fabric. Preparing, cutting, washing and ironing the fabric comes first. Next, we must begin the alum process and make the marbling bath. All this takes place in our garage so we must set up and clean afterward to get our cars back in their home. However, we have refined some of our processes, developed a packaging system, created forms, etc."

Do you consider raw materials when you set your prices?

Yes, fabric price determines our base price. Five pounds of carrageenan costs more than $100 so we must know how much fabric we can marble with that amount of carrageenan.

We looked at other choices to use as a marbling base but most contain Methyl Cellulose which requires good ventilation. We stay with Carrageenan because it is made from seaweed and is environmentally safe, natural and found in many foods as a preservative."

How do you determine overhead?

"When we worked from home we only considered increased water and utilities as overhead. But, when we move to our studio attached to our home, this will change. If we look at studio space that is not a part of our home, we will find other artists to form a co-op where we can share space, utilities and cost."

How do you determine profit?

"For now, we mark up everything we sell at least 100% to compensate for our labor.

Where do you sell?

"We decided not to sell at craft shows requiring too much money up front without a guarantee of return. Establishing a reputation for fine-art fabrics and the financial return we need for labor makes us choose our venues carefully. We do not consider our product as "craft" but as "art" so general craft shows would not portray the image we wish to project."

"Quilt shows present a dichotomy for us. Shop owners see our fabric and say they don't like the colors and don't feel their customers would buy. On the other hand, quilters themselves buy on impulse when they see our fabric so we wish to remain visible to sewers as well as quilters."

"Retail shops and boutiques have become one of our key markets making us also consider the upscale fashion market for our marbled scarves, our most popular item. Selling by consignment means we must make sure of our wholesale cost so we can set the ultimate selling price allowing for the percentage taken by the shop."

"One of the interesting issues to us is that people see marbled fabrics differently," says Linda. "They may love them but don't know what to do with them. Think of marbled fabric as you do about any fabric to use for wearables, craft projects, table runners, jewelry and wall-hangings—and yes, we do have pieces so beautiful that we can't bear to cut into them so we frame them instead."

QUICK REVIEW OF PRICING METHODS IN THIS CHAPTER:

X   Professional machine quilters charge for their services differently. Some charge by the hour, the square yard, the square inch or by the overall size of the quilt. Some even charge by the bobbin of thread used to quilt the item.

X   Provide updated price sheets every six months advising customers of higher prices for machine quilting. If you find you underpriced yourself, you have six months to find a more equitable price for your services.

X   Consider charging a flat fee based upon the sheets of paper in a pattern package. $10 per package for five sheets can include postage.

X   You can total raw materials, labor and overhead then multiply by six to determine your retail price and by five to set wholesale and distributor prices.

X   Calculate how much fabric you can dye in an hour. Divide the total into the amount you need to earn per hour and add this amount to other expenses to arrive at a final price.

X   When you quilt for others, add the cost of materials, (including thread and pattern) and prorate the following: insurance, advertising, correspondence, phone calls, packaging &

miscellaneous expenses. Figure these by the year and divide by the number of quilts you reasonably expect to complete.

X   Determine how many hours you spend quilting for others, based on an hourly rate. Include record keeping and paperwork. Make sure the resulting sum is one the market will bear for comparable work. This total becomes your wholesale price to sell outright to a shop, but add 30% if you quilt on consignment which will cover your fee to the shop-owner.

X   Take into account the complexity of design, time involved and supplies used when setting a fee. Add overhead costs such as electricity, phone, depreciation of equipment, insurance, advertising including e-mail and Website maintenance on a yearly basis.

X   Charge $20 per hour for restoration or finishing work and $25 per hour for complex projects.

X   Unsure what to charge when you begin quilting for others? Raise your price just a bit. Check in three months to see if you are losing money. If not, raise your price again to find the final ceiling guaranteeing a profit.

X   Check current, online auction prices for quilts. Subscribe to newsletters and follow quilt values in antique shops and flea markets. Make sure when you see any quilt for sale, to get the asking price to remain in touch with the market.

X   Determine basic costs to produce marbled fabric including paint, carrageenan, alum, distilled water, trays, pre-treating, heat setting and cutting. This helps you determine a base price for the fabric itself. Next, set a range for your marbling labor depending on the type of fabric used. Make sure your price remain in line with current market prices.

CONTRIBUTORS TO THIS CHAPTER

Cliff & Patsy Monk
Monk Ink
3622 US Highway 301
Ellenton, FL 34222
Phone 941-721-9438
Fax: 721-9415-fax
E-mail: pcmonk@get.net
http://www.monkink.com

Monica Norvini
24111 Olivera Drive
Mission Viejo, CA 92691
Phone: 714-951-4730
E-mail: mnovini@webworldinc.com
Website: http://www.webworldinc.com/perfectsquare

Kelly Baird
9658 Plano Rd
Dallas, TX 75238
Phone: 214-343-1440
Toll Free: 1-888-494-0291
Fax: 214-343-2223
E-mail: KBaird4939@aol.com

Emma Graham
The Crowning Touch
3859 South Stage Road
Medford, OR 97501
Phone: 800-729-0280
Fax: 541-772-5106

Marjorie Lee Bevis
Marbled Fabric and Accessories
325 4th St.
Petaluma, CA 94952
Phone: 707-762-2548
E-mail: MARBLEFAB@aol.com

Alice Furrey
Star Struck Quilting
Rural Route 3 Box 101
Carter, SD 57526
E-mail: starstruck@gwtc.net

Susan Nixon
Desertsky Machine Quilting
10445 W. Flower
Avondale, AZ 85323-4403
Phone: (623)877-3127
E-mail: Desertsky@arizonaone.com

Marilyn Maddalena
Quilt Appraiser and Judge
1435 Oak Nob Way
Sacramento, CA 95833
Phone:(916) 921-9632
E-mail: marilynquilts@jps.net
http://www.jps.net/marilynquilt

Nancy Kirk
The Kirk Collection
1513 Military Avenue
Omaha, NE 68111-3924
Phone: 402-551-0386 or 1-800-960-8335
Fax: 402 551-0971_
E-mail: KirkColl@aol.com
Website: http://www.auntie.com/kirk

Linda and Dean Moran
Marble-T Design
3391 South Nastar Dr.
Tucson, AZ 85730
Phone: 520-571-8397
Fax: 520-571-7578
E-mail: marble@marbledfab.com
Website http://www.marbledfab.com

Chapter 5

Pattern Designers

Pricing Template: Lori Nixon
In-depth interview: Jo & Jos Hindriks

Quilting Today is BIG Business! Producing patterns for other quilters is becoming an even greater business. Travel to Houston in the Fall each year and you will find out what I mean. *The International Quilt Market,* is the largest trade show in the world for the quilting industry. Shop owners, teachers, writers, designers and manufacturers come from all over the world to buy from more than 550 merchant booths in the 250,000 square foot exhibit hall at the George R. Brown Convention Center each Fall. Quilters, demanding more tools, books and especially patterns have created a spin-off industry to meet their demand. Quilt addicts cannot seem to own enough quilting patterns which is why those who make patterns have a chapter to themselves.

      *   *   *

Lori Nixon, *Northern Star Co,* produces what is known in the quilting industry as "Paper Piecing Patterns." These special pattern sheets enable quilters to piece and sew intricate designs by sewing directly through printed paper bearing complex shapes and guiding numbers to facilitate sewing small shapes that would harder to sew with fabric only. Lori shares her Pricing Template for pricing 1000 of her 17"x22" paper pattern sheets printed:

Total Printing Costs: $352 per 1,000
Shipping and Handling 11.30
Total $371.30. $371.30 divided by 1000 sheets = 0.3713 or .37 cents per sheet

"I figure per item cost for each component of packaged patterns the same way" says Lori. "I total printing costs plus shipping and handling and divide by the total number of items in each different pattern I produce. Here is a sample."

Foundation Sheet	.37 cents each
Cover Sheet	.07
Photo	.30
Pattern Bag	.03
Insert / Instruction	.00
Total	.77 cost per pattern

Lori sells her patterns both at wholesale to distributors and to consumers at retail and explains how she arrives at her prices. "Since wholesale and distributors figure their cost on your suggested retail price, I must know what discounts wholesalers and distributors expect before I set a retail price for each pattern. Wholesalers expect a 50% discount from the retail price when they buy a minimum number of patterns. Distributors expect to pay more than required by wholesalers. They pay 70% less than retail so this means I must work backward and must at least double my cost of the pattern (if not three times the cost) when selling to distributors."

Lori continues, "For example, if I sell a pattern retailing for $6, I sell it to wholesalers for $3 and to distributors for $2.10. My original cost per pattern, is 77 cents. Selling to distributors for $2.10 means I've at least doubled my cost and almost tripled it. I compare $2.10 with my cost per pattern (.77) and ask myself if this is a sufficient profit. If 'yes', it becomes my suggested retail price. If 'no', I start the math again working with a higher retail price. I try to keep my pattern prices set at $6 or $6.75 depending on how many foundation sheets and instruction sheets a particular pattern requires," explains Lori.

*   *   *

Before continuing with more pricing ideas from pattern designers in this book, I want to share with you the concerns of well-known and respected shop-owner, **Trudie Hughes** who buys many patterns for her shop. She feels dismayed with the quality of a few patterns received in her shop. "I am upset" declares Trudie. "Recently, I picked up new pattern companies to sell in my shop and have been making models according to the pattern-maker's directions. It amazes me how much new home-grown pattern companies want for their patterns. Yet, when I read and follow the directions, I am appalled with the inaccuracy of most of these patterns which are not typeset, properly illustrated and most of all—a rip-off to my customers," she declares.

"For example, I made up a paper piecing design that appeared very attractive in the photograph, but the numbers were not in proper sequence and some were missing altogether" Trudie explains. "Though the pattern was printed in color on light weight paper, usually an advantage, a customer could only use this design one time as the layout sheet had to be cut up to make the pattern. The price?—$12 dollars for a tiny design. Yet another pattern company sent an attractive brochure requesting $35 for shipping. We ship every day and know that 48 patterns do not cost that much to ship. This new pattern company does not have a distributor so if we want their patterns, we must pay their inflated, over priced cost of $20. For that price, we prefer to sell a book that looks more professional. Where do these unprofessional people come from?"

*   *   *

Nancy Roberts, contributing editor for Chitra Publications, freelance writer and pattern editor has been quilting since 1980, and editing since 1990, Nancy adds comments about pattern designers. "Like Trudie, I believe that quilters who purchase patterns deserve quality written instructions and clear diagrams and have said so in my series of articles, "Pointers for Pattern Writers" published in *Professional Quilter Magazine*. Often, when new designers tell others how to make a quilt, they overlook important details known only to them. Since most pattern buyers read patterns literally, pattern writers must put a pattern together with care. I can ask questions of the writer that she or he may not have considered when I edit. Another pair of eyes helps when preparing a pattern for publication."

Nancy continues her professional advice to pattern designers/writers. "While pricing quilt patterns is important, high quality standards so are directions and diagrams. Providing buyers with clear, step-by-step instructions ensures success by encouraging repeat customers. Patterns should be written so novices can use them. Test your patterns in classes or among quilting friends. Make your instructions complete and accurate. Have your pattern reviewed or edited prior to publication to identify areas that need clarification. Taking these steps will help satisfy buyers that your pattern is worth the price they pay."

*   *   *

Judy Garden started her pattern design company in 1996. "I researched patterns on the market to learn how to price my patterns. Average patterns cost $7.99 for quilted wall hangings or simple quilts so I price my patterns competitively. Today, patterns cost from $9.99 to $14.99. I am concerned about poorly written patterns. From personal experience, I believe quality control should be the pattern writer's major concern. I have a kind friend who edits my patterns. She's meticulous and so detailed, she even tells me when I should capitalize a word. Believe me, she is so careful that I know when she's read my pattern, it will work!" says Judy.

"Pattern writing is time consuming" Judy acknowledges, "But when I look at a quilt that someone made using one of my patterns, I get a great feeling but I still must cover production expenses and earn a profit for my work"

Judy Garden closes with her advice to new pattern writers. "Designers should not demand high prices for a simple applique block containing only a 6x8 inch piece of muslin. Perhaps quilt store owners should refuse those over priced patterns and let pattern producers know that their patens are too expensive."

*   *   *

Beth Wheeler, produces patterns for both quilting and sewing. Below, Beth's Pricing Template:

The example below is a pattern in a 6"x9" Polybag pattern with color photos on the front plus three pages of instructions, actual size patterns and diagrams inside.

Creation

Design (½ hour @ $20)	$ 10.00
Construction (8 hours @ $10)	80.00
Materials	20.00
Marketing	20.00
Photography	20.00
Film	5.00
Developing	5.00

100 copies of photo	15.00
Trim photos (½ hr @ $10)	5.00
Glue (100)	3.00
Assemble (100)	5.00
Stuff bags (100)	3.00
Polybag (100)	4.20
Printing (400 pages)	20.00
Folding (400 pages)	12.00
Instructions (and diagrams)	120.00
Total for first 100 patterns:	$347.20

Reorder (in 100s)

Photos	$ 15.00
Trim	5.00
Glue	3.00
Assemble	5.00
Stuff bags	3.00
Polybag	4.20
Printing	20.00
Folding	12.00
Total for each 100 after first 100: $ 67.20 = .67 each	

Break Even Point

Distributor price	$2.61	134 copies
Wholesale price	$3.48	100 copies
Retail price	$6.95	50 copies

Beth concludes her Pricing Template saying, "My pattern division sells patterns at $4.95, $5.95, and $6.95, depending on complexity and number of pattern pieces."

*   *   *

Ann Anderson designs, sells and distributes patterns from her e-commerce Website. She says, "I understand that shops always mark up a pattern100%, so if it costs $8.00, the shop buys it for $4.00. The remaining $4 is split 30%/70% with $1.20 to the distributor leaving the designer with $2.80 from an $8.00 pattern. Covers need color which is costly. For 1, 000, 8½" x 11" color pages cost about $500. Black and white pattern pages cost about 5-7 cents per sheet. Plastic hanging bags cost 5-6 cents. If a pattern contains 10 sheets, the total cost to produce the pattern ranges from .80 to $1.00," Ann explains.

"Next, consider the labor to assemble patterns including all the final printing arrangements," she says. "Most designers use a computer and graphics software costing as much as $700 plus expensive computers and color printers. Pattern designers must amortize all these costs and consider design time, testing time for making one or more samples, then the cost to hire someone to proof the pattern."

Another question Ann asks is this: "How does a person determine the value of the intellectual content? From my experience, I know it takes a long time to work out a design then write the pattern. It is tedious work with much rechecking of figures and measurements." She reminds readers to consider the amortized cost of equipment, office costs, communications, advertising, show costs, and unsold inventory. "Designers must sell a large number of copies of each pattern seeing much profit," says Ann. She is sympathetic to independent designers and charges less than 30% charged by other distributors. E-commerce makes this possible for her.

Today Ann combines her love of making quilts with her knowledge of the Internet, computers, sales and marketing. Ann explains her pricing ideas. "I design and make specialized fabric patterns based on a photo transfer process. I price the pattern based on complexity, the total number of pages, production costs and the time required to create the pattern. I check my costs against 50% of the potential list price. If sufficient margin remains, I go forward. If I find I cannot make any money on a product, I don't make it."

Ann produces a special Photo transfer preprinted paper pattern of the well-known design, "Sun Bonnet Sue." She says, "There's not much competition for this product but the process of making it is expensive. In this case, I take my cost, mark up 50% and take total costs of $8 for materials only. I charge $12 to shops who mark it up to $24."

Ann, has developed more uses for her Internet Website offering much more than patterns. She took her first quilting class in 1976 and adds, "When I left graduate school, I thought of starting a quilt business and made many sample pillows but did not believe I could not make a living doing this so I went to work in the computer industry —selling and marketing. Quilting rested in my life for ten years, then I lost my job. Again, I took up quilting but this time I persevered."

Ann worked in the computer industry for another ten years but kept quilting. Today, her quilting venture differs from most; she wants to become all things to all quilters and is doing so. She explains, "I began thinking that many quilters have patterns and ideas not presently being marketed. I decided to provide a place where they could earn money doing what they love if I combined my 22-year love affair with quilting with my 33 years of sales and marketing experience with computers. *QuiltWoman* was born." Only Ann can describe *Quilt Woman.* "*Quilt Woman* has several functions," she explains:

1   "*QuiltWoman,* an online, e-commerce site permits shop owners and individuals to purchase quiltmaking products. We list all shops that carry our designers' products on *QuiltWoman.*

2   *Quilt Woman* provides services and information to the entire quilting community. We serve quilters, shop owners, designers, guilds, teachers, judges, appraisers and quilt-tour operators.

3   Quilters find free patterns on the site.

4   *QuiltWoman* permits teachers, appraisers, judges, quilt shops and guilds to create their own pages by simply entering their information into my online form.

5   Search engines allow anyone to find shops, guilds, teachers, judges and appraisers.

6   We feature a gallery for those who want to look at or exhibit quilts.

7   Soon, I will include information about publications, shows, trip/tour information, workshops." Is there a doubt that Ann Anderson is a new-age entrepreneur in a traditional industry?

*   *   *

Jo Morton of *Prairie Hands Patterns in Nebraska,* shares her thoughts about minimum costs and shipping charges for patterns. "I have patterns handled by distributors, but after four years of adding new patterns, found some shops do not carry my full line so I decided to implement changes with the shop-owner in mind. After a shop opens an account with me (a total of 12 patterns in multiples of 3) I no longer require minimums on reorders and I do not charge for shipping. My minimum order is only 9 patterns," Jo explains.

"I do not charge for shipping so that I do not have to give the distributor a discount, and that amount more than covers shipping charges," she adds. "If I were a shop owner, I would appreciate such cooperation. I considered both sides carefully before implementing this policy and it has worked out very well—a win-win situation. We are all partners in this wonderful industry. My policy has not slowed distributor pattern orders. They keep growing."

*　　　　　　　*　　　　　　　*

Patricia Hammond of *Hearthstone Designs* owns a successful appliqué pattern business. In business for three years, her patterns have appeared in *The Keepsake Quilting Catalog* managed by two large national distributing companies. "If a pattern costs me $1.00 to print, I usually retail that pattern for $7.00," says Patricia. Local shops purchase patterns at an industry standard of 50% of retail or $3.50 per pattern. I must wholesale my patterns to distributors for retail less 50% plus an additional 30%—a net cost of $2.45. (Refer to Lori Nixon's explanation of this system at the start of this chapter.) Most distributors do not pay additional freight/shipping charges so that comes from my profit. To attend quilt markets, distributors suggest you send actual models of new or existing patterns. The cost to the designer ranges from $50-$100 per sample plus shipping and insurance to and from distributors. Most also demand that each pattern-maker send additional cover sheets for each new pattern for each representative they employ. Often, this amounts to 30-40 cover sheets with photos for each pattern. I must sell several hundred patterns of each design before I show a profit! Remember, if you have several distributors, they may each have three dozen of each of your patterns sitting in a warehouse. That means I have thousands of dollars in inventory all over the country waiting to be sold," she explains.

"Raw materials for me include, paper, ink, photos, plastic bags, copies of pages and glue sticks to attach the photos, etc.," she adds. From this amount, I make my pricing decisions. The pattern designer has a responsibility to find the best deals, so that they can offer the consumer a quality product at a fair price. Overhead for my business is fairly small as I keep printing and packaging of the patterns in-house with my husband and family pitching in," she adds. "I do my own bookkeeping, arrange my own travel (the Internet makes it easy to book airline flights) and deal directly with my clients. I have an answering/fax machine in my office, use e-mail and maintain my web page," she says.

"Most representatives can't sell for too many pattern companies at one time," Patricia adds, "You hope they like your designs and will try to show your cover sheets and promote your designs." Presently, Patricia is considering whether she herself should go to all the markets and sell directly to shop owners, eliminating the middleman distributor.

Patricia shares her positive experiences in this arena so far. "I have been fortunate to vend at many national quilt shows. Even with booth fees, travel and hotel costs, I make a good profit selling my designs this way. Quilt shows also lead to guild lecture/workshop contracts and more vending opportunities. Quilters love to speak with designers personally at shows and want to see demonstrations of techniques the artist uses to create her designs. Stitching on small projects while in my booth keeps it crowded all day. Visitors to my booth often buy additional patterns from me via mail order or when I visit their guild. Marketing myself results in more customer knowledge, overall profit and satisfaction that my designs please others. Small business owners like me appreciate every little pat on the back to keep going."

Patricia offers advice to new pattern designers. "Plan, research and price it right the first time and you won't have to make changes later. I researched the cost of other patterns of projects the same size as mine and estimated what printing and packaging costs would be if I printed in volume. Today, I receive the best printing prices and only print three to four times each year. Bringing large, regular business to my printer keeps my design costs down. I took the time to form a good relationship with a small local printing company as some will not work with a one-person business. Research local printers until you find better pricing. My patterns would have to cost $10 each rather than $7 had my local printer not been so accommodating."

*　　　　　*　　　　　*

Barbara Vlack, quilt teacher, designer, lecturer and author, continues the topic about patterns and those who design them. "Patricia's excellent explanation of what it takes to produce and distribute a pattern couldn't be said better. It takes lots of time and money on the production end. Many pattern designers I know are not themselves, publishers or distributors thereby earning the least percentage of a pattern's retail price. Pattern publishers, wholesalers and retailers make the most per pattern—more than designers who receive only royalties though they too have overhead and other costs," she explains.

"When we buy shops or produce patterns, we cross the line from quiltmaking as a hobby to a professional level. Demand for our services exists and we should all earn a fair price," says Barb. "Quilting would not be the big business it is today if we all did all we do just because we love quilting. The industry has grown because it can support people who choose it as a profession teaching, designing and producing quilt goods and tools."

Barb asks, "What is fair compensation, minus production costs, to a designer for the anticipated sale of 500 patterns, which have a successful run?" Don't think of the cost of a pattern with the idea that it took 10 cents per page to copy. After all, calico used to sell for 50 cents per yard and dress patterns cost 35 cents. We must advance our thinking in today's market terms."

*   *   *

Nancy Restuccia explains, "When I determine a price for my books and patterns, I start with two estimates. I figure the first in the usual manner. I add up the costs and profit and divide by the number of units. The second method I derive from competitive products that sell well. The first number reflects internal factors; the second is an external reality-check of what the market will bear. If the two figures are close, I feel confident that I've got a fair price even though I may tweak it a bit to convey a particular image. However, if I find the two estimates significantly different, I look closely at my product and pricing equation," Nancy says.

Nancy explains. "If I find a competitor's price higher than my cost-based estimate, I question why I can sell this product for much less than anyone else. Did I select competitors who are truly comparable, or missed something essential that they offer and I do not? For example, if I'm selling a foundation-piecing pattern, perhaps the competitive products include several dozen printed foundations while mine contains a single master pattern that consumers must photocopy. Perhaps the differential means I've forgotten something in calculating costs, such as professional photography, advertising, overhead, including computer software, bank charges, credit-card fees, Website host fees or even profit. Perhaps I overlooked that distributors will demand an additional 30% discount off my wholesale price," she acknowledges.

Nancy offers her advice to those just starting. "Calculate costs based on quantity pricing even if you aren't big enough to sell in quantity yet. This will help you to sell competitively" says Nancy. "I published my first pattern and based my pricing on costs for 10,000 patterns, even though I initially produced only 1,000. When I saw that the product would be successful, I published the larger quantity. Had I based my pricing on costs on a smaller quantity, it may have been perceived as overpriced," she concludes.

Nancy suggests that pattern makers examine their product value. "If cost-based estimates seem high, perhaps I'm including something that my competitors are not. In one of my patterns, I give consumers four designs, full-size quilting patterns, start-to-finish instructions and professional illustrations. My competitors' patterns generally offer only one design, a block pattern and piecing instructions. Thus, my product has a higher value than competitive products justifying my slightly higher price and I make sure my customers perceive the added value.

In the final analysis," Nancy adds, "Sales occur when the value meets or exceeds the price you ask. To make a sale, you must communicate the value your product delivers."

*   *   *

Readers met **Elsie Vredenburg** in Chapter 2. Here she explains her latest venture, pattern making. "I felt fortunate in the early stages of considering whether or not I should produce my own patterns," says Elsie. "A small group of quilting professionals on an online quilt group shared their system with me helping me learn to figure production costs, designing time, making pattern models and packaging the patterns themselves."

"First, I divide my costs by the number of patterns I plan to produce, 1000 for example. Next, I multiply the per pattern cost by 10 to arrive at the retail price. Yes, I said TEN. This may sound high, but by the time you realize that you may sell a large quantity of patterns at distributor prices, you still need to make a profit. In reality, only a small number of patterns will probably be sold directly by the designer at retail prices. Most will be wholesaled to shops at 50%."

Elsie sold quilts at craft shows for ten years before selling patterns to retail shops. She no longer vends at quilt shows as she has tired of hauling booth supplies. Today she has an agreement with a shop-owner to take her patterns as part of their setup at shows. Elsie provides the patterns on consignment and the shop-owner pays her for what they sell and return the remaining patterns after the show.

"Early in early 1995, I designed a pattern for a wall hanging featuring a lighthouse," Elsie explains. *Keepsake Quilting* included it in their catalog which validated my work and gave me nationwide exposure. I now have seven lighthouse patterns on the market. Here is my Pricing Template for patterns."

Retail Price:

Wholesale = 50% of retail, minimum: 3 of one title

Distributor = 20% off wholesale, minimum 3 dozen of one title, up to 7 dozen

30% off wholesale, more than 7 dozen of one title.

I pay shipping on orders of 12 dozen or more."

Elsie continues. "When I designed my first patterns, I thought I would only sell them when teaching. I did not expect that my pattern business would take over my whole life. I still sell a few quilts but want to decrease the number of hours a day I spend hand-quilting. After 20 years, my body is feeling the effects of sedentary work and I need to make lifestyle changes. I plan to continue teaching and will keep on designing new patterns as long as they sell well."

*　　　　　　　*　　　　　　　*

Barbara Seidlecki of Cabin Fever Crafts, whom you met in Chapter 2, adds her comments about designing patterns. Today, most of the distributors and some of the stores want a bar code on the pattern to make it easier to scan for sales or inventory. This means that you must have your own unique bar code number and the facilities to add it to your pattern. You can purchase software to produce your own or order one from a company that does that kind of work."

*　　　　　　　*　　　　　　　*

In Depth Interview: Jo and Jos Hindriks of Dutchman Designs

Jos and Jo Hindriks came to the U.S. from The Netherlands and fell in love with quilting immediately. Jo accepted a job as an economist in Wash., D.C., but they decided to spend their first American Summer in Lancaster County, Pennsylvania in 1994. Admiring the geometric quilt designs of the Amish and Mennonites, the Hindriks could not resist quilting for long. Five years and many quilts later, the Hindriks developed their own Website inviting quilters and admirers to contribute to their site.

Today, *Dutchman Designs*, a home-based business owned and operated by the Hindriks, produces and sells original quilt patterns designed and written by Jos. He describes his company as young, but he and his wife, known as "The Dutch Quilting Couple in America." plan to produce more patterns in the near future than the three which began their business.

How much time do you devote to your business?

Jos replies, "My wife Jo has a day job in Washington, D.C., so she can only help a few hours per week. As an economist she helps in practical ways, from figuring prices to handling our state sales tax payments. For me, running *Dutchman Designs* has become a full-time business. I maintain contact with other web hosts and exchange links with them plus I design and write all the quilt patterns, both free patterns and those we offer for sale. We began our Website in 1997 offering quilters free patterns when they visited our site," Jos explains. "But in January of 1999, we felt we had gathered enough experience to begin designing and selling a line of commercial patterns. We are indeed fortunate to complement each other as a quilting couple. I am the one who thinks out patterns and does all the writing. Jo, who has a degree in economics actually enjoys bookkeeping and marketing. We brainstorm together and once we decide which way we want to go, we each focus on our individual strengths."

Please describe the quilting patterns you enjoy creating.

When I saw the Hindriks' patterns for the first time, they reminded me of the delightful, optical illusions by M.C. Escher. In both cases, the secondary space of a design is completely filled in by color value reversals from the primary design. I did not think anyone in the quilting world could face the challenge of this intricate type of designing but Jo and Jos Hindriks have done so. They describe their patterns.

"We love geometric designs and quilts providing an optical illusion—especially quilts based on puzzles such as one Jos calls, 'Pentominoes'. The pattern envelope describes the design as inspired by Solomon Golomb, an American mathematician in 1953. He reckoned that if a Do-mino has two squares of equal size laid side to side on a flat surface, then a Pento-mino has five. Pentominos offer twelve different constructions of a puzzle design. A full set of these includes one piece for each way, which makes twelve Pentominoes and a total of sixty squares." Voila! The Hindriks *Puzzling patterns for Quilters* series began.

"Solving a Pentomino problem requires one to fit twelve pieces together into a given shape like a jig saw puzzle," Jos explains. "Using them in different shapes have become my favorite way to design quilts. Our free, online quilt patterns include a series of Mystery Quilts complete with detective stories. I like to share my new design ideas with the quilting public as they form a part of my marketing research. Feedback from readers helps improve my pattern writing."

Please describe your process for making quilt patterns.

"I develop all my images using precision drafting programs like *AutoCAD LT*™. I write the instructions and then negotiate with a local print shop where my patterns are duplicated by *Xerox DocuTech*™. This process allows presentably yet affordable black-and-white printouts directly from computer files. Color covers of each copy are printed at home on an inkjet printer, then sprayed with a fixative. Currently we offer four pattern titles for sale. All have one color cover and sixteen instruction black and white pages. All are letter-size pages, 8½"x11". Each pattern comes in a transparent plastic zip-lock bag with a hang-hole."

"Three of my four patterns belong to my *Puzzling Patterns for Quilts* series, which feature two-dimensional brainteasers, Pentominoes," Jos continues. "I plan to expand this series. Like quilt blocks, the puzzle solutions can be incorporated in all quilts whether traditional or innovative. My fourth pattern, *Checkered Copycats* depicts a tessellation design of poised cat silhouettes projected onto a field of squares. Our next pattern, will have a tessellation theme too based on an earlier Mystery Quilt of mine. All patterns contain precise step-by-step instructions to sew the quilt top in various sizes. My patterns allow quilters to choose their colors, calculate yardage, cut strips/patches, order of assembly and quilting suggestions. Customizing the pattern in order to create new, personal designs is my favorite aspect of the process. Numerous tables and black-and-white diagrams further clarify the text."

Do you sell both retail and wholesale or just directly to the ultimate consumer?

"We sell to both but keep a sharp distinction between retail and wholesale. Our retail prices are publicly accessible. We only forward wholesale prices to business owners after they verify their business. We maintain our wholesale prices at about half the retail price having learned that this is the accepted standard among designers, publishers and retailers. Our pricing system targets both individual buyers and retailers."

Where do you buy your supplies?

Jos says he uses local shops to buy, printer ink cartridges, labels, paper for the color covers and spray cans of fixative all of which he needs in modest amounts. Manufacturers provide him with plastic zip-lock bags which they do use in large quantities.

Do you ever buy raw materials at retail prices or "on-sale"?

"It depends on how much we need of certain materials," says Jos. For example, we buy printer paper and self-adhesive address labels at our local Office Depot. Spray cans of fixative come from a local art supply where we receive a special price on twenty cans when we ask for it."

How long had you been crafting before you began to sell what you made?

"Our specific interest in quilts began shortly after we moved from our native Holland to the U.S. in 1994. We do not have a quiltmaking tradition back home, but Jo's mother has a degree in dressmaking. However, we both have always liked doing crafts, such as spinning, woodworking and making clothes."

Have you ever lowered prices because you found they were too high?

"Yes, I lowered pattern prices on our Website in January 1999 by $2 after comparing our price to retail prices of similar quilt patterns that I found in quilt shops.

Do you have a system for pricing your items? Please describe.

"Our pricing is simple. We try to maintain uniform prices, both for the consumer and retailers. We are, however, open to negotiation when someone wants to buy in larger quantities.

Do you consider labor when you set your prices?

"No. Developing quilt patterns differs from making and selling quilts, for example. The bulk of my labor occurs before producing the patterns begins. My labor is compensated after a critical number of copies have been sold."

How do you determine overhead?

"I add up all general overhead costs per month or per year and divide that by the number of copies I expect to sell in that period."

How do you determine profit?

"Once I have a production price per copy and add the overhead per copy, I compare it with prices of competitive products to arrive at my profit margin."

Where do you sell your patterns?

"Retail shops and our own Website have become our primary selling points. The Internet was, and still is, our first and foremost source of sales. Compared to other pattern publishers, we started our business backward: First we went to the Web and later began sending literature to quilt shops," replies Jos.

"We are also considering teaching and lecturing," he adds. "We are preparing schedules and materials for quilt classes and lectures based on our patterns and offered at quilt shops and guilds. We plan to offer classes, workshops or retreats where participants will purchase a package, including the pattern they select. When we begin to give lectures, we plan to offer the audience the opportunity to buy patterns directly from us at reduced prices in lieu of shipping and handling fees."

Do you plan to employ a sales representative to sell for you?

"We are negotiating with one who is active both on the Internet and on the road. Retailers of quilt patterns prefer not to spend time and effort dealing with publishers individually. We hope that more shops will order via the Internet as increasing numbers of businesses offer e-Commerce transactions." Modestly, he adds, "Your readers are witnessing first-hand, a new pattern designer and publisher feeling his way on the market! I post questions on QuiltBiz frequently to stay in touch with quilters from around the world." (QuiltBiz information in the Appendix).

Quick Review of Pricing Methods in this Chapter:

X   Consider pricing patterns by taking 1000 sheets as a single unit. $$371.30 divided by 1000 sheets = 0.3713 or .37 cents per sheet.

X   Average patterns cost $7.99, for quilted wall hangings or very simple quilts. Today, average patterns cost $9.99 and some as high as $14.99.

X   Use a Pricing Template to Set Your Own Break-even Point:

Distributor price	$2.61	134 copies
Wholesale price	$3.48	100 copies
Retail price	$6.95	50 copies

X   Price patterns based on complexity, number of pages, production costs and time required to create it. Check costs against 50% of the potential list price. If sufficient margin remains, go forward. If not, don't make the product.

X   Take total costs and add a 50% mark up. If total costs come to $8 for materials only, charge $12 to shops and mark it up to $24.

X   If pattern costs $1.00 to print, retail it for $7.00. Local shops purchase patterns at an industry standard of 50% of retail or $3.50 per pattern. If you sell patterns at wholesale to distributors for retail less 50%, + an additional 30% for a net cost of $2.45.

X   Use the arbitrary figure of printing 5,000 versus 10,000 copies for four-page patterns which may total $1,000 and $1,200, for example. By spending $200 extra, you can reduce the per-pattern printing expense from 20 cents to12 cents if you sell all you print. Similar economies of scale can be gained by purchasing bags, envelopes and postage, in bulk.

X   Divide costs by the number of patterns you plan to produce, 1000 for example. Next, multiply the per pattern cost by 10 to arrive at the retail price as you still need to make a profit. In reality, only a small number of patterns will probably be sold directly by the designer at retail prices. Most will be wholesaled to shops at 50%.

X   Pricing Template: Consider retail price, wholesale should be = 50% of retail, minimum 3 of one title. For selling to distributors take 20% off wholesale, minimum 3 dozen of one title, up to 7 dozen, 30% off wholesale, more than 7 dozen of one title. Pay shipping on orders of 12 dozen or more.

Note to readers: See chapter 8 for more details about producing patterns.

CONTRIBUTORS IN THIS CHAPTER:

Lori Nixon
Northern Star
P.O. Box 409
Kauneonga Lake, New York 12749-0409
Phone: 914-583-0228
E-mail: lnixon@warwick.net

Trudie Hughes
Patched Works
13330 Watertown Plank Road
Elm Grove, WI 53122
E-Mail: trudiehughes@msn.com

Nancy Roberts
Quilt Legacy
148 Lake Road
South New Berlin, NY 13843.
E-Mail: robertsn@norwich.net
(does not want phone number listed)

Judy Garden
The Patchwork Garden
296 Cairncroft Rd.
Oakville, Ontario L6J 4M6, Canada
Phone/fax: 905-337-1457
E-Mail: patchwrk@cgocable.net
http://www.patchworkgarden.com

Beth Wheeler
Beth Wheeler Creative Services
9165 Laurelwood Ct.
Manassas, VA 20110
Phone: (703) 368-8642
Fax: (703) 335-1973
E-Mail: 14K@prodigy.net

Ann Anderson
Quilt Woman
612 Lighthouse Avenue, Suite 217
Pacific Grove, CA 93950
Phone: 831-644-0100
Fax: 831-644-0933
E-mail: ann@quiltwoman.com
Website http://www.quiltwoman.com

Jo Morton
Prairie Hands Patterns
1801 Central Avenue
Nebraska City, NE 68410
Phone: 402-873-3846
Fax: 402-873-3848
E-mail: jmorton@navix.net

Patricia Hammond
Hearthstone Designs
1136 Clover Valley Way
Edgewood, MD 21040-2186
Phone:-410-676-6419
E-mail:hearthst@erols.com
http://www.vcq.org/images/patricia_hammond.htm

Barbara Vlack
Sweet Memories Publishing Company
36 W 556 Wild Rose Road
St. Charles, IL 60174-1149
E-mail: cptvdeo@inil.com

Nancy Restuccia
Make It Easy
2112 Queen Avenue South
Minneapolis, MN 55405-2350
Phone: 612-377-7560
E-mail: nancylynne@aol.com
http://www.make-it-easy.com

Elsie Vredenburg
Quilts by Elsie
Box 301
Tustin, MI 49688
Phone:(616)825-2572
E-mail: elf@netonecom.net
http://www.netonecom.net/~elf

Barbara Seidlecki
Cabin Fever Crafts
P.O. Box 7604
Kalispell, MT 59904-0604
Voice/Fax: (406) 257-0434
E-mail: cbnfvr@digisys.net

Jo and Jos Hindriks:
PO Box 2989
Manassas, VA 20108-0906
Phone/Fax: (703) 791-3661
E-Mail: qdutch@dutdes.com
Website: http://www.dutdes.com/

Chapter 6

Dolls and Stuffed Animals

Pricing Template: Gail Platts
In-Depth Interview: Eileen Garrett

Do you believe that dolls and stuffed animals exist primarily for children? Think again! Today, most hand-crafted dolls and stuffed animals are purchased by collectors. Doll shows all over the country bring throngs of collectors not only to buy exquisitely made and dressed dolls by today's doll artists but to buy or trade yesterday's dolls such as Story Book Dolls, Shirley Temple Dolls, Barbies and the perennial Raggedy Ann & Andy dolls.

Eileen Garrett, the dollmaker interviewed at the end of this chapter explains that she rarely sells her dolls of yesteryear to children. Adults buy the nostalgia in her old-fashioned, double-ended dolls. Grandmothers and loving aunts also like to make and give dolls to their loved, small relatives. They want them to love dolls as they did when they themselves were small. Where do buyers go to find just the right doll or stuffed animal? Why to the Internet of course! Note that all but one of the dollmakers in this chapter sell their dolls online.

I do not actually make doll bodies as do many of the doll artists in this chapter but I do sell many crocheted and knitted doll outfits to magazines regularly. What do they want most often? You guessed it! "Please design an old-fashioned little girl doll or an angel," they ask, "…and please use lots of laces, ribbons, bows and ruffles." Today's computer literate, business-minded editors of craft and doll magazines want that old-fashioned look. How do Barbie dolls fit in? Let me remind you that Barbie turned 60 this year so in spite of her perennial, youthful appearance. She too brings nostalgia and charm to doll lovers. Teddy-bears these days, are rarely nude anymore. They come attired in fancy outfits as well.

No, today's dollmakers are not always women. Two men who make and sell dolls as their full-time business, dress them in nostalgic outfits from the *Upstairs Maid Dolls* dressed in the fashion of the old PBS series, *Upstairs, Downstairs,* to the heirloom dolls dressed by Clift Wathen. You will find them in this chapter.

*　　　　　　*　　　　　　*

Gail Platts, of *InCalico,* began her business in 1986, selling doll patterns and whimsical soft-sculptured, cloth figures. Gail works full-time making dolls but confesses to stretching her days to fourteen hours during the holiday rush. She sells both at retail and wholesale, purchasing most of her raw materials at wholesale prices from catalogs and websites though she prefers to buy fabric at local shops. To make a profit when she began selling at wholesale, she had to raise her prices to get in line with her production capabilities. Gail explains her pricing system.

1 "I gauge the cost of raw materials and how much it takes to make a dozen dolls."
2 "I note how long it takes to create an individual doll, though it takes less time to work production style."
3 "I total utility costs and overhead then divide the sum by hours worked per month."
4 "Next, I total labor and material costs and double that sum to arrive at my estimated wholesale price. Next, I add in overhead costs and divide by the total estimated price. I try to have at least 40% of the asking price reflect profit. If profit isn't enough, I tweak the asking price until it is. Gail provides her Pricing Template:

Raw Materials	$5.
Labor	$15.
Total:	$20 (Estimated wholesale price: Doubled: $40)
Overhead	$1.50
Total	$21.50

"Total costs: $21.50 divided by estimated wholesale selling price of $40.00 = 53% markup," says Gail. "If the doll wholesales at $40.00, it costs me 53 cents of every dollar to earn a profit-margin of 47%. To arrive at the retail price, I double the wholesale price = $80. Next, I subtract the total costs of $21.50 from $80.00 = $58.59. My profit percentage becomes about 73%. This may seem like an illusion but my overhead selling at a show is much higher than selling from home. If I figure my profit percentage on selling 10 dolls, I end up with a profit of around 60%, which factors in show expenses. I try to have a profit of at least 40% built into the wholesale price," she adds.

Gail considers another important factor to set a price on her time. "I try to maintain my hourly wage, and I have an injury factor to consider. I battle to keep tendonitis under control so if I accept work that makes my hands and arms hurt, my hourly wage goes up. Putting a value on my time this way helped me learn to delegate work appropriately. For example, when I found it was time to prepare my yearly Federal Income Tax Return, I calculated it would take me 40 hours to do it myself. At $10 per hour, it would cost me $400 to leave my work. I only have to pay $200 to have someone else do this for which gives me forty extra hours to make dolls."

Gail mentions another often overlooked factor. "I used to sell at craft shows but I moved from Maine to Texas. My new state is a whole new ball-game," she acknowledges. "The craft environment is different and support networks for artists, less."

Commenting that her dolls sell best at retail stores and on consignment, Gail defines how she sets her prices considering the percentage that goes to the shop owner. "I double my wholesale costs," says Gail, "but though my profit margin initially appears larger than wholesale, in the long term, costs may be higher on consignment if my dolls don't sell and become shopworn."

Gail has a website and adds, "Online doll clubs for dollmakers help me to sell from the Internet. A group of people already interested in doll patterns share information about where to buy online." Participating in craft cooperatives has also been successful for Gail. She pays a fee, which entitles her to shelf space in a group booth with others artisans. "I mail them samples and needed paperwork and they take the orders for me. Lovely," she concludes.

*   *   *

Lee and Judy Maltenfort, of *The Upstairs Maids,* began selling life-size dolls in 1984. Together, they devote about 70% of their time to their business. Of that, they spend 85% producing dolls. The Maltenforts sell most of their dolls at wholesale but occasionally sell a few at retail.

Describing their dolls, Lee explains, "Our 60″ tall dolls are soft sculptured characters with rigid armatures of 36″x18″. I build my mannequins on a unique wooden platform and use soft sculpture techniques and proprietary ceramic heads to complete the body."

Purchasing raw materials differs from many other dollmakers. Lee explains, "We buy from local vendors for armature parts and pieces. We also visit vintage consignment shops and thrift stores for fabrics and trims but use websites to buy vintage clothing to dress our dolls." The couple buys other materials at either retail, wholesale or "on-sale."

Judy attended The Fashion Institute of Design and opened her first design studio thirty years ago but joined forces with Lee to begin their doll business fifteen years ago. They acknowledge they have had to reluctantly raise prices at times. Lee explains, "I raise my prices when suppliers raise theirs forcing us to increase ours. We want the volume of business that keeps us busy but don't want to raise our prices by nickels and dimes," he says.

When they began their business, the Maltenforts hired a showroom representative, Isadora Frost of Isadora and Mizrahi in New York, who said, "When a new item sells fast, keep raising the price until you hit resistance then back down two increases." Judy Maltenfort says, "She taught us how to find the limit a specific market will bear and how to arrive at the most profitable prices," she adds.

Describing their pricing system, Lee says, "We figure our costs and labor at $15 per hour and triple the total. We determine overhead costs by calculating rent, utilities, amortization of equipment and part replacements."

The Maltenforts sell primarily to retail specialty stores and decorators through agreements with showrooms throughout the country. Today, they look forward to expanding their new Website where people enjoy visiting a community of lifelike dolls!

*   *   *

Marty Donnellan, owner of *ClothArt* started her business in 1996 but for ten years prior to that, made and sold dolls under her own name. *ClothArt* sells original cloth dolls and cloth doll patterns Marty and other designers create. Marty also sells art and dollmaking supplies. Recently she jumped onto the ever growing technological boom and began teaching online dollmaking courses on the Internet.

Says Marty, "I have been crafting since childhood but sold my first doll in 1983. Afterward, I began doing commission work in nylon needle-sculpture dolls. These were small, whimsical dolls made of ladies' nylon house, stuffed with cotton and heavily needle-sculpted and embroidered. They had acrylic flat, black eyes and were meant to represent a specific person or a theme. This did not prove profitable for my time investment so in 1993, I began to design for what I perceived to be the artist's collectible market. For a time I wholesaled to stores and did commission work," she explains.

Marty makes dolls for sale or as prototypes for patterns which consumes 70-75% of her time. She also designs and creates text and graphics for patterns and Internet correspondence courses. Designing print ads for two national magazines and managing a mailing list associated with her Website keeps her busy. She maintains her site, processes and fills orders, performs accounting chores and still sets aside time to educate herself about her market.

Marty explains her decisions about whether to sell at retail or wholesale. "When I began producing cloth dolls for sale in 1993, I realized that though a wholesale market existed for my dolls, it was not profitable. I decided against wholesaling my work and began to explore other ways to make a profit. My search led me to pattern making, instructional design and Internet teaching which is where my greatest success now lies," she explains.

Marty still accepts occasional doll commissions, but her reason for doing so is to keep her dollmaking skills as current as possible. Profit from dollmaking commissions is negligible for Marty. She prefers to make dolls as prototypes for patterns. Catalogs, local shops and manufacturers provide Marty's raw materials.

Internet selling has become the most successful for her. As soon as she began to offer products from her Website, her orders doubled. "Having a Website not only gives me international exposure but brought my work to the attention of another doll artist, Kezi Matthews, who did a feature on me for *The Cloth Doll* magazine," Marty says with delight.

"Working on the pattern for this magazine, I discovered that I really enjoyed pattern work which in turn led to selling other patterns and offering my courses on the Internet. Pattern making uses not only my dollmaking skills but I can tap into my background in writing and graphic arts as well. Teaching on the Internet takes my design work a step further—integrating text and graphics with a special mailing list to make communication possible between teacher and student," she adds.

*   *   *

Sarah Yarema, of *Cabin Bears & Friends*, started her business in 1991 designing original teddy bears, primitive dolls and animals. Sarah spends 90% of her work time producing items for sale reserving 10% for bookkeeping and correspondence. She sells at retail, wholesale and directly to the consumers. Sarah says, "I think each method has its place in the craft business world now. I restrict wholesale business to 25% of my sales since I make more selling at retail but wholesale sales can account for group sales at specific times of year," she explains.

She continues; "Making a profit in this business requires you to find the most inexpensive sources to buy raw materials. Sometimes, you must buy in bulk but in the long run, you save money and increase profits."

Sarah freely admits that pricing challenged her more than any other business issue. Like many, she began by setting her prices too low. Now, I have learned to figure my production costs rather than constantly looking at what others charge. She points out that you need to know what the market will bear but knowing your bottom line before you price matters more.

Today, Sarah has an efficient method for setting prices. She determines the total costs of making her product as if she had to buy supplies at full retail. Next, she multiplies total costs by 3 to arrive at a wholesale price and by five to determine her retail price. Says Sarah, "I only lower prices if I feel the market won't support them. My profit is what remains after material and overhead costs. I don't factor a dollar value on my time because if I did, my prices would be astronomical. When considering pricing my labor, I also consider that I work from home without daycare, travel and clothing costs," she says.

Craft malls, troubling to other contributors in this book, are successful for Sarah. She explains, "Maintaining sufficient inventory is my only problem selling at craft malls. If you are going to sell this way, you can make good money if you keep a high inventory of products and make sure that your sales cover booth rental fees."

Consignment selling appeals to Sarah so she consigns in two shops but always examines whether or not the percentage paid to the shop owner falls within her wholesale price. "If so," says Sarah, "I leave the retail price as is but if not, I raise the price slightly to accommodate the owner's percentage so I don't lose money myself."

Sarah closes by saying that though she does not sell much from her Website, she finds that it lends credibility to her business and gives her recognition."

Clift J. Wathen, Sr., of *Clift & Evelyn's Heirloom Dolls* gets right to the point about pricing "I multiply my material costs by four, then do any adjusting from there," says Clift.

"My goal is to earn at least $20 per hour for our labor. This way, if Evelyn and I each work for ten hours, we have $400 dollars in labor to build into our pricing. Next, I add the cost for raw materials and the costs involved in selling our products. This totals about $600 dollars," says Clift.

Usually, we cannot determine the cost to make each doll until tax time each year," Clift explains. "Then we divide the total number of dolls sold in a year by the total costs of motel stays, travel, meals and show fees as we sell at craft shows exclusively."

"Most dollmakers prefer to work on one doll at a time, but we do not," says Clift. "We always have several dolls in production at one time and some take longer to make than others."

"In the beginning," Clift explains, we thought we could arrive at a selling price by arbitrarily choosing a price we thought buyers would pay. If a particular doll 'sold like hot cakes' we recognized our price was too low and raised it gradually until it would not sell at all. This taught us what our market would bear. At that point, we lowered the price to where it would still sell, having found the maximum selling price."

Clift continues. "Right now we have dolls that sell too quickly and we could probably raise the price but choose not to as these particular dolls have become our 'bread and butter'. We have come to expect that we can count on these to pay expenses," he acknowledges.

Santa dolls have become popular sellers for the Wathens. Unlike many crafters, they have a strong off and on season. Says Clift, "We give an off-season discount if a customer orders a Santa doll in February rather than just before the holidays. Today we sell Christmas Dolls all year but I remember when other crafters laughed at us when we showed up for April shows with Christmas inventory to sell. When we walked out with the most sales, they changed their view. We may charge slightly less in April than in July and more in October than in July but November has become our best month," he says firmly.

Clift agrees with other crafters in earlier chapters who say, "We have found that when our items do not sell well at a particular show, it does no good to lower the prices hoping for sales. We tried this and it never works unless you want to give your products away. We will not work for nothing." Clift sounds philosophical when he says, "Beginning and established dollmakers have two different mind sets. Our first year was mostly guess work," he admits, "but today, since we make one-of-a-kind dolls, we think of ourselves as 'Doll Artists.' We are well established and recognized and can draw on past experiences and instinct now," he concludes.

       *   *   *

Anita Arias, of *Teddy Bear Junction* has been making and selling teddy bears since 1975 when she began making them for her children. Anita recalls selling her first bear when she attended her first craft show. A customer approached her and said she wanted to buy a small rat that Anita had displayed with her cloth dolls. Politely, Anita replied that she did not recall having made rats. The customer picked up one of Anita's small teddy-bears, and said, "This is the rat I want to buy." Says Anita, "I felt bad that she did not know exactly what she wanted but at least, I made my first sale."

Anita's original patterns are unique and collectible. She uses unusual fabrics like mohair, tapestry, upholstery, antique and chenille fabrics in addition to the traditional plush used for stuffed animals. "Now I am working on designing an elephant and a giraffe but I also make Raggedy Ann and Andy dolls and ethnic dolls too," says Anita.

Employed as a full-time nurse, Anita works on her dolls and bears in the evening with the help of her husband who helps with stuffing and attaching joints. They sell only to individual consumers exclusively at craft shows. As Anita began selling her dolls and bears, she too began by undervaluing her time and setting prices too low. Charging only $20 for each bear, Anita says she learned a valuable lesson. "When I was selling that cheap," she admits, "people thought my products were cheaply made and of poor quality." Today, Anita prices by totaling all her costs and tripling the sum to arrive at her retail price.

In-Depth Interview: Eileen Garrett

Eileen Garrett, known to many online crafters as "The Fairy Grandmother" began her business in 1974. No other crafter I have interviewed has been crafting as long as Eileen has—twenty-five years.

Please describe your business, Fairy Grandmother.

"I create, design, and fabricate cloth dolls and animals. Almost all my dolls are what I call, "play dollies" suitable for kids two years old and up. I also make decorator type dolls, which I describe as 'look—not play'. Most of my dolls remind me of those we had as children such as Flip-Dolls, featuring Red Riding Hood on one end and the Grandma/wolf at the other or Cinderella's scullery maid at one end, with the Fairy Godmother/Cinderella at the ball at the other end. I also make Raggedy dolls, awake/asleep dolls, Topsy and Eva Flip dolls," she adds.

Eileen provides an interesting history about dollmaking. "Concerning her black/white flip dolls, few people realize that these were made pre-Civil War on plantations by black Moms for their daughters who were forbidden by slave owners to play with black dolls. Dolls had to be blonde and pink skinned ONLY. So, the moms devised a flip doll that was black/brown on one side for their daughters to play with when the slave owner was not around and when he appeared, the little girls flipped over the skirt and a pink dolly appeared. Without this story, very few people understand black/white flip dolls.

"I've been using the same two basic designs since I started making flat and gusset-headed dolls with just a front and back," says Eileen. "Over the years, the dolls have ranged from 5" up to 30" but most measure 16"-24". They all have yarn hair and fetching outfits."

How much time do you devote to your business?

Eileen may stagger some readers when she answers, "I work fifty weeks a year, approximately 72 to 80 hours a week."

Of the total time you spend on your business, how do you devote producing something to sell?

"I spend between 50-60 hours a week just designing and producing," Eileen says.

Do you sell both retail and wholesale or just directly to the ultimate consumer?

"I do both; approximately 80% of my business is retail and the other 20% is wholesale."

Where do you purchase supplies?

"I buy most of my notions from *Home Sew Catalog* in Bethlehem, PA, even though I live in California. They give a 25% discount on wholesale orders more than $100. We have very few, local shops where I live but I will drive a distance to a fabric store out of town when they have 40% off fabric sales. Manufacturers provide me with body fabrics such as tea-dyed muslin and broadcloth. I buy direct from Roclon Mills in Maryland and buy bolts of fabric from fabric wholesalers in Los Angeles."

How long had you been crafting before you began to sell what you made?

"I'd been sewing about three years before I had the courage to approach a shop to attempt to sell one of my dolls. I didn't learn to sew until I was in my twenties and took classes. I discovered I had little skill making garments but fell in love with stuffed animals and dolls. Ultimately, my career began when I asked myself, just how many animals does one little boy (my son) really need?"

Have you ever lowered prices because you found them too high?

"Oh yes, many, many times," says Eileen, "but I leave any new item on the market at least six months before lowering the price."

Have you ever raised your prices?

"I have found it necessary many, many times. The old adage, 'If you can sell them faster than you can make them—the price is too low', works well for me. I live in an economically depressed area but when I do shows in Southern or Northern CA, I always raise my prices as big-city buyers have no qualms paying a bit more."

Do you have a system for pricing your items?

"Actually I have two. I have used the formula to multiply 5-6 times the cost of materials for years. Most of the time this covers materials, labor, travel and miscellaneous expenses. On some items, for example, my dolly purses, the materials cost only $1.50 but sell at shows for $10 each. I can make about four an hour which earns a nice profit. On the other hand, my stuffed/gesso/painted animals, materials cost remains low but involve significant labor. For those creatures, I multiply 10-15 times the materials cost."

Do you consider labor when you set your prices?

"Absolutely! Since this is what I do for a living, it is imperative to factor in my labor correctly. December is the month when I determine how much I need to earn to support myself comfortably in the coming year. I start with my yearly figure and work backwards to determine real expenses and salary. For example, I can realistically expect to sell 100 pairs of Raggedy dolls per year. At $45 a pair this comes to $4,500. Eight hundred dollars of this cover material expenses. Next, I determine fixed expenses and labor. I do not determine labor by the hour, but by the year as some designs are very laborious and some I can do quickly."

"Once I have done this with my seven to eight bestsellers, I know exactly how much I have to sell at every show and how many of each item I must sell to meet my modest living expenses. Needless to say, these figures are not set in concrete so I reevaluate every four months to see how I am doing."

How do you determine overhead?

"I keep every receipt and maintain mileage records and go over these once a month to see where I am in relation to where I want to be at the end of the year."

How do you determine profit?

"Once again, I study my yearly budget and goals and build in a 10% profit margin. Sometimes I make it and sometimes I don't. Some years my profit margin was down to 3% but during others, I felt guilty because it swelled to 20%."

How do you determine the value of your time?

"I value my time by determining how much I need to earn to live comfortably a year at a time. I do not figure a per hour wage since I do not work in a factory or office. I figure the value of my time as artists do—not by how much per hour I earn, but if I can live in a manner which allows me to pay the bills and have a bit of money left over. I am not "bookkeeperly" and cannot place a dollar value on something I love to do."

Do you sell at craft shows?

"Indeed I do," Eileen responds enthusiastically. "For years and years, I followed the craft show circuit successfully. For the past two years, due in part to foreign, low-quality imports, attendance at craft shows declined. I am fortunate to live in Santa Barbara County and received acceptance in July of 1998, to sell at the Arts & Crafts Beach Show which takes place every Sunday of the year and Saturday on holiday weekends. This show is open only to Santa Barbara County artisans and is heavily juried by other vendors who do not accept cheap imports. Because we get more than 5 million tourists a year in Santa Barbara, I find this a splendid and lucrative show in which to participate," she says.

"Other than the beach, the only other shows I plan to attend this year are, The Flower Festival here in Lompoc and the Spring Arts show here in town. Laughingly, Eileen says, "I could go on for hours about my previous show experiences."

Eileen tried craft malls, but like many, found them unsatisfactory for a variety of reasons such as poor or dishonest management, shop lifting, unkempt environment and low pay. Retail shops and specialty stores work more successfully for Eileen, especially nationwide, ethnically owned shops. "Few doll makers make black and Asian cloth dolls with which one can actually play," Eileen says, "and I love making these."

A number of shops that deal exclusively with cat items buy from Eileen too. She has a half dozen painted, embroidered, "fetchingly dressed kitties" she says. "I have learned to be cautious selling to shops more than I once was. Today I only accept payment by check or credit cards." Eileen has not tried commission dollmaking yet but feels strongly opposed to selling on consignment due to her many sad experiences. "My product line is now a proven line," she emphasizes, "and I do not feel it necessary to do consignment for any reason. I urge anyone considering such a manner of selling, to deal with only one shop to get one's foot in the door so to speak—but not to sell this way regularly."

Do you employ a sales representative to sell for you?

"I have a show-rep who sells my items at the LA and San Francisco Gift shows. He doesn't sell much, which is fine with me, and charges me 15% of the retail price. Years ago, I had sales reps on both coasts and it was a nightmare. I much prefer retail customers at shows to buyers from catalogues and shops because I detest production type work."

Do you sell via the Internet or from a Website?

"Yes, I sell via the Internet from two Websites and both have increased my business. My target market consists of women more than 45 years of age who are themselves professionals (or have husbands who are) providing them an ample supply of discretionary income. Most buy for grandchildren or nieces and nephews. Within two to three years, once everyone gets used to buying online, I expect my customer base will expand. Shop owners have discovered the joy of shopping at their computer as opposed to attending trade shows," she adds.

In closing, our charming Fairy Grandmother says, "In the past six months, I have finally done something I contemplated for several years. Now, I have *The Stuffin Place* in Southern California do doll-body stuffings for me. This is the most tedious, uncreative part of this work and their prices are reasonable. They will stuff a pair of Raggedy dolls for $2.50 compared to $5 when I take the time to do it myself. This has eliminated buying 100 boxes of fiber-fill at a time and keeps from ruining my hands/wrists/arms with that sorry task. I finally followed the advice of an SBA manager who told me once, 'Consider how much you will pay to not have to do a particular task yourself.' His advice has proven true. I encourage other artisans who craft for a living to seek out all possibilities that will eliminate the dreaded boredom factor by having someone help, assist or just do some of the thankless drudge work."

QUICK REVIEW OF PRICING METHODS IN THIS CHAPTER

X   Gauge the cost of raw materials and the time it takes to make a dozen dolls. Determine overhead by totaling utility costs and dividing the sum by hours worked per month.

X   Total labor and material costs and double to arrive at estimated wholesale price. Add overhead costs then divide the total by dolls made.

X   Have at least 40% of the asking price reflect profit. If profit isn't enough, adjust final figures to insure profit.

X   Figure costs and time at $15 per hour, for example. Then triple the total and compare totals (3x costs vs. costs + time). Choose the formula that yields the most to set wholesale price. Determine overhead costs by calculating rent, utilities, amortization of equipment and part replacements.

X   Restrict wholesale business to 25% of annual sales since you will make more selling at full retail.

X   Determine the total costs making a product as if you bought supplies at full retail. Next, multiply total costs by 3 to arrive at wholesale price and 5 to determine retail price.

X   Using a goal of $20 per hour for labor, if two people work for ten hours, they earn $400 dollars in labor to build into pricing system. Next, add the cost for raw materials and the costs involved in selling your products to total $600 dollars per doll.

X   Check your profitability at the end of each tax year. Divide the total number of dolls sold in a year by the total costs of motel stays, travel, meals and show fees to make sure your profit remain stable and within what the market will bear.

X   Avoid selling too cheaply. If you sell a stuffed bear for $20 each, people may think your products are cheaply made and of poor quality.

X   Consider totaling all costs and tripling the sum to arrive at your retail price.

X   Use the old, reliable formula: multiply the cost of materials, labor, travel and miscellaneous expenses by 5 or 6.

X   When material costs remain low but involve significant labor, think about multiplying by 10-15 times the materials cost.

CONTRIBUTORS TO THIS CHAPTER

Gail Ireland Platts
1415 Shores Blvd
Rockwall TX 75087
Phone: 972-722-7015
E-mail: GEPlatts@aol.com
http://www.incalico.com

Lee & Judy Maltenfort
Upstairs Maids
King George Blvd, #7
Savannah GA 31419
Phone: (912) 927-6417
E-mail eljayem@earthlink.net
http://www.avillageontheriver.com/upstairs-maids

Marty Donnellan
455 Grayson Highway, Suite 111-183
Lawrenceville, GA 30045
Phone: 770-466-9405
Fax: 770-466-9405
E?mail: marty@martydoll.com
http://www.martydoll.com

Sarah Yarema
320 Broken Arrow Circle
Indianapolis, IN 46234
Phone: 317-271-3551
Fax (561) 365-5739
E-mail: say@iquest.net
http://sallyanne.hypermart.net

Clift & Evelyn's Heirloom Dolls
RR4 Box 1175
Westfield, PA. 16950
Phone: 814-367 5047 or 1-888-XMASDOL
E-mail: Clift@xmasdolls.com or santaman@penn.com
http://www.xmasdolls.com

Anita Arias,
27874 Mandarin Ave,
Hayward, ca 94544
(510) 887-6369,
E-mail: Aarias3564@aol.com

Eileen Garrett
610 E. Pine Ave., #1
Lompoc, Ca 93436
(805) 735-4022
Fairegrma@AOL.com
http://www.idahoquilt.com/fairegrma.htm and http://www.www.cscrafts.com

Chapter 7

Knitting & Crochet

Pricing Template: Sylvia Landman
In-Depth Interview: Diane Sack

My crafting career began thirty-five years ago when I began embroidering, dressmaking, knitting and crocheting on commission. Knitting and crochet remain popular crafts today. Thousands of yarn shops throughout the country in addition to mail-order catalogs and Websites fulfil the wishes of knitters and crocheters for yarns in every price category, color and fiber. Several online mailing lists today serve so many knitters and crocheters that each one receives and publishes more than 100 posts each day asking questions about techniques, tools, yarn and thread sources.

Knitting is making such a comeback that for a full week in October 1999, The Second Annual "Knit Out, Crochet Too" was held in Union Square in New York City. National television coverage followed the event as knitters and crocheters handed out free patterns, provided "Show-and Tell" of projects in progress with intermittent fashion shows of hand-knitted or crocheted clothing. New York, home of many of the most illustrious, well-known knitting experts simply took a week off to extol the virtues and pleasures of knitting and crochet.

The Hobby Industry Association, in its annual Consumer Study states that needlework is the top craft category preferred by the most crafters in the U.S. Broken down by category, crochet takes third place, practiced by 29% of all crafters surveyed while knitting takes seventh place practiced by 18% of crafters.

This has not surprised me as I have taught several weekly classes in knitting and crochet at our local college since 1962. In fact, I am now teaching children and grandchildren of my first students. The industry is large enough that is has its own annual trade show, The National Needlework Association, combining manufacturers, vendors and publishers in crochet, knitting, needlepoint embroidery and cross-stitch, all defined as "needlework."

The Knitting Guild of America, The Crochet Guild of America, The Professional Knitting Designers Guild and *The Stitches Seminars* also provide annual workshops attended by thousands of aficionados eager to learn more techniques and styles and to see the work of the "Super-Stars" in this field. Knitting and crochet, having such large consumers of yarn, have a spin-off organization, *The Yarn Council of America*, which promotes the use of yarn crafts and supports the industry. The latter also played a big part in charity work by sponsoring such events as "Warm up America" gathering knitters and crocheters to make afghans and blankets for the poor and homeless.

Though I design and publish in several crafting arenas, I must confess that I never watch television without knitting or crocheting. For more than half of my life I have maintained at least four projects in-progress, ever eager to try new stitches or work with new yarns. The rumors many have repeated are true. I do knit/crochet at meetings, theaters and in the dental chair. The repetitious, soothing movements come highly recommended by psychologists as a way to combat stress and bring on relaxation. I'll attest to that!

Pricing Template

Though I have branched out into other crafts over time, my original knitting and crochet Pricing Template still serves me well. Following my system, I can set prices quickly and easily for custom sewing, knitting and crochet—then and now. I based my system on the time consumed to work up a single skein of yarn. This system makes it simple to calculate price:

Start your own pricing schedule by making note of everything the customer asks of you. Ask yourself a few questions before you commit to the work.

- Will you make garments for men, women and children? Do you prefer to make afghans or dolls and stuffed animals?
- How easy or complex do you find a particular design someone has requested?
- Is the yarn or thread the customer wants fine and thin? Remember it takes longer to knit or crochet with fine yarn or threads which require small sizes of hooks and needles.
- Is the yarn heavy? If so, you will find it faster to knit or crochet but it may be harder on your hands and fingers.

Customers should *always* provide and pay for the yarn separately from your labor charges even though he or she may buy it *from* you if you own a shop or order it wholesale. Yarn or thread cost is *not* considered in the system below. I intend only to help you set a price for your labor, excluding the cost of materials. If you don't adhere to the policy of separating these two basic costs, you may find yourself in a mess, as I did years ago.

One of my first customers asked if I had included the yarn in my price. I said "yes" since up to then, all my customers wanted common, worsted-weight yarn, easily and inexpensively available. She then told me that since I included yarn in my price, she wanted me to use imported angora instead, a very expensive fiber. We had to negotiate uncomfortably until we arrived at a fair price. Choosing and paying for yarn or thread became the customer's responsibility from that point on when working on commission from my studio.

The Pricing Template below is based on a single skein of worsted-weight yarn, any fiber.

Simple Patterns:	Intermediate Patterns	Advanced Patterns
3½-4 oz Skeins $12	$14	$16

For a woman's simple sweater requiring eight skeins, I would charge $96 ($12x8 skeins = $96.)

If the customer requests a sweater made up of intermediate patterns such as easy cables, small repeat laces or easy textured patterns, I charge at the $14 rate as these techniques require more time and skill. (8x $14 = $112), an increase of $16 for more intricate work.

What about customers who want a complex sweater made with cables or a Fair Isle sweater in multi colors and motifs requiring a high skill level and take more time? A garment like this would consume more yarn so I move to nine skeinsx$16 and charge $144 for the labor alone.

Many years ago, a new client came to see me after seeing three sweaters I had made for a friend who wore size 12 garments. She already knew the price I had charged my friend and expected the same price. However, the new customer weighed 300 pounds and wore a size #24!

Fortunately, I had my list ready and could show her that knitting the identical garment for her would take not 7, skeins but 11 or 12. She could see this would take more time, involve more stitches and effort. The price sheet helped her understand that it was fair to raise my price based upon the materials consumed in making the project. Everyone felt satisfied.

I suggest that in addition to your basic Pricing Template, you also list all the extras that frequently come up in hand-knitting or crochet. These examples would be in addition to making the sweater itself.

A set-in zipper for a cardigan: $5 to insert the zipper in place of buttonholes.

Lining a sweater: I charge for the lining fabric plus $6 per hour for the time it takes me to cut the fabric, assemble it, allow for stretching and to set it into the garment by hand.

Beads or other embellishments: I charge for materials cost plus the time it takes me to add these. However, if the garment requires knitting or crocheting beads into the garment as I go, I double my price as this is very slow, laborious work limited to short periods of time due to the strain on hands and fingers.

Design options such as detachable hoods and sleeves: I charge based on the additional yarn used.

Handmade buttons rather than store-bought: I charge based on the additional yarn used.

Features like these should trigger moving your base "single skein" price upward but the total still must remain within what the market will bear in your geographical area.

One last thought—what if you use a knitting machine for all or part of the work? Consider this a "whole, new ball-game" and have another price sheet prepared as you cannot charge the same amount for knits created by machine as you do when you knit by hand. As of this writing, crochet machines do not exist yet.

Speaking of crochet, I frequently make doilies for publication. Pricing has become easy for this now that I charge based upon the diameter (or other shape). The smaller, the doily, the lower the price. Large table centerpieces work out just as well. Once again, I have three pricing levels: very easy, intermediate or very complex. I begin at $65 for small and easy and work up to $200 for very complex laces for table centerpieces. If you follow this system, consider stitch gauge. If you work with heavy cotton yarns, similar to worsted weight, you will have fewer rounds than you will need to make a doily using #20 or #30 fine thread.

Today, my primary knitting and crochet customers are magazines—both specialty knitting and crochet publications and general craft magazines. All my handmade items are returned to me after publication which allows me to literally sell each item twice. Magazines pay me for the design and instruction then individual customers pay me to take the item home. I also do repairs on knit and crochet garments (usually dog-bites or moth-holes) and base the fee on the time it takes to complete the repair. Now, let's hear from others who also do custom knitting and/or crochet.

                            *   *   *

Darlene Buckel shares her experiences doing custom knitting and crochet. "In the past, I made knitted, crocheted and cross-stitched items for sale. I did not charge by the hour as worked while watching television and relaxing. I considered this downtime. I tried to figure what the market would bear and charged accordingly. For example, at one time afghans sold for a maximum of $100. Depending on the degree of difficulty, I gauged my price based upon that. When doing custom work for a client, I charge by the hour. I do this because many customers just want someone else to make them a specific project because the required skill exceeds theirs. Other customers buy the supplies and start the project only to learn they don't want to finish it or perhaps, they have come up against a deadline, like someone's birthday, and need help. I made several items for a customer who wanted to give someone who was dying a special gift and she simply could not make it in time. Under that kind of pressure I was glad I could charge by the hour."

*   *   *

Tonya Caudel crochets baskets from fabric strips, a task very hard on your hands. "I found a good wholesale supplier where I could buy rolls of fabric," says Tonya. "I decided to charge $5 per hour for each basket as I could make one per hour. I added the cost of the materials plus 20% to cover stripping, knotting/sewing. I doubled the total to sell at wholesale and tripled it to sell wholesale. This method kept my prices even and easy to maintain."

Tonya explains that since her products are labor-intensive, making them more inexpensively is impossible. "I choose a day when I am completely free, organize all my supplies, and crochet till my fingers drop" she explains. The continuity cuts down on my time."

*   *   *

Nazanin (Nazee) Fard, of *Nazee's Designs* began her business in 1992. She designs and makes knitted and crocheted garments primarily for craft magazines for publication. She crochets or knits the items and writes the instructions so readers can reproduce them but only gets paid if a magazine buys the design.

Crafters who write for magazines generally do not purchase raw materials. Nazee explains this system. "I receive complimentary yarns and threads from manufacturers and in return, I endorse their product when I write the instructions, mentioning them by name."

Nazee learned to knit in her native Iran when she was only five years old and learned to crochet in high school. Today, in America, Nazee found craft information so plentiful, she taught herself Silk Ribbon Embroidery three years ago and has since become a teacher. She sells these designs to magazines too. (More about this aspect of Nazee's business in the following chapter.)

"Lowering prices can be challenging when the customer is a magazine editor," Nazee says. "Sometimes, an editor likes my design, but does not have the budget to pay my asking fee. I may lower my price to maintain the relationship and hope for more business in the future," she adds.

Raising her prices comes easier to Nazee as she explains, "I have raised my prices on several occasions when one of the following situations occurs."
1-If the design is complicated and requires more time to produce and write instructions.
2-When the publisher or manufacturer wants to keep the project to use in shows and demonstrating rather than returning it to me.
3-If I must work on a very tight deadline because the editor wants it in a rush.

Nazee shares prices for some of her basic items:

Knitting/crochet afghans: $400 to $500
Vests: $300 to $400
Sweaters: $400 and up

Nazee only considers labor when setting prices. Since manufacturers provide her raw materials, this is not a pricing issue. Her small overhead consists only of postage costs when mailing items to editors. E-mail has helped Nazee with her relationships with editors. She says she has received specific design requests from editors because they can contact her readily by e-mail.

Today, Nazee sells her designs from her Website but says her site is not profitable yet. She makes good use of e-mail for correspondence which cuts response time considerably. "Now, I can send proposals with photographs of my designs to overseas editors and receive a response in two days rather than the weeks it would take otherwise. This has become very important to me," explains Nazee.

*   *   *

Marguerite Nabinger says "I learned to crochet two lace patterns one summer when I was seven years old and still use them today. About ten years ago, I stopped using commercial patterns and began sculpting with crochet—designing as I went along. I make character dolls or whatever strikes my fancy just letting my hook wander where it will. Of course, I rip out now and then."

Marguerite says she likes working with fine threads such as size 20 or 30 thread. She continues, "I like to try new concepts. For example, once I made a round bedspread by translating a doily pattern requiring fine thread into heavier wool. Because of the time it takes, I don't feel it is practical to make many crocheted things for sale. I have a sweater pattern that I can crochet in one day. I make and sell it for $35 if I can buy the yarn for less than $10. I feel okay about earning $25 per day for my labor," she concludes.

"Selling lace, I would have to charge $5 a yard, so that is not practical. You can make good money making intricate heirloom-styled pillowcases with crocheted lace insets and striking lace along the edges. Sometimes, I add embroidered butterflies. A good crocheter who follows these ideas and makes a high quality product in quantity would find this profitable," she adds.

"When I make pillowcases like these, I use fine linen and delicate thread and sell them for $50 a pair, boxed and shrink wrapped," Marguerite explains. "Because of the great investment in time and materials, these are more satisfying for me than profitable" she says. "I find joy in creating something beautiful and selling it to invest in more materials." Marguerite says she can make three simple sweaters per week when using simple stitches. She sells these for $45-$55, depending on the yarn.

Marguerite says she prefers knitting afghans with an intricate design based on needlepoint graphs. She knits with two long circular needles used as regular knitting needles. She explains, "I like to spread my work out and watch the colors develop. Since this takes weeks to finish, I sell them for $350-$500 and up. I finish these special afghans with a very elaborate border to add richness to the overall effect. Afghans like these are for interior designers as they are one-of-a-kind," says Marguerite.

She also knits pleated skirts and dresses and sells them for more than $300. She continues, "Fashion doll sweaters sell best for me. I have designed a simple pattern that I can knit front to back in two hours, and an additional 30 minutes to add finishing touches. I sell these for

$7.50 to $12.50." Marguerite says that today, she likes to design and make patterns for others to knit or crochet most of all.

In-Depth Interview

Diane Sack's enthusiasm for knitting and crochet, took her from a prolific hobbyist to teaching, designing and selling her creations. Working both from home and part-time in a yarn shop, she remains well informed, continually exploring the yarn market nationally and internationally.

Do you sell both retail and wholesale or directly to ultimate consumers?

Diane responds, "I sell both to consumers and also on consignment at a local yarn shop. I design, make and sell knitted and crocheted garments for babies, toddlers and adults. Recently, I started a line of garments for small children called, "UNDER-4's." These have become more popular and successful than I expected. I sell them at on consignment in specialty shops and at Christmas Fairs where my unique, whimsical hats for children sell immediately."

Where do you purchase supplies?

"Though I prefer to support local shops, buying this way adds to the cost of a project. I often use catalogs as they have the widest selection. I prefer to buy from manufacturers who sell me yarn in smaller quantities as they provide the lowest prices of all. Balls of yarn in many colors for a multicolored project must be purchased at a shop since catalogs and manufacturers set a minimum of 10-12 balls of a single color which creates overbuying for a single project when you only want single balls of yarn," Diane explains.

Have you ever lowered prices because you found they were too high?

"Yes," Diane says. "This happens when people choose very expensive yarns which raises their overall price including my labor. Customers do not always understand the difference between generic, dime-store yarns and high-quality imports for example."

Do you have a system for pricing your items?

"When I knit baby garments, I double or triple the price of the yarn for my labor. Knitting adult garments under this system, however, raises the price to more than $500, more than the market can bear. Using cables and fancy stitches takes longer to knit but I only charge $100 more than the price of the yarn to remain competitive in the market."

Do you consider raw materials when you set your prices?

"Yes. I start by considering the price of the yarn and go from there to other details such as size, style, level and intricacy but I set prices based upon the cost of the yarn."

How do you determine overhead?

"I prefer not to consider it as I enjoy knitting so much that friends and family think of me as a compulsive knitter."

Where do you sell your products in addition to the yarn shop where you work?

"I sell at craft shows. This is the best place to get my prices easily. County fairs work differently for me. My work is more upscale than items sold at county fairs so they are not appropriate for me. I also researched craft malls but found that buyers who come to craft malls want to buy at flea-market prices. I cannot even recover the cost of the yarn by selling in craft malls. It is simply too labor intensive to sell so unreasonably low," Diane replies.

Diane does well selling on consignment in the yarn shop where she works. She explains, "I am fortunate that the shop-owner who allows me to display my garments on consignment does not charge me though we both recognize that most shop owners do. She says it pays her indirectly to display my garments when she stocks the yarn in her shop. Seeing my work has proven to encourage customers to buy the same yarn I use in a specific garment and to make their own version. This arrangement satisfies us both," Diane concludes.

Recently, Diane explained that her new line of crocheted and knitted clothing for toddlers, "UNDER 4's" has taken her business in new directions. A specialty boutique shop nearby has set up a "living room" in the back of the store for Grandmas and proud aunties to shop. The shop-owner buys each item from Diane at wholesale and resells them. Diane has discovered a specialized "niche" in the market as she continues to make adorable fairy or flower caps for very small children. People seem so enchanted with how cute these items that they keep Diane's fingers flying. She can make three per day, each, one-of-a-kind.

However, we might say Diane has gone "International" in one sense. On a recent trip to Mexico she took a bag full of these little hats to trim and finish while on vacation. Not one hat made it home. Tourists bought them as they saw Diane making them on the beach. As I have said many times in this book, "Never stop marketing…even on vacation."

QUICK REVIEW OF PRICING METHODS, KNITTING & CROCHET

X   Use a Pricing Template plus an add-on list of possible, additional details to arrive at a full retail price. Customers pay for all supplies.

X   Charge by the hour to cover simple to complex projects. Customers pay for all supplies.

X   Charge $5 per hour per item completed in an hour. Added cost of the materials plus 20% to cover stripping, knotting/sewing and doubled the total to sell at wholesale, tripled it to sell at wholesale.

X   Charge by the project for principle products, afghans, vests and sweaters. Only consider labor when setting prices since manufacturers provide all raw materials.

X   Charge by the particular project based upon earning $25-$55 per day but charge more for making one-of-a-kinds when selling to dealers.

X   Double or triple the cost of the yarn to set the final retail price.

X   When selling very elaborate adult garments and afghans, price would exceed what the market would bear so knitter charges $100 more than the price of the yarn to remain competitive in the market.

CONTRIBUTORS TO THIS CHAPTER:

Sylvia Ann Landman
Sylvia's Studio
1090 Cambridge St.
Novato, CA 94947
Phone: 415-883-6206
Email: Create@Sylvias-studio.com
http://www.Sylviasstudio.com

Darlene Buckel
DKK Associates, The Clay Factory
54310 Pleasant Valley Dr.
Osceola, IN 46561
Phone: 219-674-0521
Fax: 219-674-0649
Toll Free: 800-622-5131
E-mail: padbuckel@juno.com
http://www.clayfactory.com

Tonya Caudel
The Added Touch: Unique baskets and gifts.
E-mail: tcaudle@spock.ctsi.net
http://www.ctsi.net/addedtouch
(Prefers not to list street address and phone)

Nazanin S. Fard
1644 Novato Blvd.
Novato, CA 94947
Phone: 415-898-7072
Fax: 415-897-3568
E-mail: nazee@craftland.com
http://www.craftland.com

Marguerite Nabinger Winfield
Rural Box 108
Kirbyville, TX 75956
Phone: 409-423-5730
E-mail: mktgmvn@juno.com

Diane Sack
657 Cherry St.
Novato, CA, 94945
Phone: 415-897-8067
E-mail: dianjohn@sonic.net

Chapter 8

Needlepoint, Cross Stitch & Embroidery

Pricing Template: Sylvia Ann Landman
In-Depth Interview: Anita Tinlin

Preparing to write this chapter baffled me for a time. Crafters whom I interviewed for this book inundated with me with wonderful, original and specific pricing standards for their particular craft. They exhibited eagerness to share with others what they had learned about pricing issues *before* I began Chapter 9. Reality hit me when I realized I had not found a single person other than myself who embroidered for others. Had threaded-needle crafters vanished?

I have sold needlepoint and crewel designs to magazines and clients and expected to find many others who did the same. Soon, I realized that the advent of computerized sewing machines had displaced embroiderers who worked by hand. Several companies advertised in the yellow pages of my local phone book offering commercial, *machine* embroidery services. Most indicated they would embroider on shirts of all types and on the bill of caps.

Later, I asked questions of crafters who offered machine embroidery services online. Most agree that hand embroidery had become unprofitable as they could not compete with those who could do the same work faster and cheaper by computerized machine.

"Setting prices for commercial machine embroiderers like myself remains very difficult," a friend told me. "It's easy for us to embroider by machine when the font and design a customer wants already exists within stock computer files and its software. But when customers request a specific letter size, pattern, design or font that I don't have stored in my computer, I must digitize what they want before I can begin the embroidery itself," she concluded. We must wait to see if hand embroidery will continue to diminish as embroidery machines drop in price. Nonetheless, national organizations such as *The Embroidery Guild of America, The American Needlepoint Guild* and the trade show, *The National*

Needlework Association continue to provide seminars and classes which continue to have enrollment.

*   *   *

Pricing Template: Sylvia Ann Landman

A few years after I became established as a dressmaker, knitter and crocheter, I began to receive requests from customers to work canvas embroidery for them, popularly known as "needlepoint."

Canvas embroidery differs from my other crafts. Tremendous variation in style, size and complexity are a part of the three crafts above, but canvas embroidery is more consistent especially when using variations of traditional Tent Stitch. Traditional canvas embroidery varies only in the size of the canvas used which in turn, determines how many stitches. I must fill the canvas. I worked out my Pricing Template below:

1   Consider the size of the canvas mesh first.
2   Determine the total number of stitches per square inch by multiplying mesh width by mesh length. Example: Canvas mesh sized at 14"x14", = 196 stitches per square inch.
3   Determine the time it takes to work one square inch carefully. It takes me 12 minutes to cover one square inch of #14 canvas.
4   Determine dimensions of the stitching area. Example: For a 12" square working surface, multiply 12"x12" = 144 sq. inches.
5   Multiply the number of stitches per square inch by the total dimension area you will work. 144" total square inches by 196 stitches to the inch results in 28,224 stitches overall.
6   Divide the total number of stitches by the time it takes you to work one square inch. In our example: 28,224 stitches divided by 12 minutes per inch means it will take 2,352 total minutes. Divide by 60 minutes per hour and you will find it will take you 39-40 hours to do the work.
7   To earn at least $6 per hour, you would charge 40 hoursx$6 per hour or $240 for labor.

Everything changes if the size of the canvas mesh changes. Using the Template above, see what a difference there would be if you were to work on #10 canvas.

1   10 stitches = 1 square inch
2   10 stitches x 10 stitches now equals 100 stitches in each square inch.
3   I cover 1 square inch of #10 canvas in seven minutes.
4   For a 12" square working surface, 12" by 12" = 144 square inches
5   Now, multiply 144 square inches x 100 stitches to the inch = 14,400 total stitches.
6   Divide total number of required stitches, 14,400, by seven minutes per inch = 2,057 total minutes, divided by 60 minutes = 34-35 hours.
7   35 hours x $6 = $175.

Many artisans in other media can adapt this system to their own craft. For example, this may be useful to those who bead, crochet squares, make quilt blocks or other crafts where size and time remain static throughout the project.

Cross-stitch is another matter. In this case, all stitches on the surface are not necessarily covered with stitches as in needlepoint or canvas embroidery. In fact, only the design itself is embroidered with cross stitches but the background surface remains plain or unstitched. Now, you have variables to consider.

Calculate the number of stitches in the worked design. Most cross-stitchers can make about 100 stitches per hour depending on how many color changes and re threading the work requires. Using the example of $6 per hour, divide the total number of stitches by 100. Last, multiply by your hourly rate and you have determined a fair price.

When you hand-embroider for others, make sure the customer pays for canvas, yarn, fabric and thread. If the client chooses a painted canvas or a commercial cross-stitch graph, the system above works well. However, if you must create a design from scratch, everything changes again. You must now consider design and layout time, time to select colors, painting a canvas or making a graph and selecting threads and yarns yourself. Add these charges to your total fee.

Don't forget this point. When you time yourself, do you only consider your absolute best pace? In reality, we seldom work at a super tempo nor at a snail's pace. If you only time yourself at your fastest speed, you are not being fair to yourself as you set prices.

A last word about pricing your time: Determine the income you would like to have in a specific year. Divide it by the number of hours you plan to work. For example, if you want to earn $52,000 per year, working forty hours per week, using this system, you would find that you should earn $25 an hour. Price as if you were paying *yourself*, $25/hour.

*   *   *

Tana Taylor embroiders primitive folk art samplers for her customers both at retail and wholesale. "When I first began making primitive samplers, I priced by the letter," explains Tana. "My system worked well at the time as supplies used in this work remain relatively inexpensive. Labor is the greatest expense involved in producing my samplers so when I began, I charged 25 cents per letter. Tana explains that using her old system, a sampler containing 60 letters would sell for $15."

Today, Tana determines prices by the size of the frame the customer wants. "You may wonder what frame size has to do with my actual embroidery," Tana explains. "Larger samplers containing more words, therefore, more letters take longer to embroider and therefore, require larger frames" she says.

Tana says her wholesale system remains simple if she prices all 5"x7" samplers at $16, all 7" x 9" samplers at $20 and so on, to larger frame sizes. "This system works well for me," she adds.

*   *   *

Lyn Sethna began doing counted-cross-stitch 16 years ago inspired by a friend. "Years ago, pre-stamped cross-stitch on fabric provided little "x's" that were not a uniform size and lines of them were never straight," Lyn explains. "Counted cross-stitch worked from a graph and stitched on an even-weave cloth such as Aida cloth, always turn out perfectly!" says Lyn enthusiastically.

"My daughter turned sixteen recently. When she was four years old, I bought a leaflet showing an alphabet with each letter depicting an object such as "A" for apple, "B" for balloon, etc. I made my daughter a cross-stitched pillow featuring her name. Soon, her little friends also wanted them when they turned four. My pillows became so popular with Moms that the birthday party invitations began to arrive with the child's first, middle and last names carefully printed in anticipation of a pillow as a gift. I decided to sell them then and I still make them today," Lyn says.

Lyn works on white Aida cloth measuring 11 threads per inch which makes counting threads to create uniform letters easy. "Most orders I receive," says Lyn "are very traditional. Blue for boys, pink for girls. Each pillow measures 14"x12" which includes a ruffle around the edge. I charge the whopping price of $35 for each she says. "I have made about 250 of these alphabet pillows over the years using this particular pattern," she adds. "Recipients receive such enthusiastic 'thank you' notes from my customers who give my pillows as gifts, that they call me to read the notes to me!"

"Everyone, no matter their age, enjoys seeing their name in print," says Lyn. "Since each pillow is custom-made, it is not possible for me to make them ahead of time. Word-of-mouth advertising has worked well for me. Usually, Moms who receive a pillow as a gift will order a pillow when their friends have babies. I even get orders from overseas," Lyn comments. "As long as the recipient speaks English, the alphabet pillow works. Unusually spelled names are never a problem. These are special gifts that will be cherished for years to come," she concludes.

*   *   *

Nazee Fard, whom you met in the last chapter, sells silk ribbon embroidered items to magazines but she says this differs from designing knit or crochet pieces. "Selling knitting and crochet designs, I usually send in a swatch of the pattern stitches along with a brief description and sketch of the design and interested editors call me, we set a price and I go to work," she says.

"Selling embroidery items, means I must work on speculation and make the item first since editors do not accept drawings for these," Nazee explains. Like knitting and crochet, Nazee rarely buys products for design work as manufacturers provide it at no cost while she endorses the products by name in her instructions.

Nazee continues. "To me, the most important aspects of preparing items for publication are the design and instruction writing. Stitching does not seem like work to me, because I love doing it so much. A good design that becomes a beautiful project makes editors and readers happy," she adds. "In addition to the appearance of the project, editors want easy-to-follow, accurate instructions" Nazee emphasizes.

Nazee shares specifics about her pricing when she says, "I have sold a small silk ribbon embroidery box, which takes three hours of stitching time for $50 but a design in a picture frame with a much more sophisticated design pays $250. Prices may seem high to readers but keep in mind that I can sell an item just once. No editor will permit the same design to appear in another magazine."

*   *   *

Janet O'Brien, began her business, *In Cahoots* with a partner in 1993 and has taken her embroidery skills in another direction from other embroiderers in this chapter. Janet says, "I believe my present love and expertise for embroidery has evolved to machine embellishment rather than hand embroidery. I have taught machine embellishment for more than five years after many years of hand embroidery. I use the term machine embellishment because too many people today think of machine embroidery as using preset embroidery motifs programmed into their software. I teach students how to use decorative and unusual threads to embellish fabric that may become a wall-hanging, quilt, garment, or linens. This is certainly in the tradition of embroidery but I use a machine as an extension of my hands. I tell my students that any stitch will create beautiful embroidery. I do not limit techniques to those based on beautiful preset stitches of the top-of-the-line machines. I teach how utility stitches can be used in combination or alone to manipulate stunning embellishments," she explains.

"I am proud of the patterns we designed and books we wrote together, especially our book, *Point Well Taken,* still the most complete guide to needles and threads for home sewers on the market. We also wrote *Two Needles Are Better than One, a* workbook describing twelve different machine embellishment techniques using twin needles. Our popular vest pattern, *Great Squares,* offers different machine embellishment techniques plus an adaptation to use machine embroidery motifs. Our books and patterns have been featured in publications such as *Sew News, Quilters Newsletter, and Open Chain Newsletter."*

Designing has brought Nancy to national prominence after exhibiting her garments during a fashion show sponsored by the American Quilting Society and various quilt shows and an Atlanta gallery. Nancy and her partner were invited to design two ensembles for the prestigious Fairfield Fashion Show as well. (See next chapter for details about this important show.)

Teaching at national quilt shows, quilting retreats, groups of sewing machine dealers and The International Quilt Festival add to her professional status. Says Nancy, "Since my partner retired this year, I have returned to my roots in designing and teaching spending about six hours per day on my business. Many days run longer depending on deadlines or inspiration. My time includes designing, sewing, marketing, administration, and teaching."

Nancy demonstrates her respect for running a business as she says, "One must always perform a certain amount of paperwork. Without the infrastructure to support your business, you will eventually fail. Growth will be overtaken by poor management. Artisans who bring creative talents to their business, must still develop the business skills. Sometimes I feel that my business runs me. One of the difficulties is that when you try to do everything in the business, you experience a significant drop in the amount of time available for creating. Balancing your time plus good decision making brings about enough time to create," she adds.

Nancy sells at both retail and wholesale and through distributors. She explains, "Each market requires a different approach and different rules that drive decision. Retail customers are sometimes hard to reach by small companies because advertising is expensive. Another expense to consider in retail sales, especially mail-order, is shipping and handling. Packing a box of fifty books for a distributor takes less time than packing fifty single retail orders. On the other hand, home sewers and quilters love to share their latest finds; so getting products in their hands remains an important marketing tool. Distributor sales far outpace wholesale orders which outpace retail orders," she explains.

"Purchasing through sewing distributors who permit designers to open wholesale accounts has been helpful," she says, "but I needed good, established credit information and must purchase a minimum number of supplies each time. I prefer to buy fabric at local specialty shops as I don't need large quantities. Since I like to work with silk, I have found national sources who require low minimum orders for a discount. Creative people can tap into many sources of supplies locally and through the Internet to keep production costs low," she suggests.

Nancy explains she chose to lower her prices when a gallery in Atlanta found them too high. She also had to adjust the colors she uses and the sizes of garments. "I had to use more cool colors and sew larger sized garments," she says, "But spending time on a few prototypes saves a lot of wasted time and materials," she adds.

"Time is very valuable to me so I must decide how I want to use it," says Nancy. "My accountant once said not to do anything that didn't bring in money. He suggested I focus on designing, making strategic decisions and marketing. I admit it takes awhile to have the cash flow to do this," she explains.

Nancy discusses pricing in detail. "When selling on consignment, the gallery gets 30% of the purchase price of the piece to cover their overhead and I find this reasonable. Distributors and catalogs who sell my products certainly work for me and they get a special rate for large quantity orders—a negotiable discount within a certain range."

"Pricing must include all production costs and account for all discounts to wholesale customers and distributors must remain within the range prices of competitive products in your market," says Nancy. "You may not be able to discount certain items because your costs are too high. If you depend on discounted outlets, you may have to rethink your product. Make sure to include all production costs including packaging, photography, copying and materials. I don't think development costs except materials are considered by small businesses like mine," she adds.

Nancy says that if you produce multiples of an item as she did with patterns and books, you have to consider the amount of inventory you want on hand versus the discount for ordering large quantities of a single product.

Pricing her work in the beginning, Nancy charged $125 for a pieced, embellished vest for a gallery. "This was too high," she admits. "The best price turned out to be $90. Today, my vests sell for $65 to $75 but when I make larger sizes and use cooler colors, I get my best price of $90," she adds.

Nancy discusses pricing patterns. "There are several costs involved in determining the costs of garment patterns. There is the hang-hole bag of about $.05 when you buy large quantities, several thousand per order. The color, cover slicks should be around $.05 when you buy 5,000. From large printers, you should get your directions printed or copied within a range of $.02 to .05 per double sided copy for a quantity of 5,000," she advises. "Remember to multiply this number by the number of pages of your directions," she adds.

"With the increase of paper and shipping costs and the length of our pattern directions, *In Cahoots* never reached that goal," says Nancy. "Because *In Cahoots* patterns often have 12 to 16 pages of instructions, garment patterns range in price between $9.00 and $12.00."

"Although you may never use 5,000 cover slicks," she continues, "You can staple cover slicks from all your patterns together with a price list to provide potential customers a color catalog of your work. Tissue patterns have a great advantage because they are light weight for shipping and make a thin pattern for storage and for merchants who hang them on racks."

Pricing her books differs. Printing and binding can become expensive and using coil binding can equal printing costs. Nancy says that to photocopy a small run of your book, you can test the waters without investing a lot of money. You must pay copying costs of between $.08 and $.12 per double sided page if you print 100 copies. Folding is a small, extra charge, or you fold your own. Costs of printing heavier, cover stock paper can run between $.05 to $.10 if you provide a special cover stock. Nancy reminds readers that binding is labor intensive; so it can cost $1.00 or more per book. Offset printing reduces the cost per book but raises the initial outlay because printing runs are generally for 5,000 copies plus there are set-up charges. If your cost is $2.00 per book, your initial investment is $10,000. *"In Cahoots* books sell for $14.00 each," she says "But *In Cahoots* pricing has to account for sales to retail, wholesale and distributor buyers," she adds. "Some pattern designers do not sell to distributors for various reasons, but often, the reason is that they combine production costs with a competitive selling price, not allowing for a comfortable profit after subtracting the distributor discount," she adds.

Nancy concludes with advice for other embroiders and sewers who also sell patterns. "In your product research, determine how many of an item you can sell. If the cost of one item is low but you must invest a lot of resources and store a large quantity of the item, producing based on short-term demand makes more sense. You may pay more per item, but you do not tie up a lot of funds on a single item. Remember when tax time comes, inventory counts as assets upon which you pay taxes. In other words, you may have to pay twice in hopes your item sells."

Informal Interview: (Anita preferred an essay style interview rather than questions and answers used by other contributors in this book.).

Anita Tinlin and her husband were both working at a large computer company in 1990 when they decided to change their lifestyle. Anita explains that she and her husband each gave a month's notice and took off on a sailboat for points south, with one entire berth on the boat reserved for fabric and hand-cranked sewing machine. Says Anita, "We planned to return in about six months but didn't return until two years later after many adventures and a strong sense of satisfaction at having realized a dream. We returned to Atlanta ready to be responsible."

Continuing, Anita says, "We started a consulting and training development company called SKILLS, which has grown during the past seven years. We create customized advanced-project management training for a large telecommunications company and write software for a retail sales training company." Anita explains.

"During all this time I continued to pursue my passion for collecting and restoring vintage quilts. In 1996 I was looking for specialty papers for my printer (preprinted paper with some sort of quilt-related images) when my spouse suggested I create my own. Our business, SKILLS Graphics was born. Using digital photography and vintage quilts in my collection, a graphic designer and I created several collections of preprinted stationery for laser and inkjet printers, featuring high-quality, four-color images of vintage and contemporary quilts," she adds.

Recently, Anita became interested in another form of needlework popular during the late 1800s and early 1900s, called "Redwork Embroidery." Anita loved it immediately as white and red were her favorite colors. "I have a red and white sewing studio filled plastic items from the 1930's such as a red and white Hoosier cabinet, red/white enamel tables, etc.," she adds.

Working with an artist, Donna Brennan, Anita created a collection of embroidery patterns suitable for Redwork. "My designs are based on a quilting cat, and named Pawleen, who enjoyed a lot of attention at Quilt Market. Based on the response to Pawleen, we are now at work creating designs featuring Pawleen's kittens," Anita says. "I work with a silk screener to create preprinted fabric squares for Pawleen and her children."

The response for Pawleen patterns at *Quilt Market* was so great that a shop owner told Anita that many of her customers were red-work enthusiasts and has reordered three times. "Feedback from shop owners suggests that at first, customers display mild interest but when they see samples and someone else embroidering, they decide to try it," Anita explains. "Hand embroidery is highly portable, which is part of its appeal. Many customers who come to my show booths told me they wanted embroidery designs suitable for baby quilts. Only one person asked if the designs were available for machine embroidery. I hope to have tee shirts available in the fall with Pawleen designs," Anita relates. Today, Anita's business includes:

- Making preprinted stationery for laser and inkjet printers
- Designing and making note cards and gift cards with envelopes featuring designs suitable for embroidery,
- The company will soon have embroidery kits (including the designs transferred to fabric, floss, needle, etc.), and tee shirts.

Anita vends at retail shows, featuring vintage textiles, sewing and craft items for sale. "In the course of scouring antique shops, flea markets, thrift shops and yard sales in search of vintage fabrics for my collection, I came across many things that I felt compelled to purchase and save from some awful fate," says Anita. "I love seeing and using old sewing and craft items and thinking about the role they played in women's lives. Often, little value is placed on them. A half-finished wool sweater still on the knitting needles for only $1.00? Someone worked hard on that and perhaps saved awhile to purchase the wool. I want to give all of these things a second chance to be finished and valued. At some point, when I am no longer working full-time in SKILLS, I would like to become a certified quilt appraiser," she says.

I asked Anita if she thought that embroidery in the U.S. was in decline. Says Anita, "I cannot speak about needlepoint and cross-stitch but I do not think hand embroidery has lost favor. In fact, I think I expect to see a resurgence of it. I belong to a large quilt guild in the Atlanta area, (approx. 275 members) subdivided into stitching bees of 10-25 members each. At the last meeting, I noticed that over half of us were doing hand embroidery while the rest were either hand-quilting or hand-piecing. Most of the embroiderers were working on block-of-the-month style blocks for quilts or wall-hangings. Many were doing Red-work, a traditional form of embroidery where all stitches are made in red thread on a cream background.

Anita is preparing to be a vendor at a large, well-attended show. This year she plans to make embroidery a main theme of her booth. Says Anita, "In addition to featuring Pawleen and two additional embroidery design collections, I will have a wide variety of vintage embroidery items for sale including old textiles which are stamped for hand-embroidery. Based on my discussions with vintage textiles dealers, I find a lot of interest in collecting old needlework and recreating needlework from the 30's, 40's and 50's" she explains.

"Pricing embroidery is a little harder than other crafts," explains Anita. First, I created an Excel spreadsheet to include all costs associated with developing my products. My first expense was product research. I purchased one of every product on the market similar to what

I was planning to create. This helped me understand what was currently available, to avoid overlap and assess the quality of what I had found."

Anita continues, "Next, I considered design fees. Over a period of several months, I worked closely with an artist to give her a sense of what I wanted, feed her ideas and provide feedback on her preliminary sketches. While she continued her work, I spent considerable time researching copyright and drafting an agreement which would allow me to purchase the designs and copyrights from her for specific uses. Our agreement states that if I want to utilize the designs for products other than those specified in our agreement, I will compensate her for any and all modifications which may be necessary to the designs. After I decided which of her designs I would use, I spent considerable time converting them to electronic media" says Anita.

Continuing, Anita explains her process. "I scanned, sized and colored the designs using Corel software. I created front and back package covers and wrote comprehensive instructions. I spread the cost of all of these activities across what I estimated to be the number of packages I could reasonably expect to sell during the first year which gave me a creative cost per package."

Always alert to improving her system, Anita began another Excel worksheet. She says, "I calculated the cost of printing, paper and toner for each package and added the cost of the packaging which yielded my cost per package. I doubled that to cover overhead expenses such as office supplies, hardware, software, marketing and advertising to arrive at my wholesale price. Using that total, I doubled it again to arrive at my retail price," she explains.

A thorough researcher, Anita created yet another Excel worksheet to list all the competing products she had purchased during her research phase. She explains, "I noted specifics such as; type of product (book, booklet, paper pattern, etc.), number of pages of written material, number of pages of design material and quality of the material. This was judgment on my part but I found misspelled words, grammatical errors and poor layout in the products I reviewed both layout and creativity. Additionally, some bore inflated retail prices. (See chapter 5: Pattern makers.)

"I compared my retail prices to similar products and found that I was on the low side. Next, I did an informal survey of other embroiderers to learn out how much they would be willing to pay for a hypothetical product which was in fact, the one I had developed but which they had not seen. This survey suggested that the retail price I chose resulting from the exercise described above was in fact too low, so I raised it 10%. I reasoned that if the market would bear a slightly higher price, I will try it. After all, there is no guarantee that I will sell as many packages as I originally estimated I would need to in order to recover my development costs. Besides, it is easier to put a product on sale (show specials, etc.) than it is to raise the price after ads and other marketing materials are already in circulation," she adds.

"Many people in the industry whose opinions I value advised me to package my fourteen patterns separately. I entered every bit of information associated with this product on my computer so I am free to do whatever I wish as I consider the suggestions of others. I print on demand, i.e. I print on a regular basis and have someone help me package orders to keep up with incoming and anticipated orders, but I do not maintain a large inventory. In the county in which I live, you must pay taxes on inventory. I learned the hard way that maintaining a large inventory, which I had done with other products manufactured in large volume, to get a cost per piece that the market would bear.

Anita continues her astute observations. "My methods may be time-consuming but I am surprised at the number of industry associates who, when asked to describe their costs for a particular product, say they do not really know. I advise them to use software similar to Excel with one worksheet connected to another so that when prices of one product component changes, it is easy to recalculate the cost. I like the way that Excel recalculates for me when I change just one number. I can even do modeling, (i.e.) look at creative costs if I were to sell 1000, 5000 or even 10,000 packages in my first year. I prefer to remain in very close touch with my business," she concludes.

QUICK REVIEW OF PRICING METHODS FOR EMBROIDERY

X   Consider the size of canvas mesh size and determine the total number of stitches per square inch by multiplying mesh width by mesh length. Example: Canvas mesh sized at 14"x14", = 196 stitches per square inch. Work 1 square inch of canvas embroidery to time yourself.

X   Determine the stitching area dimensions. Example: For a 12" square working surface, multiply 12"x12" = 144 sq. inches. Multiply the number of stitches per square inch by the total dimension area you will work then calculate the required labor.

X   To earn at least $6 per hour, you would charge 40 hoursx$6 per hour or $240 for labor. Everything changes if the size of the canvas mesh changes.

X   When embroidering samplers containing alphabets, price by the letter.

X   Consider setting prices by the size of the frame that will hold your embroidery. Larger designs in larger frames take more time to embroider.

X   Sell an easy to make cross-stitch pillow measuring 14"x12" which includes a ruffle around the edge but no background embroidery and charge a flat rate.

X   Think about the complexity of the embroidery. A box which requires three hours of stitching may sell well for $50 but a design in a picture frame with much more sophisticated, elaborate, detailed designs may sell for $250.

X   Consider having three Pricing Templates; one for selling at full retail price, a second for selling at wholesale and a third when selling on consignment when you must pay a commission fee.

X   Create a spreadsheet to include all costs associated with developing the product including product research. Purchase one of every product on the market similar to yours and observe style differences in what you find to avoid overlap and assess the quality of the market.

X   Consider design fees if you work with an artist. Tell them what you want and listen to feedback while they make preliminary sketches. This will help you decide on the complexity of the design, the time it takes the designer plus the time it will take you to embroider the design. All of these costs must be included in your final retail price.

CONTRIBUTORS TO THIS CHAPTER

Sylvia Ann Landman
Sylvia's Studio
1090 Cambridge St.
Novato, CA 94947
Phone: 415-883-9426
Fax: 415-883-6206
E-mail: Create@Sylvias-studio.com
http://www.Sylvias-studio.com

Tana Taylor
(Prefers not to list address and phone)

Lyn Sethna
10 Sawmill Trabuco Canyon
CA 92569-4205
FAX 949-459-7578
BtlQuilt@cs.com
http://www.best.com/~amethist/pt/home.html

Nazanin S. Fard
1644 Novato Blvd.
Novato, CA 94947
Phone: (415)898-7072
Fax: (415)897-3568
E-mail: nazee@craftland.com
Website: http://www.craftland.com

Janet O'Brien
PO Box 72336
Marietta, GA 30007-2336
Phone: 770-971-2675
Fax: 770-565-6324
Atlanta, GA
E-mail: janetfobrien@mindspring.com

Anita Tinlin
SKILLS Graphics,
3905 Twin Leaf Place,
Marietta, GA 30062.
Phone: 770-565-0889
Fax: 770-971-7970
E-mail: anitat@mindspring.com

Chapter 9

Art-to-Wear & Sewing

Pricing Template: Linda Schmidt
In-Depth Interview: Margo Gallinoto

"Seamstress" or "tailor" used to describe a person who altered or made clothing for others but how things have changed. Seamstresses and tailors still alter or make clothing for customers but we call the exciting development now so popular, "Art to Wear," "Wearable Art" or "Decorative Clothing."

People do not ***need*** Art-to-Wear garments to stay warm or cover themselves. From hand-painted T-shirts to dresses made in gossamer layers of silk embellished with pearls, they make or buy such garments and wear them as an "artistic statement."

The present craze of decadent, embellished clothing received a giant boost twenty years ago when the Fairfield Processing Company in Connecticut decided to sponsor a fashion show and staged at different quilting events throughout the U.S. to expand sales of their batting products. Before then, batting was what quilters used to fill their quilts, placing it between the decorative quilt top and its backing or lining. Fairfield envisioned greater sales—and rightly so—if the same people who used batting to make quilts would also use it to make clothing.

Early Fairfield Fashion Show garments *did* look like wearable quilts at first. Sewers simply adapted traditional quilting patterns such as *Dresden Plate, Texas Star* and appliqué techniques to garments. Soon, they found that inserting batting between the decorative outer layer and a garment's lining. The clothing acquired more body without losing its shape. Batting also helps support the weight of added embellishments so it did not take long before sewing artists added ordinary sewing notions such as textile paint, beads and ribbons to their garments. Feathers, dolls, jewelry, fur and heavy metallic threads, cords and tassels soon became a main-stay of garments described as "Art to Wear."

Each year, talented textile artists receive a personal invitation from Fairfield to submit a garment of their own design with no limits to embellishment as long as the company batting was included. A collection of the best garments became a sort of traveling fashion show, moving from one side of the country to the other. As artists competed to be included, they began to outdo each other showing no restraint in imagination and creativity.

The Fairfield Fashion Show soon spurred a spin-off industry which the craft industry embraced heartily. Manufacturers of beads, ribbons, thread and other embellishments began to offer invited artists unlimited supplies of their product on a complimentary basis. With no financial limitations on their use of such items, sewers increased their skills and creativity choosing increasingly more expensive, luxurious embellishments for their clothing.

Traditional quilting patterns in Art-to-Wear gave way to costumes and fantasy garments not seen since seventeenth century European courts. Demand grew from quilt show sponsors to show the collection at their event every year. Meanwhile, the interest in such incredible embellishment spawned not only new manufacturers of threads, beads, etc., but also caught the eye of sewing machine manufacturers. Using computer technology, we now have sewing machines than not only mimic hand-embroidery but also sew on beads, trims, cords and silk flowers. Today, the sky is the limit in Art-to-Wear. One look at this year's collection, more lavish than ever to celebrate Fairfield's twentieth year of sponsoring such shows, brings to mind wardrobes from illustrated art books of Grimms' Fairy Tales. They are beautiful beyond belief but alas, where does one wear these outrageous garments in today's fashion world of jeans, sweatshirts and running shoes for every occasion no matter how formal? Well, if you are as creative and talented as the artisans in this chapter, why not model your Art-to-Wear at a Fairfield Fashion Show?

*   *   *

Linda Schmidt chose an unusual name for her thriving business. She calls it, "*Short Attention Span*" explaining she always listens intensely and works fast because her attention span is short! Looking at Linda's quilts and especially her decorative clothing, one comes to doubt that. Linda's garments have appeared in several Fairfield Fashion shows.

Only outstanding clothing designers from around the country receive an invitation to submit their original fashion statements for this prestigious show.

Linda formally started her business in 1993 but had been sewing at an incredible rate since she was a child. Today she works about twenty hours per week making quilts and garments and another ten hours developing classes, filling out exhibition entries, correspondence with quilt guilds and exhibition promoters, writing lesson plans, writing articles for magazines, writing a book, developing handouts and figuring taxes.

As if this were not enough, Linda teaches a quilting class every Tuesday morning for two hours and also spends time traveling to guilds and quilt shops to speak or present workshops. "However," explains Linda, "When I receive a commission from a client, I devote all of my quilting time to creating a work to sell."

Linda sells only at retail to the ultimate consumer but has recently received an invitation by a museum shop to create Art to Wear as exhibits. "Lately," she says, "My opportunities feel overwhelming. Right now I have a commission to make a large quilt for a city, another one for a fabric company, several people want to buy the clothes off my back, which makes me think about cloning myself."

Linda buys most of her fabric and notions including dye and paint through mail-order companies, but prefers to attend big quilt shows and buy directly from the representatives to stock up. She explains, "I try to buy things on sale, but some specialty items I use never go on sale such as hand painted fabric and glass fused buttons. I have begun painting and dying some of my own fabric, making my own jewelry and dying my own shoes. My friends know me as the person to whom one takes fabric one no longer wants. One quilting friend gave me five boxes of linings, velvets, brocades and sheer fabrics. Another gave me five bags of fabric which I shared with Seniors at a local center. Another gave me the buttons and zippers her Mom left behind when she died. I have incorporated all of these into my quilts and art-to-wear garments," Linda says with pride.

Though she has never lowered her prices, she has raised them. Linda explains. "When I received a public art commission from the City of Dublin, I charged the City of Dublin $75 per square foot for my quilts. Later, I charged the City of Newark $100 per square foot plus expenses of $700 for making a 60"x80" quilted wall-hanging. I just sold two more pieces to a medical center for $130 per square foot. I guess I'm moving up in the world," Linda exclaims.

Describing her pricing system Linda says, "I talked to other, well-known fiber artists and asked how they set their prices. One said she uses a per square foot rate because it seemed a reasonable, businesslike way to price when approaching members of the corporate business community and for private commissions. She had a fairly high rate, but she is quite famous. I set my per square foot rate about 1/3 less than hers and based my current commission rate on that figure. It works well for quilt commissions because one can determine the square footage easily but it doesn't work very well for garments!" Linda explains.

Today, Linda makes fabulous wall quilts so detailed, that they appear to be oil paintings. She says, "I charge $100 per square foot plus expenses and recently received $750 for a long, ethnic vest." Using the vest as an example, Linda offers her Pricing Template and how she arrived at it.

1   Travel time and mileage back and forth to Oakland for meetings and fittings: two trips, 50 miles each, $.32/mile = $32.00

2   My design and pattern were original but size was determined by an existing garment provided by the customer.

3   Times to develop the pattern, draft the design, get it approved and laid out in proper size,
4 hours @ $15/hr = $60.00

4   Cost of thread and ethnic fabric using snippets from at least 500 different fabrics: Approximately $75-100.

5   Labor to sew and finish the garment. Linda explains, "I work fast, but something of this nature takes a lot of time. This garment had eight vertical rows of fabrics on an angle, individually string pieced, and it had a complex frontal design. I estimated it would take approximately three weeks to complete the project. 16 hrs x 3 weeks = 48 hoursx$15/hr = $720."

6   "I liked my client and her good will was important," says Linda. "I knew the garment would please her and create good press for me. I discounted my total price by $100 and charged her $750."
Linda explains her intrinsic values. "I choose to work only on projects that interest me and help me grow as a wearables artist and quilter. As creator, part of my reward is simply personal growth. Making garments to specifically fit one person interests me; making garments for myself is great fun but I don't think I will ever make garments

for the general public. I might wind up with twenty jackets in various sizes of the same pattern that don't fit me or suit anyone else," she says.

Approaching a topic many contributors to this book expressed, Linda explains how she values her time. "I price my work at a level that makes me feel I can bear to give up a design. I want people to know how much I think my work is worth and how much time and effort goes into creating a thing of beauty. If I don't get my asking price, I prefer to keep my work. As it is, I become attached to my pieces and can always use them when giving talks and demonstrations or base classes on them. Thus, I still make a profit from making my garments without giving them up unless I receive my price," says Linda firmly. Though Linda says she loves her work, she says, "Labor is time and time is my life slipping away through my fingers."

Working four part-time paying jobs, Linda says she earns an average of $20 per hour. "So" she explains, "I figure my sewing time is worth that too. Fortunately, I work fast. But how do you measure time you spend in meetings doodling about the garment you're going to make or the time shopping for fabric or the time meeting with the person you're going to sew for or the time you spend pre-washing fabric and finishing? I will not undertake a project unless I will enjoy doing it and feel well paid. If not, what's the point?"

Asked about how she determines overhead, Linda replies, "I keep accurate records of all the fees I receive from speaking, all the prize money I've won making quilts and the commissions I've earned. From that total, I subtract the fabric and raw materials I've purchased, sewing related repairs, any equipment I've had to buy such as my scanner, computer programs, etc., classes and conferences I attended, fees for shipping quilts to and from and entering exhibitions and the percentage my accountant says I can write off for utilities. If a balance remains, I consider that—my profit."

She closes by saying, "Make a name for yourself, do good work and get noticed by winning exhibitions, teaching, wearing and showing your work. People will then come to you and you can price your work to your own and their satisfaction. Everything you fashion must be charged with the breath of your own spirit, or it isn't art so put a bit of yourself into everything you make, believe in it, value it, and others will do the same."

*   *   *

Maral Good, of *Maral Good Designs* is new to making decorative clothing. She designs and makes art-to-wear garments such as jackets, vests and coats usually from Batik or hand-dyed fabric—her favorites.

Recently, she designed a basic vest to use as a foundation for similar garments. She began with a muslin-basic garment to use as a fitting pattern for customers. Once she acquires the correct fit, she applies multiple layers of fabric. The layers become unified when she embellishes them with decorative yarn, ribbon, beads and other trims. Maral sells her garments at retail, directly to the consumer but sells her patterns at wholesale to pattern distributors.

Maral purchases raw materials at large quilt, bead and embellishment trade shows where she can find unusual and hard-to-find items though she purchases needed notions from local retail shops. Maral favors Batik fabrics made by Hoffman and discovered that the popular fabric appreciates in value over time. Says Maral, "My Batik collection in my own stash makes me feel as if I am gathering interest in a bank. Rare Batiks enable me to make one-of-kind garments for my customers."

Maral says her pricing system is simplicity itself. "I add together the cost of raw materials (based upon retail cost), thread, fabric and embellishment. I multiply the total by three and this becomes my retail price for the garment. I allow 1/3 of the price for labor, 1/3 for raw materials and 1/3 for my profit," Maral explains. "The only time I raise my basic price is for a complex technique, hand-dyed or imported fabric or if I hand paint the fabric and add expensive beading or embellishment materials," she adds.

Maral sells most of her garments at quilt or embellishment shows but also sells on commission. At times, customers see her work at a show and see something they like but would prefer in another color or size. Says Maral, "I try to accommodate their personal taste to make sure my work pleases them." However, when Maral sells on consignment, she reverts to her basic pricing formula. She stays with that allowing the shop owner to raise the price for their own percentage.

*　　　　　*　　　　　*

Millie Becker, of Quilted Creations makes lap and baby quilts and quilted wall-hangings but her flagship product is unique and much needed. Wheel chair-bound herself, she reaches out to others designing a practical line of one-of-a kind, quilted bags to fit the backs of wheelchairs. Today, we find her making adjustable, waistband purses not only for disabled customers but the open market as well.

People in wheel chairs found a friend in Millie when she began her unique business in 1992 after a diagnosis of Myasthenia Gravis. Today, she devotes about 80% of her time to designing and making products for sale. Shopping has limitations for Millie so she purchases most of her supplies from catalogs or directly from manufacturers at wholesale.

Millie's pricing system is one we have seen frequently in this book. She calculates total costs of raw materials and triples the total to find her retail price. People with disabilities are Millie's primary market so she attends shows and expositions for the disabled. She also sells at craft malls and at times, on commission or consignment. In the latter case, like Maral, she adds the shop owner's percentage to her full retail price. "This works well," says Millie, "because people are willing to pay more in a shop than directly from a crafter."

Millie has made good use of her website but not as substantially as she would like. Says Millie, "With my website I can reach many more people than I would otherwise and have sold my bags all over the country for much less than it cost me to advertise in disability magazines which I did in the past."

Millie closes with her advice to others. "Try to make items not currently being sold, so you can create a unique market for your product. Duplication floods the marketplace so think about what you can make that looks different enough and yet appeals to customers."

*   *   *

Dale Rae started her small sewing and design business making doll clothes for the 18" *American Girl Doll* and the15" *Bitty-Baby Doll.* Dale was more than qualified for her new business as she had been designing and sewing for more than thirty years with a B.A. degree in theatrical costume design. For twenty years she worked as a dressmaker and for eight years, she designed and made exercise, dance wear and dance costumes.

Pricing always concerned Dale. "Recently, a friend told me about her problem determining a fair price," Dale explains. "She told me that stating a price to her customers always made her feel as if she was asking too much—especially if she knew the customer couldn't afford much. I used this analogy in trying to help her," says Dale.

"If you go to a Cadillac dealership to look at a car but can only afford a small economy car, do you ask the dealer to give you the Cadillac for the price of the lesser car because that is all you can afford? Of course not. You know the Cadillac is a fancier, better designed and probably better made than small economy cars. Think the same way when you do custom designing. Why would you charge them the small car price for a Cadillac automobile?", asked Dale.

"Others with whom I shared this philosophy tell me that they had never thought of it that way," Dale explains. "I don't say I always know best when it comes to pricing, but I certainly look at all the elements that go into making the item such as materials and labor."

Dale buys raw materials both retail and wholesale and remains on the lookout for sales and closeouts. Manufacturers however, must provide her with special accessories, such as doll shoes.

Like many crafters, Dale has had to lower her price now and then. She says, "If I produce a product that I thought would sell well and it turns out that customers won't buy, I lower the price." She has raised her prices more often. "When the item is unique or involves a higher level of skill, e.g., an Aran doll sweater with kilt and feather pin, etc., customers didn't flinch at my price even though I thought my price was too high for my area," Dale says. "Thus, the next time I produce an item like this, I raise the price. Sometimes, I also raise the price on an item easy to produce but in great demand." Dale shares her pricing system:

X   "Raw Materials: I cut out several items at a time from my fabric. I determine how many I can get from a yard of fabric and note what I paid for it. This gives me a "price per garment.""

X   "Next, I add in the cost of notions, elastic, ribbons, thread, flowers, etc. Last, I add a small amount to cover thread and other small notions that I cannot price individually such as snaps and buttons."

X   "Labor: I figure a "price per hour" cost. I am continually developing new designs so I try to keep track of the time it takes to make an outfit the first time through."

X   "Overhead: I add in costs such as booth rental and the commission I pay at a craft mall. I total these to determine the final retail price to the customer."

Dale says that determining profit is difficult just now for several reasons. She explains, "First, my business is still new and I am exploring options for obtaining materials at lower prices. Second, it is still a part-time business as I work full-time during the day. Consequently, the time I sew—evenings and weekends, is not my most productive time of day. Right now, my full-time job income subsidizes my part-time business while I build a stock of fabric, trims, patterns and notions. I earn enough to pay craft-mall fees and shows but still, I cannot accurately gauge my profit for probably another year," Dale says.

Determining the value of her time is easier. Dale charges $10 per hour for her labor in constructing the garments. "But," she adds, "When I order the accessories, my markup helps account for the time used to order, package, label and shipping. When my business becomes full-time, I will reevaluate how I work to come up with consistent fair prices."

Dale is quick to point out what she calls "intangible profits" in her new business. "Seven years ago I felt forced back into the corporate business world. After years of pushing paper, answering phones and not producing anything I look at and appreciate the chance to produce beautiful items. Customers who say, 'I have not seen any other doll clothes so unique and well made as yours' thrill me. Most of all, I like to see the faces of young ladies that fill up my booth at a craft fair or doll show, hearing them 'ooh' and 'ah'. When they describe how their imagination will run wild thinking of all their new dolly can do while wearing one of my outfits, I feel rewarded and consider this, a very real profit for me," Dale says.

Dale expresses her biggest frustration. "When I look around at other booths at craft fairs, I am well aware of the time and cost involved. I recognize that some of these vendors only earn one or two dollars per hour! Crafters and artists have a responsibility not to undervalue their work as this leads the public to expect a low price on every handmade craft they see, never appreciating the artist's time and creativity," she exclaims. "Many potential customers express the attitude, 'well, you do this while you watch television'. Often, they do not consider that a crafter should be paid for their skill and time," says Dale. Like several crafters in this book, Dale specifically requested that I include her comments that crafters who produce items to sell should always consider their time as a valuable commodity and that this time should earn a reasonable wage.

          *   *   *

In-Depth Interview: Margo Gallinoto

Margo Gallinoto, of *Mind's Eye Creations & Hand-painted Apparel* started doing custom work in 1993. A talented, fine artist, she designs and makes garments which she embellishes with hand-painted images. She sells her one-of-a-kind products directly to the consumer at retail prices.

Your garments are so beautiful and original. Please describe your process?

"Before I work a sketch into a final drawing or pattern, I analyze how labor intensive it may be to paint. I may rework some design elements to simplify then and make the garment cost effective without sacrificing quality. Next, I choose a suitable style of garment bearing in mind that I must balance the labor and cost of the garment to keep the projected retail price in line. I have learned to use only the least labor intensive designs on T-shirts, since most people have a preconceived idea of how much they will pay for a T-shirt, no matter what is on it."

Next, Margo transfers her pattern to the chosen garment and determines the time it takes her to paint. "I make notes of the colors and mixtures used to speed up the process for the future. Once the painting is complete, I analyze the costs again. Depending on the figures, the design may become a one-of-a-kind, or I may change the type of garment for future renderings or it may become part of my regular line," she adds.

Is your work affected by seasonal buying?

"Budgeting money for a seasonal business like mine requires planning. I attend craft shows from early May through the beginning of December. From January until Spring weather arrives, people are not motivated to purchase where I live. Though this may not be so for all crafts, it holds true with apparel. When the weather stays cold into Spring, people feel that warm weather will never arrive so they feel it's too early to purchase short sleeves and Spring designs. They also tire of Winter and have little interest in purchasing more Winter clothing."

Where do you purchase your raw materials?

"I purchase from distributor catalogs as I do not buy raw materials at retail prices," Margo says. "I order most of my supplies in quantity from distributors, however, I also scout the ads for retail store sales. Since I am an individual professional artist, I do not receive the most favorable discounts from distributors. Large chain stores receive the deepest discounts and can buy in large quantities to keep prices low. When craft chain-stores have a sale on supplies I use frequently, I find their prices are often lower than my wholesale prices so I buy while there," Margo adds.

When did you begin selling your work?

"I began to sell my designs about eleven months after I developed my wearable line."

Have you ever lowered your prices?

"No," says Margo. "If one of my designs does not sell at the price I established, I take a long, hard look at ways to reduce the cost of making the item or discontinue making it. My retail prices are not inflated therefore, reducing them takes away my profit," she explains.

Have you ever raised your prices?

"Yes." Margo acknowledges. "Attending my first craft show as a vendor, I realized my prices were too low. I didn't lose money but didn't make much either. It was a good learning experience bolstered by the fact that I nearly sold out all my merchandise. This added to my confidence, so it wasn't a total loss! I went home and immediately repriced most of my line."

Margo continues. "Over the years I raised prices on some items, not because the prices were too low, but as a method of inventory control. I felt swamped with orders for a popular part of my line. Keeping up with inventory needs was becoming a problem. Increasing the price of that particular line, decreased the volume slightly but my income and profit went up. Experience has taught me that prices on some items can be raised beyond the formula I use, if the item is unique. I have also found that some items sell better when I raise my prices," she acknowledges.

How do you determine the retail price of garments you make?

"I double the cost of raw materials, add my labor and add 20%, rounded up. Since I paint apparel, I also double check myself by pricing the same unpainted garment in local department stores, if available. If store prices are set low for that item, I am careful not to do labor intensive painting on that garment," Margo explains.

How do you determine overhead?

"Overhead is everything related to your business that is not part of the product," Margo explains. "There are show fees, commissions, initial and replacement costs of display materials, packaging, office equipment, office expenses, telephone, fax, computer, car, insurance, self employment taxes and more. I have seen too many crafters ignore this category, spend what they thought were profits and find themselves in debt!"

Margo calculates overhead and divides by the number of items she expects to produce and sell. "I knew this would make my overhead costs high initially since I was not yet experienced enough to produce and sell maximum quantities. It also made my retail prices too high initially, so I marked up a bit less and considered the difference as part of my initial investment. I recoup my overhead now completely through my sales," she adds.

How do you determine profit?

"Profit to me is what remains after totaling materials, labor and overhead."

How do you place a value on your time?

"Initially, I set this figure too low," says Margo. "I thought if I paid myself $5 to $6 dollars per hour, it would be fair since I work from a home studio. However, I only counted the actual time I worked on inventory. That price made me an unpaid worker in my office and my shows. I finally began to track the average time I spend in my business wearing ALL the hats, not just actually painting. Knowing how much inventory I produce in an average week allowed me to figure my labor accurately," she explains.

Where do you sell your work?

"I sell at craft shows, have sold at craft malls in the past and some on consignment. Since my prices already include overhead because I do craft shows, I add very little if anything to my prices for other markets. I have increased postage for remote locations or extra travel to check on my booth, but this is offset by my not needing to maintain a booth in a consignment store," Margo replies.

Do you sell via the Internet?

"I have not sold on the Internet, but setting up a web site is a primary goal. Meanwhile, I have entered into an agreement with a fellow crafter to have my designs featured on her website for a small commission," she explains.

Please be precise and describe your product in detail.

"Art-to-wear garments I make are hand painted usually, and using purchased apparel. I think hand painted clothing lends itself to standard pricing methods but there are other things to consider. Most people have what I call a 'Perceived Value' attached to apparel—a ceiling to the amount they will pay for certain garments. For example, I did a very detailed, realistic painting on a T-shirt. I put a higher price than usual on it because it was labor intensive. The shirt sat unsold in my booth for months while receiving many compliments. I realized most people have a limit they are willing to pay for *any* T-shirt! Later, I duplicated the same design on a blouse that only cost a few dollars more to buy. I sold it immediately at almost twice the price I'd asked for the T-shirt," Margo said.

How do you test your market to determine what it will bear?

Margo replies. "Adjusting your prices from one show to the next with a new item is one way to test the market. You certainly should know your costs to avoid lowering an item's price to the point of not making a profit! However, sometimes an item that just sits at one show, will sell to beat the band at the next! Strange as it sounds, another idea to consider if a design is not moving, is the possibility that you have priced too *low*. I have raised the price on a design at times because it didn't move only to find it began to sell well. Customers often feel if your item seems like too much of a bargain that it is cheaply made, won't last, or has a defect," she says.

"Learning about the market and buying habits in your area is critical, Margo advises. "I moved to Texas from the East Coast and must adjust my show schedule to take advantage of the market here. Margo closes by sharing her schedule and budgeting system with readers also affected by uneven seasonal changes in their business. "In January I prepare taxes, schedule the upcoming season's shows and reorganize my work area as needed. February through April is used for creating new designs and building inventory. Except for telephone and mail orders,

I do not have much cash flow during these months. To compensate, I put my earnings in a savings account at the end of my season except for anticipated expenses such as show fees, telephone and car expenses. Expense money remains in my business checking account. I then budget the savings to provide income during the four off-season months. Discipline is required but it is well worth it. I have seen too many professional crafters spend the money that should be set aside for business at the end of the season, only to find themselves struggling to start their businesses over again year after year," Margo concludes.

QUICK REVIEW OF PRICING METHODS IN THIS CHAPTER

X   Consider charging by the square foot rate when creating wall-hangings on commission. Creating garments requires more careful, individual pricing.

X   When starting out, think about charging 1/3 of what a well-known famous designer of art-to-wear receives. Then, as your experience increases, raise your prices until you are competitive.

X   Develop a pricing template considering:

Travel time and mileage,

Design time,

Pattern making, development and drafting at @ $15 per hour for example.

Fitting time,

Cost of thread, fabric and other raw materials.

Labor to sew and finish garment.

X   Total raw materials (based upon retail cost), thread, fabric and embellishment. Multiply the total by three to determine the final retail price for the garment, allowing 1/3 of the price for labor, 1/3 for raw materials and 1/3 for profit.

X   Calculate total costs of raw materials and triple the total to find your retail price but add the shop owner's percentage to full retail price when selling on consignment.

X   Total raw materials and notions at full retail cost. Add a "price per hour" cost plus overhead such as booth rental and commissions paid at a craft mall. The total determines the final retail price to the customer.

X   Double the cost of raw materials, add labor plus 20%, rounded up. Check the same unpainted or unembellished garment in local department stores. Proceed only if you can make a profit or lower the complexity of detail added to the garment.

CONTRIBUTORS to THIS CHAPTER

Linda S. Schmidt
7695 Sunwood Drive
Dublin, CA 94568
Phone (925) 829-4329
E-mail: shortattn@home.com
http://members.home.net/shortattn

Maral Good
Maral Good Designs
488 Ethel Ave
Mill Valley, CA 94941
Phone: 415-361-0540
E-mail: mginmv@hotmail.com

Millie Becker
Quilted Creations
31 Clark Street
Danvers, MA 01923-1912
Phone and Fax: 978-777-2613
E?mail: MILLIEBECKER@prodigy.net
http://pages.prodigy.com/milliebecker/qc.htm   and,
http://pages.prodigy.net/milliebecker/jt.htm

Dale Rae
Dale Rae Designs
1177 N. 230 W.
Logan, UT 84341
E-mail: dalerae@champ.usu.edu

Margo Gallinoto
1120 Oakhollow Dr.
Corinth, TX 76205
Phone: (940) 321-2125
E-mail: mcgallinoto@theoffice.net

Chapter 10

Woodworking

Pricing Template: Pete LeClair
In-Depth Interview: Kathy Anderson

People have appreciated the luster, grain and color of natural woods for centuries. Even Joseph and his son, Jesus, were known for their clever ways with wood. In the beginning, wooden products were utilitarian but it did not take long for them to become works of art as well. Traditional, carved decoration remains of great historical importance in our lives today. Its classic beauty ranges from the ancient Greeks through Gothic, Renaissance and Rococo, from beautiful redwoods from Northern California to the gorgeous colors of Purple Heart from tropical countries. Wood appeals to everyone.

In today's craft industry, wooden items are enjoying tremendous popularity. Not only do we love it in its natural state, but modern artisans paint it, sand it and decorate it in myriad ways. Wooden chests and cabinets, yesterday's treasures and today's antiques are more prized than ever. Today, we even have special paints and finishes to make new wood look old! Unfinished or stained, new or old, large or small, furniture or toys—and people still love wood.

*   *   *

Jean-Pierre "Pete" LeClair of *Quality Wood Products*, a family-owned business since 1991, says "Three generations work in our business," Pete explains. "My father, mother, wife, son and I work together. My Father and I cut wood. My wife paints it and my son helps out at shows. Mother does the bookkeeping, filing and makes our patterns. Though my Father is retired, he spends all day cutting and assembling items. My Mother, my wife and I all work full time. I work with wood about 70% of the time, relegating about 30% of my time to business issues such as advertising, promoting, database and website maintenance and photography. Most of our waking moments not actually working with wood, in one way or the other, relate to the business. Our business has taken over our lives and we love it!", Pete says enthusiastically. We focus on making functional items," Pete explains. The LeClaire family products includes but is not limited to:

Scroll sawn Shelves
Scroll sawn Book racks
Scroll sawn Desktop Clocks
Bread Boxes
Napkin Holders
Welcome Signs.

Pete's Pricing Template offers crafters of all types, solid information about setting up a pricing system such as the one he offers below using a shelf as an example.

Shelf Type	Material Type	Material Cost/ bf	Units of Material	Cost of Materia	Cut Time	Finishing Time	Labor Cost @$10/hour	Minimum Price
plain 24"	pine	$1.50	2	$3.00	0.5	1.0	$15.00	$18.00
painted	pine	$1.50	2	$3.00	0.5	2.0	$25.00	$28.00
Scroll sawn	pine	$1.50	3	$4.50	3.0	1.0	$40.00	$44.50
Scroll sawn	oak	$6.00	3	$18.00	4.0	1.0	$50.00	$68.00

Currently, the family sells its wood products directly to the consumer but they sell wholesale finished wood pieces at shows. Pete says, "This allows us to maintain a single price list and sell raw stock to anyone that wants to embellish it. We offer quantity price breaks to buyers that want to purchase for resale."

Pete's family buys their painting supplies from catalogs, trade-shows and local shops when the need is immediate or they have a sale. They purchase their hardware by mail-order from catalogs which includes scroll sawing supplies. Their wood comes from local yards where they established commercial accounts. They have the equipment to resaw and plane their own materials so rather than purchase thin woods for fretwork, they make their own.

Pete's Dad actually started the business in 1991 selling his wood-crafts through Craft Malls. "Sales were great from the start," says Pete. "We went into business with him before we started crafting but as soon as we began producing, our sales were immediate."

The LeClairs have lowered prices but only to clear out of a line that did not move. "That tells us not to make that particular item," Pete explains, "and allows us to focus on the items that generate revenue."

The company raises its prices when they experience rising raw materials cost or in response to high demand. Pete says, "We like to have a wide variety of items in our booth. If an item sells like hot cakes, rather than focus only on that item and neglect the rest we bump the price up until we find what consumers will pay."

Pete describes the family products. "Our work is labor intensive while material costs remain relatively low. We cut most of our pieces from pine. We consider the cost of materials and would not think of making an oak scroll sawn shelf for the same price as one made from pine. We base our prices primarily on labor. To determine a price for a specific line, our shelves, for example, we begin by determining the average time required to make one unit. Overhead includes costs for: show fees, postage, supplies, fuel, mileage, etc. not directly related to making our products. We price our time at $10 per hour," he adds.

The LeClairs sell their products from their website or while vending at shows. Pete explains, "We have tried various other outlets but if we mark up our prices to cover commission we don't sell much and only the shop owner profits. Internet sales do very well during the holiday season. We receive large, custom orders from businesses that we could not have gotten any other way than from the Internet. Besides using our site as a store front we see it as an adjunct to other advertising."

* * *

Bill and **Pat Lawson,** of *Owl Enterprises* enjoy making small, decorative wood items which can be labor intensive. Pat explains, "Our wood items are usually hand painted with very detailed artwork, and sometimes elaborately shaped taking a lot of cutting time with a scroll saw. Our hand-turned wood lathe items are labor intensive too. Although a small decorative wood item may cost only $2 to $10 worth of wood, the hours of labor involved in cutting the wood, turning it, assembly and/or decorative painting may add up to more than $100 in labor."

The Lawsons sell only at retail and describe their formula for pricing their items:

Materialsx2 + labor + production/selling expenses per item. Pat explains, "We double the cost of our materials first as this becomes the profit we expect to make if we did nothing except buy materials and resell them to our customers. We pay our wood cutter(s) and artists (in this case, ourselves), $10 per hour for basic cutting and painting. We charge $15 per hour for base-coat painting or for more elaborate scroll saw cutting, wood-turning, intricate construction or highly skilled and detailed decorative painting."

"Our expenses," Pat explains, "Include everything it takes to run our business and sell our crafts, such as our tools and equipment, business licenses/fees, office equipment, website fees, advertising, shipping, craft show time and displays. We total them for a year, then divide to arrive at an approximate per-item cost. We consider what the market will bear for any particular item. If we price our items too far above the current market price, we may not be able to sell the item. On the other hand, we cannot price our items below formula or we will lose money."

Pat explains that sometimes, they cannot afford to make and sell a certain item and make a profit at all. "But occasionally," she says, "We find an item that we can sell for more than we need to make a profit. This gives us leeway to make and sell another item which may not be as profitable. In other words, the two balances each other. In this case, we get to make and sell something we enjoy making and the customer who buys it gets a bargain," she concludes.

*   *   *

John Dunney's business, *J&L Folk Art, Garden Folk Art & Rustic Country Decor* began in 1973. Says John, "I just dove in and right from the start began to sell my crafts within days of making my first items. I learned along the way and improved as I went."

He describes his business as a full time operation averaging 8-10 hour days, five days a week. "However," John states, "During the holiday season I often work till midnight or later trying to keep up with the increased demands for my crafts. I work in my studio averaging forty hours a week but spend the rest of my time making supply runs, bookkeeping, errands, deliveries plus working two days in my gallery."

Explaining his sales ratio, he says he sells about 95% retail in his shops and 5% at wholesale. "I want to increase my wholesale sales and add more Internet business," he says. "Lumber is my primary raw material. I purchase locally when the prices are right. I buy tools and other supplies from catalogs and have everything delivered. My time is too valuable to spend all day running around trying to get the best deal on a box of nails or a gallon can of paint, so sometimes I pay a little more to save that precious commodity—time."

John reports that occasionally, he will lower his prices and have a "sale" to generate needed capital. "After all," he says, "A beautifully finished product isn't paying a bill or putting food on my table while sitting in a showroom."

"On occasion," he continues, "I raise prices on particular items when they sell too quickly and reconsidered my labor in making them. The only other time I raise prices is when material costs increase and I can no longer absorb the increasing costs," he explains.

John honestly admits a small problem when he says, "I have tried breaking down my costs into tiny details to get an accurate figure but it doesn't seem to work for me. Instead, I total the actual material costs of the item and multiply by four. I make necessary adjustments from there based on other items in my line. It's simple and I feel I am getting a fair return on my investment of time and materials," he adds.

Currently, John sells retail at two craft galleries but his wholesale accounts have increased over the years from time spent at craft shows or word-of-mouth from other shops. In the past, John sold at weekend craft fairs but grew tired of the travel and related expenses and found them declining in profitability. He has sold at wholesale trade shows and used sales reps but is not currently using these methods to reach the wholesale market. He says, "I am not sure if wholesale would be good right now as I prefer selling directly to the retail customer. I can create lots of one-of-a-kind items along with a few production items and avoid getting stale from producing a few selected items by the hundreds to satisfy the wholesale market. Focusing on the retail side of my business keeps my creativity fresh and challenging as I strive to continually update my line. I have customers who come back every few weeks so I try to have something new to show during each visit. This has become very rewarding for me, especially if they buy it," he adds, smiling.

*　　　　　　　　*　　　　　　　　*

Tom and **Chris Cooper,** of *Paperways*, a husband and wife team, use woodworking methods to manufacture picture frames. Chris designs prints, makes etchings, decorates frames and assembles the final product. They both sell their products at shows using their method Pricing Template below. They begin with Cost, Profit & Analysis, (CPV) telling how much they must sell to earn a specific amount of money. "If you have a goal such as making a living wage, CPV Analysis will tell you how many pieces you must sell to support yourself," says Tom. He offers his Pricing Template.

1   "Determine the cost of each item you make. Several costing formulas are essentially the same; i.e., direct costs + indirect costs + labor + profit margin = total costs. Another variation on this theme involves the fixed cost of labor and variable cost of labor. Fixed labor costs include activities such as the labor cost of doing shows, running errands, marketing, advertising, talking to buyers or customers on the phone or in person, computer work, record-keeping. This particular phase absolutely eats me alive. We can become so intent upon making our art that at times, we overlook some of these important aspects. You may not be able to assess as high a per-hour figure as for doing your artwork but do consider some recompense," he suggests. Tom continues. "Variable labor costs means the time spent hands-on with your craft. Assess a value to this time in dollars per hour. We access $10 per hour for our labor. However, fixed labor costs delineated above can knock your hourly wage to pieces yet, you must count that time too!"

2   "Keep a log book of activities to see where your time actually goes. To determine variable labor costs, make several of one, specific piece and average the time it takes. Practice and grouping similar tasks improve efficiency. Your average will be your truer figure."

3   "Total materials that go into each piece. This takes time, patience and good records but you have to know eventually. The good news is that once you do it, you will only have to modify it in the future."

4   "Use CPV analysis to determine the final price for your work. Calculate from this equation: Price = Materials + Labor + Overhead + Profit Margin. We use a spreadsheet to list all costs associated with making a piece of art. The spreadsheet calculates a recommended selling price based on the materials, labor, overhead and a profit margin entered into the program. Not only is the spreadsheet useful for estimating price, it shows where the largest costs are and makes possible rapid 'What if?' calculations to help lower costs and increase efficiency. The following table lists costs associated with a framed, unlimited edition print we sell. When I enter the dimensions of the picture frame, the spreadsheet calculates the material cost. In this example, picture

frame molding is the largest material cost. The spreadsheet tells me that looking for inexpensive molding suppliers will help cut costs," Tom says.

Materials Cost Data

Cost/Foot, 2" molding($) =	$1.21
Cost/Foot, 3" molding($)=	$1.06
Glass Cost per sq. ft. ($)=	$0.72
Price/Print ($) =	$0.42
Mat Board ($/sq. ft.)=	$0.42
Mat Backing Board($/sq. ft.	$0.26
Screw Eye Cost/Picture($) =	$0.02
Wire Cost $/2 ft./picture	$0.04
Fletcher Points $/10/picture	$0.04
Backing Paper Cost($/Picture)=	$0.01

Wire Cost $/2 ft./picture	$0.04
Fletcher Points $/10/picture	$0.04
Backing Paper Cost($/Picture)=	$0.01

The table below gives assumed labor costs, profit margin and overhead calculated from the previous year's sales.

Labor and Profit Data

Art Labor Cost/Hr =	$10.00
Framing Labor Cost/Hr.	$4.25
Profit/Print($)=	$1.00
Profit Margin(%)=	15
Retail Markup(%)	50
Overhead($/Piece)=	$5.00
Frame Assembly Time(hr)=	0.42
Basing Time(hr) =	0.33
Picture Assembly Time(hr) =	0.25

Tom explains this table saying, "It lists the times required for all the stages of framed print manufacture. We determined these numbers by first preparing a flow chart of the process for making a picture and then timing each step of the process. Note the most labor intensive stage is decorating the frame."

Framing and Assembly Data

Framing Time(hr) =	0.42
Basing Time(hr) =	0.75
Assembly Time(hr) =	0.25

Decorating Times for Several Framed Prints

Name	Decorating Time(h)	Total Labor($)
The Farm	1.9	$26.59
The Fifth Day	0.92	$16.79
Noah's Ark	2.42	$31.79
Farmer's Prayer	2.42	$31.79
Market Day	2.1	$28.59
Sunflowers	1.42	$21.79

"We then put together all costs and a profit margin to give a recommended price," says Tom. Labor is the largest cost. To cut this cost, we use many strategies to improve efficiency. Analyzing the process used to make a picture will give small improvements in efficiency. Combining small improvements can substantially lower labor costs," he adds.

Projected Retail Profits for Several Framed Prints

Units Sold	The Farm	The Fifth Day	Noah's Ark	Farmers Prayer	Market Day	Sunflowers
10	$288.27	$232.95	$328.91	$319.16	$307.47	$248.59
20	$576.55	$465.90	$657.82	$638.32	$614.95	$497.18
30	$864.82	$698.85	$986.73	$957.48	$922.42	$745.77
40	$1,153.10	$931.80	$1,315.64	$1,276.64	$1,229.89	$994.36
50	$1,441.37	$1,164.76	$1,644.55	$1,595.80	$1,537.36	$1,242.94
60	$1,729.65	$1,397.71	$1,973.47	$1,914.96	$1,844.84	$1,491.53
70	$2,017.92	$1,630.66	$2,302.38	$2,234.12	$2,152.31	$1,740.12
80	$2,306.20	$1,863.61	$2,631.29	$2,553.28	$2,459.78	$1,988.71
90	$2,594.47	$2,096.56	$2,960.20	$2,872.44	$2,767.25	$2,237.30
100	$2,882.75	$2,329.51	$3,289.11	$3,191.60	$3,074.73	$2,485.89

"Profit per piece is an integral part of a costing formula. You may determine this up-front by tacking on an additional 10% to15% or you may derive it when you set a price on an item using the formula above combined with marketplace response. For example, if my base cost of an item is $20, I examine similar pieces that sell in the $40-$50 retail range. If I add 15%, making the wholesale $23, doubled to $46, I note if other pieces like it sell for around $46. In reality, we've been adding only another 50% markup for retail shows instead of the traditional doubling. Supply and demand is a hard taskmaster. In a different market, we may be able to get a 100% markup. I choose not to wholesale anything for less than a 70/30 split.

I've spent too many years working below minimum wage for 50% of my retail price. If you only sell wholesale, you must determine your profit percentage up front. Beware of buyers who try to take it away from you," he warns.

In-Depth Interview:

Kathy Anderson, a versatile artisan, designs in over a dozen craft media. She sells at retail directly to consumers through a craft mall or a gift boutique nearby. I ask each contributor to tell me exactly *what* they sell but Kathy's list overwhelmed me. Kathy replied, "I sell candle sticks, switch-plates, wood trays, terra cotta pots, bird houses, welcome signs in the shape of birdhouses, glass vases, paper maché boxes, hand-painted plaques, water color pictures, Victorian picture frames, Victorian dolls, ribbon roses attached to boxes, decoupage hand-painted rose papers, recycled jewelry boxes embellished with Victorian collage and/or roses painted on top and many other wood products. If this were not enough, she also sells patterns packages, crochets rag rugs and edgings, makes place mats, paints on T-shirts, knits, embroiders, does macramé and teaches crafts.

Please describe your business.

As one might expect, Kathy works full-time at her crafts. She says, "My retail sales pay for my designing expenses, travel, dues and membership fees to organizations, phone, etc."

Kathy buys raw materials from catalogs, local shops and directly from manufacturers. She explains, "I buy mostly at wholesale, have wood items made for me and also watch for sales."

When did you begin selling your crafts?

"I began selling in 1990 but had crafted all my life," she explains. I learned to crochet when I was eleven and it snowballed from there for forty-nine years," she says. "In that time I studied interior decorating, made all our clothing, learned to tole paint in 1978, dabbled in oil painting, macramé, ceramics and do watercolor paintings. Finally, I settled on tole painting using acrylics on wood and painting watercolors on wood as my main forte. Designing and crafting comes easy for me as I feel I have an eye for color and style."

Have you ever lowered prices because you found they were too high?

"Yes, on occasion. I think one must remain tuned to market prices. If you make a mistake, correct it. Every market has its top selling prices but one must be careful because every market has its bargain hunters too."

Have you ever raised your prices? Why?

"Yes, I raise them a little at a time until sales slow down, then back off and sometimes lower them again. I test a product this way before making too many. The price isn't always the main selling factor. Perhaps your design is outdated or the customer wants a fresh design in today's colors."

Do you have a system for pricing your items? Please describe.

"I decided to charge $1 per inch for tole-painted wood items that I cut myself but find my system works well for purchased wood items bought at wholesale too. If the finished project is 12" tall, I charge $12. If the market will bear it, and every crafter should know their market, I use a range from $12.00 to $18.00 per 12" x 6" project. It didn't really matter how I arrived at the $1 per inch because it works so well. My system is an easy way to price something without too much figuring. It even works no matter what width board I use. Generally, I use a 12" wide board and cut smaller pieces. If I add embellishments, I adjust the $1 an inch formula. Expensive embellishments include charms, expensive buttons, laces and small antique items. I use the $1 an inch plus the price of the embellishment at least doubled to arrive at a final asking price."

Kathy provides an example: "I made 9" candlesticks priced at $8.99. When I tried to go to $9.99, sales stopped telling me $8.99 was perfect but my 7" candlesticks cost $7.99. The by-the-inch rule keeps working for me."

Do you consider labor when you set your prices?

"Yes, to a certain extent. If I can't use my $1 per inch rule, I multiply the cost of all supplies by five and that covers everything including my labor."

How do you determine overhead?

"I include this in my $1 per inch or my 5X rule. If I can't price an item using these rules, I eliminate them from my inventory. Sometimes, my system results in prices too high for one market while just right for the other. Thank goodness, I have two different markets and they are both on the low side."

How do you determine profit?

"I keep an eye on whether or not I make a profit on each item I sell by scrutinizing the paperwork I receive from the two stores that sell my work. If the profit isn't good enough, I drop that item."

How do you determine the value of your time?

"I use my $1 per inch rule again. I figure my hard work will pay off. Because I love what I do, I don't value my time spent separately other than to say it's valuable to me. I love what I do and believe this comes through in my work. I love my life and everyone reaps the benefits."

Do you sell on commission or consignment?

"Both places where I sell take a commission plus I must pay rent. I'm available to help during store sales or open houses. If I demonstrate my craft in the store, the owners waive my rent. That's a big help," she says.

"About consignment," Kathy continues, "I guess both places are considered consignment as I pay rent in addition to the shop-owner's percentage. I take 100% of what I want to earn and subtract their commission. I divide the balance into what I want the item to earn for me and what they want for their percentage. For example, I start at 100%, subtract their 25% commission. That leaves a balance of 75%. Then I divide what I want that item to earn for me by 75%. That way, customers pay the commission because I add it to the total retail price."

Do you sell via the Internet or from a website?

"Yes, but selling differs from crafts. Customers don't mind buying crafts because they pay so little for them and can replace them inexpensively. But people keep a piece of art much longer. Customers may feel hesitant to buy knowing they will have it for a while as they do not replace fine art as often as a small craft item. I price according to how long I've been selling my art work but don't earn as much as seasoned fine artists. I usually triple the cost of the frame and matting to allow for my time and profit," she explains.

Kathy loves doing watercolors based on her love of flowers, especially, roses. She says, "I offer two pattern kits on my website consisting of a pattern plus instructions. One of these is for my candlesticks, the other for a switch plate. My instructions include paint colors and helpful hints. I provide line drawings for placement of flowers. I began this idea by checking to see how others price their pattern kits and started there. I didn't want to price myself out of the market nor lose money so I calculated the cost of the entire kit and tripled the total because I pay shipping." Continuing, Kathy says, "I sell lace edgings from my site though they are tough to price. Raw materials for crochet are inexpensive but take a long time to produce. I look to see what fabric stores charge for quality laces and edgings and go from there. I make mine by hand so they are of greater quality than what stores sell. I sell mine in one yard pieces to keep costs down. I give my customers ideas on how to use my edgings and provide an item number so they can order more if they wish. I always add a hang-tag identifying them as handmade and explain that I have more available," she adds.

"Decoupage, hand-painted rose papers I design and sell from my site are my best seller," says Kathy. "They are not computer generated. Rather, I hand-paint the roses directly onto the paper and use quality color copiers which show up well on my website. I priced these much like my pattern kits—determining the cost to reproduce and multiplied by three to include shipping.

Hooked rugs interest me too," she says. "I make mine with wool strips but I have plans to design and use wool yarns in a punch-needle style but haven't decided how to price them yet," she adds. What will Kathy come up with next?

QUICK REVIEW OF PRICING METHODS IN THIS CHAPTER

X   For full-time woodworking, consider a well-planned template to help you price.

X   When buying wood at wholesale for painting and decorating, consider the simple system of: Raw Materialsx2 + labor + production/selling expenses, doubled to arrive at retail price.

X   Consider paying yourself or hired wood cutters and artists $10 per hour, for basic cutting and painting, and base-coat painting for $15 per hour or more for elaborate scroll saw cutting, wood-turning, intricate construction, or highly skilled and detailed decorative painting.

X   Determine your cost of business for one year including tools and equipment, business licenses/fees, office equipment, website fees, advertising, shipping, craft show time and expenses, displays, divided by approximate per item cost.

X   Never forget what the market will bear as you price any particular item. If you price too far above the current market price, you may not be able to sell. If you price below what your formula shows, you will fail to make a profit.

X   Total your actual material costs and multiply by four which provides for labor and profit.

X   For full-time wood working, start with a Cost, Profit & Analysis, (CPV) telling how much you must sell to earn a specific amount of money.

X   A simple pricing system: direct costs + indirect costs + labor + profit margin = total costs, doubled for wholesale, tripled for retail.

X   Think about charging $1 per inch for tole-painted wood items. If the finished project is 12" tall, charge $12. The system works no matter what width board you use but when you add embellishments, adjust to $1 more per inch.

CONTRIBUTORS TO THIS CHAPTER

Pete LeClaire
4958 Jones Ave.
Riverside, CA 92505-1361
Phone 909.689.8070
Fax: 909-689-4023 (by request)
E-mail:pleclair@sprynet.com
http://come.to/qwp
For catalog requests: http://home.sprynet.com/sprynet/pleclair/catalog.html

Bill and Pat Lawson,
Owl Enterprises
Laguna Beach, CA
Phone: (949) 494-7619
Fax: (949) 494-7619
E-mail: owlgifts@users.cihost.com or patlawson@earthlink.net
http://come.to/owl

John Dunney
The Rustic Fence, Garden Folk Art & Rustic Country Decor
295 Main Street,
Yuba City, CA 95991
Phone/Fax: 530 755-3424
E-Mail: jdunney@jps.net
http://www.jps.net/jdunney

Thomas and Chris Cooper
1336 Kercher Street
Miamisburg, OH 45342
Phone: 937-847-9337
Fax: 937-847-7443
E-mail: coopertm@earthlink.net

Kathy Anderson
K. Anderson Designs
20533 SE 272nd Street
Kent, WA 98042
Phone: 425-413-1267
E-mail: KMA205@aol.com
http://members.aol.com/kdesigns.htm

Chapter 11

Jewelry & Beading

Pricing Template: Pam East
In-Depth Interview: Judy, Frank & Paul Byers

For centuries, the word "jewelry" meant gold, silver and precious stones. Jewelry has adorned people all over the world for centuries. Today, it is craft jewelry that is sweeping across the United States. No longer reserved for wealthy aristocrats, the new craft jewelry can be worn and enjoyed by everyone. Gold and silver still indicate elegance and prosperity but modern wire-wrapped jewelry with its twisting ropes of beads, pearls and glass are every bit as alluring.

I have made beaded jewelry and sold a few designs to magazines but recently, I discovered what threatens to become a new craft addiction for me. During a national craft show, I had my first opportunity to use Fimo®, a polymer clay and the incredible artistry of Donna Kato. Attending craft shows for years, I always passed booths about clay thinking it would never appeal to me. Though I am not a sculptor, the moment I saw little squares of plain clay emerge from a pasta machine, looking like rainbow-colored marble, I was hooked. The gorgeous colors and metallic variations of this humble substance appeal to many who can hardly believe their source. Donna Kato's creations make you feel you are wearing malachite marble in the style of "Millefiori," (a million flowers in Italian.)

Wire-wrapped jewelry has become incredibly popular in the craft industry. Shaping and curving special wire in many colors allow bead-makers to craft new jewelry in an innovative way, bending it or literally wrapping the wire around semiprecious stones and one-of-a-kind hand-blown glass beads. Inexpensive to make and easy to learn, wire wrapped shapes and a multitude of beads from clay to glass have made hand-crafted jewelry available to nearly everyone. Prepare to say, "I made it myself," to admiring onlookers.

*   *   *

Pam East began making jewelry for sale in 1997. Pam describes her business saying she makes, "Earrings, necklaces, bracelets and Sleeve Pinz or anything else that incorporates my handmade enamel beads. I simply love making beads! Sleeve Pinz have become my best sellers as they are such a different type of jewelry. They have become my niche in the marketplace," she explains.

"My business with Sleeve Pinz began when my mother showed me a cheap pair of sleeve pins made with plastic beads she bought at a craft show," Pam explains. "I liked the idea and decided to buy some but could not find them anywhere. I knew they would make wonderful gifts so I began haunting bead shops without success. It might have ended there but the owner of our local store intervened," says Pam.

Pam explained to the shop owner that she wanted to make something of higher quality than her mother's plastic pins to create a kilt pin. The shop owner showed her a handful of enamel beads and said the words that Pam says, changed her life. "I can teach you how to make these!'"

After only one class, Pam bought a torch and other materials. Soon, her husband noticed how much she was spending on her new hobby and suggested that she try to sell a few items so her expenses could become legitimate business deductions. "Exactly one month after taking my first enamel bead-making class, I participated in my first craft show selling Sleeve Pinz and earrings and earned $260," Pam exclaimed. "I knew I'd found my calling," she explained.

Pam considers several factors to determine prices. She explains, "My cost for raw materials remains very low. When you buy materials by five or ten 10 gross at wholesale prices, the cost of an individual part drops to almost nothing. Raw materials for a pair of sleeve pinz cost only $1.00," says Pam. "Labor became my primary consideration. I wanted to earn $20 per hour for making the beads themselves. Assembling the finished jewelry and putting it on display cards takes only minutes as I use assembly line techniques," she explains.

Timing herself, Pam determined how long it took to make beads. "Making a bead varies depending on its size but color is the most determining factor," she says. "Some colors must be worked slower than others or they scorch but buyers would not understand why a pair of red sleeve pinz cost twice as much as blue. I abandoned the idea of a varied pricing scheme and decided to set my prices to make a profit on the most difficult colors," she adds. "The extra I make on easy colors balances out. A finished pair of opalescent white sleeve pinz takes 25 minutes to make and that's the slowest color I've got," she declares. "Rounded to half an hour, I charge $10 for the pair to make my goal of $20 per hour. Calculating this way helped me decide that $10 per pair would become my lowest wholesale price. I will not sell them lower than that. I charge $15 at craft show," she explains, "but the extra $5 per pair covers the cost and time of doing the show. Vending at craft shows, I consider a show excellent if I make ten times the cost of the booth fee," Pam says, "but I am happy if I make six times my booth fee. If I earn less than five times my booth fee, I don't go back" she states.

Commission selling has proven successful for Pam. Several customers loved her work but could not find the exact color or style so Pam made them to order. "I have a special order form for this," she says. "I note all I know about the customer, pricing and provide an area for describing and/or drawing a picture of what they want. I then offer my customers two options for billing. Either they can pay 100% in advance and pay only $3.00 shipping or they can pay 50% in advance and pay the rest C.O. D., including full postage and C.O. D. costs. So far all elected to pay 100% in advance."

Pam limits herself to selling at one show per month but goes more often just before the holidays to take advantage of increased buying. She looks forward to promoting her new Website while completing a wholesale brochure to take to resort areas nearby. "I plan to talk with shop owners that look as if my jewelry would compliment their stock. I don't want to overextend myself," she says, "but I am a one-woman show and want to stay that way until my daughter starts school."

Purchasing raw materials by mail-order works well for Pam. She says, "I used to buy only from local shops but that became too expensive for me. I even went to the Los Angeles garment district and found wholesale resources there but they charge more than ordering direct from manufacturers and importers. It took me a long while to find sources for all my raw materials but I've got them all nailed down, now," she concludes. Her Pricing Template appears below:

Pricing Template

	Standard bead	Mini bead	
Bead-making time	10	5	In minutes
Labor per hour	$20	$20	
Beads per hour	6	12	
Cost per bead	$3.33	$1.67	

Raw	# standard	# mini	Cost of	Assembly	Labor		
Materials	bead	beads	beads		in minutes	cost	Total cost
Sleeve pinz	$1.00	2	$ 6.67	5	$1.67	$9.33	
Earrings	$0.30	2	$ 6.67	4	$1.33	$8.30	
Wire-wrap necklace	$15.00	5	$16.67	360	$120.00	$151.67	
Wire-wrap earrings	$ 3.00	2	$ 6.67	45	$15.00	$24.67	
Mini necklace	$1.50	4	$ 6.67	15	$ 5.00	$13.17	
Mini earrings	$0.20	2	$ 3.33	3	$ 1.00	$4.53	
Bracelet	$1.25	5	$16.67	20	$6.67	$24.58	

Cost comparison	Template pricing	Actual pricing	Profit/ loss
Sleeve pinz	$ 9.33	$ 15.00	$ 5.67
Earrings	$ 8.30	$ 10.00	$ 1.70
Wire-wrap necklace	$151.67	$ 80.00	$ (71.67)
Wire-wrap earrings	$ 24.67	$ 25.00	$ 0.33
Mini necklace	$ 13.17	$ 15.00	$ 1.83
Mini earrings	$ 4.53	$ 8.00	$ 3.47
Bracelet	$ 24.58	$ 20.00	$ (4.58)

Pam comments, "I learned a lot preparing my Pricing Template for this book. To make wire-wrap necklaces, which I love, I realized I must do it for the love of it and cover my basic costs and forget about labor and any real profit. I can never sell them for what they are worth."

Sterling silver and 12 Karat gold-fill wire-wrap necklaces and earrings, incorporating Pam's enamel beads sell well. Pam explains, "I initially set my price for a necklace at $100 for silver and $120 for gold. Each necklace represents about 6-8 hours of work, so the price remains on the low side," she says. "I love making them, but I've sold very few. I lowered my prices to $75 for silver and $85 for gold but they still haven't sold. I know the quality is good because I get compliments all the time from jewelry artists but high-ticket items like that just don't sell at craft shows. People want things they can get with a $20 bill or less. Unfortunately, it isn't worth my while to make them for less," she adds. "I think they might do better in the upscale boutiques."

Incidentally, for you readers, like me, who have not seen "sleeve pinz," check Pam's Website which I did myself.

*   *   *

Christine Gries, of *Beadmaven's Beadoir*, sells handmade, beaded jewelry at both wholesale and retail. She also sells vintage and new loose beads. She purchases raw materials primarily from manufacturers and catalogs at wholesale, but admits hunting through thrift shops looking for the best vintage items. Christine has been beading since she was twelve years old but has been selling her beaded products as a business for four years.

Discussing her pricing system, Christine says, "To earn more than minimum wage, I multiply my design and manufacturing hours by $5.00 since I work from home and overhead remains low. I bead fairly fast," she says, "but others may work slower."

Christine determines profit by totaling labor, overhead, raw materials, average cost of show fees and subtracts the total from total sales. She sells at craft shows, but chooses juried-only shows to find upscale buyers. Christine concludes by reporting that selling her beaded creations from her Website increases every month.

*   *   *

Holly Yashi Inc. began as a two-person business in a *very* small town (population, 12,000) in a *very* small, rented garage. Today, only fifteen years later, the company competes with America's top costume jewelry manufacturers, coast to coast.

Owners, Holly Hosterman and Paul Lubitz employ fifty artisans to hand craft imaginative jewelry featuring a rarely used metal, niobium. Holly developed an electronically charged method to transform its dull, gray color into refractory metal flashes of iridescent color. More than 1800 stores, galleries and museum shops feature Holly Yashi jewelry bringing the company's annual sales into seven figures.

"Jewelry production goes on daily by our full-time staff" explains Paul, "but as president, I spend most of my time in management strategy, business development and sales. We sell at wholesale only purchasing all our raw materials from catalogs and manufacturers"

Holly had been designing jewelry and one-of-a-kind metal sculpture for many years after attending fine art classes. From the time Paul and Holly joined forces, their purpose was to sell jewelry that would become recognized everywhere. Like many crafters in this book, the company has lowered prices. "When the market rules," says Paul, "we raise them when our costs increase."

Though Holly Yashi is a large company, unlike many single business owners included in this book, they use the same formula used by many. Succinctly, Paul says, "We determine our wholesale prices by totaling the cost of raw materials, manufacturing costs and administrative overhead. We take the total and multiply by three," he explains.

Holly Yashi sells goods at craft shows, boutiques and specialty stores. Unlike many contributors to this book, the company uses a network of sales representatives. Lest you think this is only because it is a large company, keep in mind that they began working alone together in a rented garage!

*   *   *

Rosanne Andreas , began her business, *The Beaded Phoenix* in 1995. She offers beadwork items at retail to consumers via direct sales, the Internet selling at wholesale to galleries. Rosanne is also a beadwork teacher and sells printed, educational materials for bead-workers called, *The Beaded Phoenix Bead & String Reference Chart Poster & Booklet Set.*

She charges an hourly wage based upon her experience and expenses and adjusts it to the marketplace in which she sells. For example, selling her work in New York City Galleries brings more than selling in isolated shops in the Midwest. "Working on a repair job or doing restoration work costs approximately 40% more per hour since this is such specialized work," Rosanne explains. Rosanne buys her raw materials from catalogs, local shops and directly from manufacturers in the bead district in New York City. Continuing, Rosanne says, "I consider raw materials, labor and profit in my pricing system but I continually watch the marketplace, comparing their prices to mine. I attend many bead shows to check market prices before raising or lowering my prices. Customers also provide feedback about my prices, and I may raise or lower them considering all these factors."

Since Rosanne designs one-of-a-kind beaded creations she sells occasionally at small craft shows to find individual buyers though she prefers galleries. Today, Rosanne focuses on her educational beading literature. Selling these through a distributor allows her to get more products in the hands of the majority of beading stores. Rosanne provides her Pricing Template for her beaded creations below but reminds readers they must charge their own hourly rates and material costs considering their geographical area.

1) Cost of materials: $30.00
2) Wage per hour: $10.
3) Labor for one of her special pieces: 3 hours (3x$10 = $30)
4) Wage per hourxtotal hours worked = total wage costs.
3) Totals: $60.00 for the retail price.

When placing her work in a high-end gallery, Rosanne adds half of her hourly wage to her price to allow for the percentage taken by the gallery owner. In her example above, she would add $15 to bring the total selling price at the gallery to $75.00.

Pricing beadwork differs from pricing her printed goods says Rosanne. Designing and printing educational materials require writing time, illustrating and design skills so printers can show her work to advantage. Professional printing companies enable her to sell both at retail and wholesale.

"I sell my charts and booklets at an introductory retail price of $14.95 per set but others must consider the time they spend writing and designing similar information in addition to allowing for production and printing costs as well," she explains.

"Shop owners receive 40% discount when they purchase a minimum order of 12 sets from me," Rosanne explains. I send first orders C.O.D. but for subsequent orders, but shop owners may pay net, 30 days. I advise readers to come up with whatever minimum they want but I suggest C.O.D. for first orders so they can confirm customers' tax numbers making sure they qualify as wholesale accounts," she explains. Rosanne also requests a photocopy of a shop's advertising in the yellow pages to eliminate people who claim to be shop owners but in reality are just seeking lower prices or other private information."

Concluding, Rosanne says, "My beading business consumes my every spare moment and I enjoy it very much. My future plans include selling beading kits, broadening my teaching opportunities and selling specific lines of beaded jewelry."

*   *   *

Jacqueline Collins-Parker, of *Angel Craft Studio* began making jewelry in 1985. "I vend at many craft shows from May to early December so my business remains quite eclectic," she begins. "Some of the shows I where I vend are general craft while others are ethnic. Offering a variety of products at different shows helps me stay in business while it keeps my mind active," she says.

"I sell Lampwork Moretti glass beads and prefer making intricate fish and goddess beads from glass but buyers on the East Coast do not seem familiar with glass as wearable art," Jacqueline explains. "Customers think of it as utility ware or for stained glass pieces. I sell small glass turtles, frogs, ladybugs and other animals made from larger beads with dichroic glass and/or metallic powders," she explains.

"To educate the public about my process and usage, I give glass demonstrations at every show where permitted which increases sales, exposure and educational opportunities. Since glass is a new medium for me, (I taught myself just 28 months ago) and because it is not familiar to my market; I augment my product line with additional items to generate sales."

Jacqueline works full-time at her art selling both at retail and wholesale with the help of sales reps. She purchases supplies wherever she can find the best prices and service as there are few Moretti glass suppliers in the country. "I buy at wholesale whenever possible," she explains, "sometimes combining orders with friends to obtain the best prices."

Fortunately, for readers not familiar with Jacqueline's raw materials, she explains them well. "I use 5-6mm Moretti Glass rods. The glass is soft enough to be melted with MAPP gas and a Hot Head torch. Moretti melts at a much lower temperature than Pyrex or Borosilicate glass which allows more control but is slower than larger torches. Beginners should use a small torch until they learn technique and control. I use a smaller one too as I don't have the space or the inclination to live with an oxyacetylene set-up," she explains.

Jacqueline uses stainless steel bead wires and bead release—a molten glass tip touched to the wire with hot glass wound onto it to create bead holes. "Bead release," Jacqueline explains, "helps remove the cooled bead from the wire. Torch temperature works best at about 1,200F and since glass rods come in many different colors, I can mix them in the heat to create even more colors. Melting clear glass over the creation adds a magnifying effect. Dichroic glass adds mother-of-pearl or pattern effects. Stringer, 2-3mm rods come in limited colors. I mentioned that I create my own along with Latticino, 2-3 mm rods twisted together and laid over the hot bead to give a lacy effect of color," she adds.

Making pieces over so many years, Jacqueline no longer adjusts prices up or down unless the cost of raw materials increase. "When I began selling crafts at small church bazaars and craft fairs, I found that my prices were higher than everyone else's," she says, "but bazaars and church-fairs are not my best markets. I did not lower prices but produce bazaar items within the price range that the market would bear. I found that I was working too hard to produce hundreds of lower-end items and vending at 20-30 shows a season to sell them all," she confides.

"When my products sell too fast, I realize the price is probably too low. I then tweak the price by $5.00 the next season and watch for customers' approval." Jacqueline also produces ceramics and shares her pricing formula:

15% of the mold price = green-ware price

green-ware pricex2 = bisque price

Bisque pricex2, 3 or 5, = the finished ware price, depending on its intricacy and market.

She prices finished pieces in thirds: 1/3 for replacement supplies, 1/3 for labor/overhead and 1/3 for profit. Jacqueline applies her Pricing Template for making Lampwork turtle beads:

X   Time to make beadx$5.00 per hour, making four turtles in one hour

X   1 turtle every 15 minutes = $1.25 every 15 minutes if the design is easy: $1.25

X   Glass:-1 medium glass green rod-1/8 rod used ($8.25 each rod) $1.03

X   Glass Stringer: for dots-6 dots total $ .50

X   Stringer cost is an approximation as she makes her own by melting the tip of a rod and pulling the molten end to a thickness of ½ inch pencil lead.

Gas:$20.00 for a full 20 # barbecue gas tank. One tank lasts a month or more with daily usage of 6-8 hours a day.

Jacqueline concludes saying, "I have met many wonderful folks through crafts and love sharing information and ideas. The craft world continues to change and adapt and we should all continue to grow and develop along with it."

In-Depth Interview:

Judi, Frank, and Paul Byers, co-owners of *The Phoenix Experience* work with gold and silver creating fine jewelry pieces. They have two distinct jewelry lines: *The Signature Collection* and *The Collector's Edition* explained in their pricing system. Each began their career differently. Judi was born and raised in a small town in Oklahoma. Her paternal grandmother was Cherokee-Potowatomee Indian and her maternal grandmother, Cherokee. This background influenced her love of life but especially animals and stones. In 1979 she left nursing to develop her own jewelry style full-time. In 1988 a friend wanted to study jewelry making classes at William Holland Lapidary School in Young Harris, Georgia. The two decided to study wire wrap jewelry since it was so flexible. Judi loved it and continues perfecting her skill today.

Frank was born and raised in the same small town in Oklahoma but was a mechanical contractor for 21 years. When the oil industry began to fail in 1984 his company, with only thirty minutes notice, closed their doors creating a year's unemployment for him. A year later he moved to Aiken, South Carolina. His wife, Judi, taught him wire-wrapping. Together, Frank and Judi created and sold jewelry at Judi's workshops and seminars and at Gem and Mineral shows as well.

In 1995, they returned to the William Holland Lapidary in Young Harris where Frank studied Silver Smithing. Imports began overtaking Gem and Mineral shows so they stopped doing shows altogether in 1996. At that time, they began wholesaling their jewelry.

Please describe your market today.

"We have been on the retail show circuit off and on for the past eight years and sell both at retail and wholesale. In 1997 and 1998 we participated in 25-40 shows each year."

Please describe your jewelry line.

"We handcraft14 Karat gold fill and sterling wire-wrap, silver smithed jewelry. Our products are upscale, unique pieces and not beginner wire wrap pieces."

Where do you purchase your raw materials?

"We purchase supplies directly from wholesale manufacturers and from wholesale catalogs. Our wire is made to our specifications and we purchase it directly from the manufacturer. We select each of our stones at wholesale gem and mineral shows and purchase at retail only in emergency situations. The larger the order, the better the price so we try to purchase large quantities at wholesale."

How long had you been producing your work before you began selling?

"We started making jewelry because our friends wanted to wear their favorite stones. We began selling right from the beginning though at much lower prices than today. We had been making jewelry for a couple of years before we tried to sell at a show."

Have you ever raised or lowered your prices?

"When we found we were not earning much, we read everything we could about pricing. We then realized we had been selling to retail customers at wholesale prices! Next, we tried the ordinary 6/5 pricing recommended by many craft professionals. (Explained in earlier chapters.) During our next two shows, we barely paid for our booth as we realized people found our prices too high. We immediately changed the way we figured our prices and created a balance lowering some items while raising others."

Do you consider labor when setting your prices?

"Yes, we try to maintain a $10 per hour basic price but this is only part of the pricing equation." As much as we would like to earn $20 per hour, to do so would price us out of the market."

Do you consider raw materials when setting prices?

"Yes. Both of our systems require us to figure the actual cost of wire, stones, etc. Our biggest problem has been that the market differs greatly among the fifty states. Trying to determine what the market will bear became impossible unless we change our prices every show which is not practical."

How do you determine wholesale cost?

"We add the actual cost per item, fixed expenses plus $10 per hour which equals our wholesale price."

How do you determine overhead?

"Last year, we totaled all fixed expenses from 1997 such as electricity, water and the cost of building a new workshop behind our home. We added truck expenses to carry our show supplies and divided the total by 2000 hours."

Do you use sales reps to sell your jewelry?

"We have looked at using reps though it means paying them a commission but have not been successful in finding one. We never consign in shops as this brought us only problems in the past."

Do you have an Internet Web site?

"We are working on it now but it has not increased sales yet. We also participate in online auctions to channel traffic to our new site."

Please describe the pricing system you use now.

"We use two different systems. One is for one-of-a-kind wire which is labor intensive. We could not possibly sell these basing the price on time invested in addition to all the smithed jewelry. We described our second system below":

Here is the Byers' first Pricing Template. Frank emphasizes he begins with fixed costs each year. "Since we added a shop behind our house, we figured these expenses by the difference in our 1996 and 1997 utility bills. We added to this, payments for the truck used to haul supplies to shows. We did not add in show expenses such as gasoline, show fees, food, etc., as these are not fixed," Frank explains.

Next, we divided this total amount by 2000 hours (50 weeksx40 hours per week). We then add our labor at $10 per hour providing fixed expenses by the hour. To arrive at our wholesale price, we add the actual materials cost of the item. (Example: $39 fixed expense + $12.50 material cost = $52.00 rounded to the next whole dollar,)" he adds.

Since the Byers' deal with the price of gold and sterling, they must adjust prices constantly as these materials fluctuate. "Yet", says Judi, "Much as we would like to make $20 per hour, it would price us out of the market. We must order both wire and sterling silver by the ounce. The larger amount we order, the better discount we get, but we must consider the price of gold and silver the day it is manufactured. We know how many inches of wire we get per ounce so we divide the number of inches into the cost per ounce of wire. We figure the cost of silver plate the same way. We always figure the cost per inch by the most we have ever paid for gold or sterling, to compensate for the fluctuating prices as well as wire or sterling that must be scrapped. Knowing the next order could cost us more or less per inch, we thus protect ourselves from having to adjust our prices with each order," she explains.

The Byers' continue. "For our *Signature Collection* line we time ourselves when making multiple items, such as 10-20 at one sitting. We divide this time by the number of items made to arrive at the least possible time per item. We then calculate that amount of time by our cost. Example: $52.x¾ hr = $39 to arrive at our wholesale price."

"To determine retail," they explain further, "We multiply the wholesale figure by 1.7 as this gives us a wholesale amount of 40% off retail. Example: $39x1.7 = $67 rounded to the next dollar to equal our retail price. We use this system only on reproducible items in our *Signature Collection.*"

"Determining the price of pieces from our *Collector's Edition* of one-of-a-kind and silver-smithed items, we take our actual materials cost and multiply by 4 to arrive at our wholesale price and again multiply that by 1.7 for retail," Frank says. "The main difference is with the *Collector's Edition* wire and the difficult silver smithed items. We can only give a 25% discount for wholesale to compensate for the extra time it takes us and still give the retailer a price with which they can work," he adds.

Pricing Template

The Byers' share their Pricing Template: "Using the system listed above, figuring the cost per piece of jewelry is simple. Once you know the cost of your wire per inch (in our case we use 20 cents per inch for 14 karat gold fill and 15 cents per inch for sterling) the rest becomes easy. Let's say you make a simple standard 8" wire bracelet consisting of four karat gold-filled wires and four sterling silver wires. The difference in actual cost of making a bracelet in the standard sizes of 6" to 7 ½" is so minute that we do not charge more unless we go over 8". Bracelets above 8" and less than 5 ½" must be figured individually," they say.

Continuing, the Byers' explain further. "We type out instructions for each item we make with a materials list at the top of the page. This makes it quick and easy to figure the cost for someone needing a larger size." Example for the bracelet listed above: Using 21 gauge wire:

2 wires @ 2 x L + 1" (L = length of the bracelet)

4 wires @ L

2 wires @ 7"

2 wires @ 3"

We use a total of 49"of 14 karat gold-filled wire including wrap wire and 29" of sterling silver wire. This totals:

49 x $ .20 = $9.80

29 x $ .15 = $4.35

$14.15 total cost of materials (If a bracelet had a stone, we add the cost here.)

Actual time to make a bracelet is 25 minutes, so we figure .42 x $39 hr fixed expenses = $16.38. Now add the actual cost of materials. $14.15 + $16.38 = $31 (rounded up to the next dollar). This gives you the wholesale price. Now multiply this amount by 1.7 to get your retail price. $31 x 1.7 = $53.

"Pricing becomes more difficult when adding a stone you must cut to the equation," says Judi. "When I cut a stone for the bracelet above, I start with a precut slab of stone for which I paid $7.00. Using a template and marking on the slab where I can cut a good cabochon, I figure how many cabochons the slab will yield. In this case I get 8, so I divide $7 by 8 and figure the cost of material per cabochon is 83 cents. Since I don't work fast, it takes me 16 hours to cut, trim, grind and polish the 8 cabochons. If I figure my time @ $10 per hourx2 hr per cabochon plus the cost of material, then each should sell wholesale at $21. If I were going to sell these stones at retail, I would again mark up to1.7," she adds.

"Many jewelers forget they are running both a wholesale and retail business," conclude the Byers. "If we made the mistake of figuring cost at only $ .83 per cabochon, we would have been paid nothing for the two hours spent getting the cabochon to become usable. Purchasing the cabochon from a wholesaler I certainly would have figured in the cost," says Judi. "In essence, I sell the cabochon to myself and add in the extra $21 to the cost of the bracelet. ($14.15 + $21 = $35.15 + $16.38 = $52 wholesalex1.7 = $89 retail). All of this requires a good bookkeeping system," says Frank "To show that although no money changed hands until we sell the bracelet, we first sell it to ourselves then show the profit made on each stone accordingly," he adds.

Paul F. Byers, their son, was an architect major in his senior year at Oklahoma State University when the architecture school was incorporated under the Engineering School. Paul would have had to attend another 18 months to graduate with a double degree in Structural Engineering as well as Architecture. He decided he too would prefer to use his creative abilities to design jewelry and moved to South Carolina in 1996. Since he has never officially been to jewelry school (Judi taught him the basics) he combined his love of stones and his architectural design background to develop his own unique style and create in wire what others do by soldering or casting.

Today, Judi and Paul create all the wire wrap pieces while Frank concentrates on Silver Smiting. Judi still cuts some of the cabochons, but they usually purchase their stones, selecting unusual ones in which they can design a piece for that stone alone. When this piece sells, that particular design is not used again defining these pieces as the *Signature Collection*. Most of their jewelry design originals are protected by copyright as most are one-of-a-kind pieces. Though many of their designs are reproducible, since all are handmade and thus slightly different, each piece remains "Unique One-of-A-Kind."

BRIEF SUMMARY OF PRICING METHODS IN THIS CHAPTER:

X   If you make the beads for your jewelry yourself, raw materials cost is small so consider paying yourself $20 per hour for your labor.

X   Sterling silver and 12 Karat gold-fill wire-wrap necklaces and earrings sell well. Consider an initial price for a necklace at $100 for silver and $120 for gold as these necklaces represent 6-8 hours of work.

X   Total your labor, overhead, raw materials, average cost of show fees and subtract this from total sales for an easy pricing method when starting out.

X   Always consider raw materials, labor and profit in your pricing system but watch the marketplace to determine how your prices compare.

X   Attend many jewelry shows to check market prices before raising or lowering prices.

X   Pricing Templates for beaded creations can make setting prices easy. Consider your own hourly rates and materials costs.

X   When a product sells too fast, the price may be too low. Tweak the price by $5.00 for the next season and watch for customers' approval.

X   Consider setting a fee based on $10 per hour and working upward as your experience and reputation grows.

X   Think about a flexible Pricing Template based on an entire year's income and expenses to make sure you make a profit.

X   If you can make 10-20 jewelry pieces at once, divide your time by the number of items made to arrive at the least possible time per item.

CONTRIBUTORS TO THIS CHAPTER

Pricing Template: Pam East
22230 Emerald St.
Grand Terrace, CA 92313
Phone: 888-335-9884
E-mail: pam@pinzart.com
http://www.pinzart.com

Christine Gries
Beadmaven's Beadoir
PO Box 47
Shohola, PA 18458
Phone: 570-296-3034
E-mail: junkdlr@warwick.net
http://www.beadmaven.com

Holly Yashi
1300 Ninth Street
Arcata, CA 95521
Phone: 707-822-0389
Fax 707-822-9221
E-mail: hyashi@northcoast.com
http://www.hollyyashi.com

Rosanne Andreas
The Beaded Phoenix
Box 292
Monsey, NY 10952
Toll Free Phone: 888-684-7248
E-mail: bphoenix@bestweb.net
http://www.bestweb.net/~andreas

Jacqueline Collins-Parker
Angel Craft Studio
3008 Stevens Street
Camden NJ 08105
Phone: 609-338-0611
E-mail: Jacquelinedol@aol.com

Judy & Frank Byers
The Phoenix Experience
Box P
Aiken, SC 29802
Phone: 803-278-1002
http://wwwcsranet.com/~phoenixe

Chapter 12

Decorative Painting

Pricing Template: Marlene Watson
In-Depth Interview: Tori Hoggard

Decorative painting has become very important to the arts and crafts industry according to a recent issue of *CrafTrends,* a trade journal for the industry. The Society of Decorative Painting is experiencing growth and interest not only from individual artists, but from corporations who want to buy paintings as wall decor for their offices.

Pricing decorative painting depends totally on the complexity and size of the design plus consideration of the painting surface. Some surfaces will accept paint readily. Others require extensive preparation of the surface before applying paint.

I limit myself to painting on silk and other fabrics and finished wood. I also use stencils and stencil cremes extensively on these two surface types. Generally, I time myself and charge by the hour which considers simple to complex designs in few or many colors in all sizes of projects. My basic hourly rate is $12 per hour for painting.

Paint manufacturers have been very generous with me. I have attended many workshops and seminars they sponsor and as a published designer of one-of-a-kind pieces, they also provide generous amounts of paint so I can try the latest colors or paint types. I find them very cooperative in answering questions. Additionally, as a teacher throughout the country, most manufacturers with whom I deal provide paints at no cost to my students when they take my classes.

Last Fall, I spent an entire day at the manufacturing plant of one of my favorite companies to see the process of making and dyeing paint from start to finish. Contact the companies you prefer and request a list of their upcoming workshops, educational seminars and manufacturer's plant tours. All well-known paint companies have websites today so use search engines to locate your favorite companies for more information.

Do not overlook the workshops provided by such organizations as The Society of Craft Designers and The Hobby Industry Association mentioned previously in this book and in the Appendix. These events generally bear no fee other than dues required by the sponsoring organization itself. And now, let's examine the pricing ideas and template of Marlene Watson, a well-known, widely respected decorative painter who has appeared on more television craft shows than I can count.

*   *   *

Marlene Watson, fine artist and demonstrator is a welcome guest on many craft shows where she illustrates how to paint simple to complex designs primarily, though not exclusively, on textiles and garments. She sells embellished clothing and patterns with her original designs and provides regular classes from her studio. Her Pricing Template is easy to understand.

First, she determines what she wants to earn per hour. Second, she tracks exactly how long it takes to paint a "T" shirt for example. Last, she adds the cost of the paint itself and totals these three elements.

Marlene explains that painters can either keep track of the amount used of each paint color but she prefers to add $5 as her basic paint cost rather than calculate how much she uses of several bottles. Rarely, does she use whole bottles on one project as she specializes in careful, intricate shading where many tints and shades of several colors may appear.

1   "Naturally," she explains, "a hand-painted shirt takes more time than a stenciled or sponge painted shirt so I track my time carefully. Don't include the price of the shirt with your time. Keep that price separate as most customers want you to paint on a special shirt or jacket they provide. However, I also sell several and variously priced shirts and jackets if they do not already have one. I add that amount last," she explains. Marlene shares her Pricing Template when painting on garments:

Hand-painted Iris and butterflies (1 hour painting time)	$15.00
Paint:	$ 5.00
Cost of sweatshirt	$15.00
Total	$35.00

Sponge painted flowers and butterflies: 30 minutes painting time $7.50   time

Paint	$5.00
T-shirt	$6.00
Total	$18.00

Since Marlene sells her blank garments to customers who want them, she explains that she makes a bit more profit from garments she buys at wholesale to sell at retail. When customers order a large amount of sponge painted "T-shirts for a specific group, for example, she lines the shirts up and sponges the design assembly line fashion cutting her painting time in half. In this situation, she offers a group discount.

Example for a 25 "T-shirt order:

Approximately 20 min. per shirt	$4.00
Paint ea.	$5.00
"T-shirt ea.	$4.00
Total	$13.00
Grand Total: 25 shirtsx$13 =	$325

Marlene says that these guidelines will work for anything you paint on fabric, wood, glassware, lampshades, walls, etc. "Remember the importance of keeping track of your time," she advises. "I make a note on the corner on my popular patterns of how long it takes me to paint that design.

*   *   *

Monica Obenchain-Janis sells furniture purchased from second-hand stores directly to customers. She refinishes with colored stains and paint and upholsters fabric pieces as well. Local hardware stores and second-hand stores provide most her supplies but for more obscure tools and other articles she purchase from catalogs. "As my business grows," she says, "I plan to get a better foothold in purchasing my supplies wholesale."

Considering her fondness for refinishing furniture, Monica explains that over the years she has come to prefer working on odd bar-stools or chairs. "Only in the last six months have I recognized this passion," she says. "Creating new and interesting accessories for people's homes and working with different types of wood, stain colors and numerous fabrics ranging from silk to leather to faux fur keep my creativity flowing."

Monica has never lowered prices but found it necessary to raise prices significantly after studying her competition and realizing she had sold herself short. She describes that her pricing system works best as she considers labor, cost of supplies and the cost of the furniture item itself. Her overhead remains low working from a home studio and she says that her business fluctuates from month to month depending on the jobs she acquires. She takes refinishing jobs from individuals according to their specifications.

Today, she charges 10-15 times what she spends to buy the piece itself in addition to adding in the supplies to refinish it. Says Monica, "I find it difficult to measure my time so I break it down into simple factors to make it easier. Some say that if you have a degree in art or formal training in art school you can technically charge $100.00 per hour. I find this figure exorbitant and do not follow this advice though I qualify in both these areas. I feel comfortable charging $25.00 per hour for my murals. Custom painting brings costs up," she adds.

Monica explains, "I am taking my business slowly because I realize that it may be easy to start a business but the hard part is *staying* in business. My clients/customers are happy with work I have done for them. I am confident in my skills though the time it will take to get my business off the ground requires significant financial stability so I am keeping my outside job until I am more financially secure," she acknowledges.

Refinishing a small chest drawers, Monica charges $100-$150 depending on the intricacy of the woodwork. Complex styles take more time so she charges $150-$200 and $200-$250 for up to enormous dressers which cost $300-$350. "It is difficult to generalize because many times certain pieces don' fit into any category and need their own price," she adds. Hand-painted pieces cost more than simple staining due to the personal detail and imagination required," she explains. Monica paints and sells four to five feet long coffee tables and prices them from $500-$1000. She finds it difficult to predict more exactly as each piece requires its own price.

Steve Matosich, a fine artist working in California paints on several unexpected surfaces from other artists. Shops, restaurants and churches hire him to paint his exquisitely designed murals and pictorial designs on their walls or store-front display windows. Passers-by walking along the side-walk can enjoy his work.

Portfolio in hand, he finds his window/mural customers by visiting shops. Word-of-mouth advertising works best for him especially during holiday periods. Dealing directly with the business owner that hires him, Steve not only paints murals in a variety of designs but also specializes in theme window designs. Christmas, Easter and other holidays come to life on shop windows from his imagination and his eye for detail.

Painting full wall murals, Steve considers several issues before giving an estimate.

X   Over-all size is important in large undertakings such as this. A square foot or two measured inaccurately affects the cost of paints and other materials critically.

X   Does the client want oils on glass or temporary paints to wash off later?

X   Will the mural include copy or lettering?

X   Labor based on many hours or even days differs greatly from labor on very small items. A few hours off multiplies Steve's loss if he does not correctly assess the time required.

X   Doing large murals and windows bring other considerations to the equation from other artists. Steve cannot work privately at home as he must work visibly on someone else's property. He must also consider how much input the client wants as the work progresses. Some shop owners merely want a Christmas snow scene, for example, and leave the rest up to Steve. Others stand around as "side-walk superintendents" making suggestions as he goes without regard to the time it takes to rework a specific area.

X   Next, Steve revises his figures with clients before closing the deal reminding them that all overhead materials will be added separately with a detailed invoice.

X   Often, grocery stores want all their windows painted which can mean painting up to fourteen windows for a single customer. He charges more if they want their windows painted on the inside as well.

Using an option I described at length in my first book, *Crafting for Dollars,* Steve offers his clients an option if they hesitate over his final estimate. He suggests that they divide his payment into three even parts—the first paid before the work begins, the second, midway through the work and full payment when he completes the work. This system makes paying for artwork more affordable for artists unsure if their budget will cover the initial outlay of raw materials. "Accepting payment in three parts works," says Steve, "because if the customer backs out, I have at least have recovered the cost of raw materials."

Steve also creates designs for company "T-shirts, portraits, album and book covers and illustrations. He is equally comfortable working with water-colors, oils, acrylics or pen and pencil drawings. Recently, he has begun doing family portraits in oils which he describes as the most challenging to price.

Customers who want portraits want to an idea of costs before committing. Steve begins his estimate based upon the number of people in the portrait. He tries to achieve an hourly estimate and discusses what the client can afford. Next, he explains his system of "re-dos" if the client wants changes or adjustments and explains that all raw materials are extra. When customers understand this, he discusses the finished size of the portrait. "Precision pricing is difficult when painting portraits," Steve says, but this system works well for him. Recently, a very satisfied customer paid him $100 more than his final asking price as he completed portraits of her children. No pricing template can beat that!

In the next chapter, readers will meet other artisans who work with clay but Steve mentioned pricing his sculpting. He considers the cost of clay and renting a kiln to fire his creations then proceeds the same way he does his murals. Since he describes himself as a versatile artist, Steve explains that working in many media keeps his enthusiasm fresh. He presents his clients with a unique outline describing his various services which he shares with readers who also work in multiple media:

Artistic Media:	*Type of Work*
Drawing or Painting:	Portraits, landscapes and design
Commercial Art:	Business cards, brochures, résumé design, book/album Covers
Sculpture:	Clay, bust or full figures, abstract design
Crafts:	Christmas ornaments and/or decor
Murals/Windows:	Painting, animation, line drawings, landscape renderings, and or portraits in realistic or cartoon format
Pen & Ink Drawings:	Any subject chosen by customers

He describes his pricing structure further when customers indicate their interest in his artwork listed above. He starts by asking and answering a list of questions for himself:

1 What media will he work in as a versatile artist?
2 How does the design rate from simple to complex?
3 What about the over-all size of the project?
4 What will the total of raw materials cost?
5 Will there be many or few colors?
6 Does the buyer insist on continual input as the work progresses?
7 What does he estimate his labor will cost?

8 If the work will be the exact likeness of someone in a formal portrait, how long will sitting fees take?

9 How cooperative will the subject be?

After making informed decisions about all of these issues, he provides the customer with an approximate estimate, giving himself "wiggle room" if unexpected changes or issues surprise him. Since, size varies greatly from a display window to a small book cover, Steve's estimates also vary from a few dollars to over $500. His attitude of working until the work is as perfect as he can make it before releasing it to a client is bringing him growing acclaim. Still holding a day job, Steve looks forward to working as an artist full-time in the future.

* * *

Kathy Anderson, of *K. Anderson Designs*, whom you met in the wood-working chapter has many other talents as well. Her specialty is decorative tole painting, particularly her hand-painted switch-plates and candle sticks. First, Kathy paints them white, adds a light green wash, mauve roses, leaves, buds and baby's breath artificial colors. She has a complete line in antique styling using, gold, dark green and burgundy roses. As a designer and decorative tole painter, she also does stenciling, faux finishes, collage work and watercolors. Kathy prefers to make home decorative and usable items. "My work appears in two stores and I teach decorative tole painting in one of them," she says.

Recall that Kathy has worked at her business full-time since 1990. Selling through craft-malls directly to consumers allows her not only to sell what she has made but to take custom painting and special orders as well.

She buys bare wood items from several well-known craft catalogs who in turn offer her 40% off from retail prices in local craft supply stores. She says she prefers to devote her time to design and paint rather than to shop personally and finds wholesale catalogs pay for shipping when she meets their minimum orders.

Kathy finds it necessary to lower prices at times because she sells her painted goods in two opposite markets right now. "I test one of each product in each market and see what happens. If things sell fast in one market and they just sit at the other market, I try changing prices. Sometimes they still won't sell so I move them to the market where they will sell. I need to know the price I can get for an item then I decide if it's worth making the product.

I measure the time spent on an item and figure it at $10 per hour. I used to make ten of something before testing its price but don't do that anymore. I make two or four for each market. If I were to try a third market, I'd make 3 or 6. Marketing matters greatly to me so I continually study it, always learning all I can," she adds.

Kathy has heard from artist friends that she should place a higher value on her painting time. She explains, "I used to think $7 per hour was great but now charge $10 per hour. I hope to raise my hourly rate to $20 now that I have had increased exposure on Aleene's Creative Living Television program and have had my designs published in magazines."

Selling on consignment motivated Kathy to set specific prices. "If a shop featuring my work charges me rent plus commission, I will not pay them more than 20% of the retail price. Though these establishments do a lot for me, I consider the shop's reputation, customer base, sales, advertising, etc., first. Next, I decide if it will benefit me to pay a percentage of the price while I make sure the owner will do what I pay him/her to do for me," she says.

To set prices for consignment, I divide what I want for an item by the remaining percentage. For example, if I want at least $5, I divide $5 by 80% to arrive at my selling price for many items such as my best-selling switch-plates and candle sticks." she concludes.

*   *   *

Susan Young, a member of The Society of Painters, began her business, *The Peach Kitty Studio, Inc.* though she has been selling her painted objects since 1978. She adds painting touches to flower pots, gardening gloves, assorted birdhouses, custom mailboxes, tavern signs, front door plaques, bunny, teddy bear, angel designs and Christmas ornaments.

Susan paints on many surfaces including wood, resin, porcelain, china, paper, metal, glass, "wood n' wire" plaques; hand painted greeting cards, lapel pins, floral wreaths, and has a line of pattern packets which include project color photos and instructions.

Designing for craft magazines and author of craft-related how-to books, she paints for major magazines such as *Tole World, Painting, Crafts, Pack-o-Fun, Crafts n' Things, Country Marketplace, Decorative Artist's Workbook, Decorative Woodcrafts, Aleene's Creative Living* and has been featured in Barbara Brabec's regular craft magazine column many times.

With so many paint-related activities in her life, Susan works 80 hours per week from her home studio. She spends half her time making items to sell to consumers and the other half, writing magazine articles and book proposals related to the craft industry.

Commenting on selling at wholesale, Susan says, "Time and materials required for my custom, decorative painting makes wholesaling cost-prohibitive for me. I refuse to mass-produce projects "assembly line style" and prefer to eliminate the middle-man as well."

Susan purchases raw materials primarily by catalogs saving shipping costs by placing large orders. She explains that many catalogs waive shipping costs if orders total as little as $50 to $100 which saves $8 to $20 in shipping charges. She offers readers a valuable tip when she says, "One of my favorite catalogs include coupons throughout their pages for up to 50% off certain items with a minimum order. I avoid impulse buying but often, these coupon items replace my regular inventory.

As a craft professional with a Seller's Permit, Susan often purchases directly from manufacturers and works diligently to form strong business relationships with many of them. "Many manufacturers and suppliers furnish my paints, brushes and wood cut-outs at good discounts, and at times, provide me complimentary boxes of assorted materials," she adds.

Discussing prices, Susan says, "In my early days I felt embarrassed once I set a price and found I would have to lower it. My mistake was my lack of confidence thinking my prices were too high. The public was buying but I was so new to the industry, I didn't understand. Today, I hold successful yard-shows under the maple tree in my front yard and earn up to $700, she says.

Like many crafters in this book, Susan had to learn how to price her items. She explains, "One must be patient in analyzing pricing. Sometimes it hinges on personal geography and local economics. I thought I was on target with a promotional idea for a gift item I'd geared toward a specific community business. I made many samples believing business owners would order these items from me to present to their customers as gifts. I felt proud of my 'inexpensive' line of goods thinking the low-cost would bring orders. Rather than place orders, people asked to see things in a higher price range. I rewrote my brochure doubling my prices and sent it out with the previous samples. Many orders followed," she acknowledges.

In her book, *Decorative Painting for Fun and Profit* Susan explains her Pricing Template she calls her "Rule of Threes" which works well for her. Her system: Cost of Materialsx3 + Hours at Desired Wage = her selling price. It's simple and has worked well for her for twenty-five years. Susan provides an example:

"If I spend .50 on a wood cut-out to paint as an ornament for an Easter wreath or Christmas tree decoration, and multiply .50x3, = $1.50. That's my "base materialx3. If it takes me one hour to paint the wood cut-out and I price my time at $7 per hour, the final price is $8.50. I also consider I used up paint and wear on my brushes. Depending on the project's intricacy, I add another .50 to $1 toward replacing my paints and brushes. My rule of threes becomes a Pricing Template assuring that I will recover the initial cost of the base materials and replace them for future projects. Raw materials costing $5 today, when depleted and needing replacement, may have gone up," Susan comments.

Susan discusses placing a value on her time. "Each crafter's approach to this issue varies depending on their previous experience, their career history (possibly in unrelated fields) and what they expect. A career professional who leaves a corporate job netting $20 hourly is not likely to command $20 in labor for painting birdhouses. Think realistically. If your local minimum wage is $7, try that as a guideline when starting out. Network with other crafters and ask what they charge as an hourly work rate. A quilter making every stitch by hand can charge more for her time than one who uses a sewing machine. You must start somewhere but don't lose sight of future options. As you become established, you can increase your hourly rate," she advises.

Selling designs to magazines has been quite profitable for Susan. She receives from $30 to $400 per accepted submission. Twice, she had a three-page spread of her designs in leading craft magazines for which she received $400 for her painted projects plus her instructions. Added to this, like most members of The Society of Craft Designers, she received three hundred dollars more in endorsement fees from paint manufacturers for specifying their company and specific colors. There is no denying that Susan, like many crafters, finds that membership in professional craft organizations worthwhile.

*   *   *

Melissa Seigfried of *Lazy Day Creations,* began her business in 1992. She paints on finished wood but often adds dried floral wreaths to complete her original home decor products.

Mothering a two-year old limits her to working evenings in a unique way from many contributors to this book. Melissa explains, "When making new products, I like to take the item from beginning to end which includes pricing, recording the item on my inventory sheets, and photography if it is a new product. This method works well for me," she says.

She sells to the ultimate consumer through craft shows preferring them because they give her direct commentary for the likes and dislikes of her customers. She purchases most of her raw materials at wholesale with the exception of clearance sales. Today, she avoids lowering or raising her prices feeling that her work is worth the prices she charges. Melissa prefers to wait for the "perfect customer" rather than change prices to keep her pricing as stable as possible.

Melissa offers her pricing system: For example, if supplies cost her $5 to make and $3.00 in labor, she arrives at $8.00. Next, she doubles that sum to arrive at a final retail price of $16.00 + tax. If a similar item sells for much less in her local market, she adjusts to remain competitive. She sets her hourly price at $6.00 per hour, a fair price in the geographical area where she vends.

In Depth Interview, Tori Hoggard

Tori Hoggard began her company, *Harmony Artworks* in 1994. She sells hand-painted furniture, floor and wall cloths, small home accessories, hand-bound, painted journals and greeting cards. She also teaches workshops based on art and craft combined with the spirituality of the creative process, something in which she believes and chooses as her life-style

How much time do you devote to your business?

"I work 20-30 hours per week but more when I have upcoming shows."

Do you sell both retail and wholesale or just directly to the ultimate consumer?

"I sell wholesale to but at retail while vending at shows or when doing custom work."

Where do you purchase supplies?

"I buy raw materials at wholesale if I can't find what I need at second-hand stores. The bulk of my materials come from thrift shops and from scavenging at stores where I can buy scraps for nothing. For example, a local building supply store had a bucket of tile scraps sitting next to the tile cutter provided for customers. I asked what they did with their scraps and they explained that they go in the trash. I was happy to become their trash woman."

Have you ever raised your prices? Why?

"I believe that higher prices convey to a customer that I do quality work but it took me a while to get to this point. Combining my products with increased quality and skill plus rising costs for raw materials has caused me to raise my prices. Pricing becomes difficult when I become too personally involved, wanting people with limited budgets to be able to afford nice things for themselves."

Do you have a system for pricing your items? Please describe.

"I add the cost of materials to my hourly wage. I am much more generous with myself now but realize this may prove to be impractical in the future."

Do you consider raw materials when you set your prices?

"Yes, but since my raw materials are often minimal, I set my price based on how much the raw materials might cost if I had to pay standard prices for them. For example, if I find a good deal on a used chair I buy for $5 in a second hand store, I consider that it would normally cost around $30 at wholesale. I think about this as I seek the ultimate price."

How do you determine overhead?

"I add approx. 10% on to each item."

Where to you sell your work today?

"I sell at craft shows, county fairs, retail shops and boutiques. I like to work on commission but find it more difficult to sell on consignment. I charge the same as I would charge wholesale since I only deal with owners that take 50% or less. I take my things from the shop after awhile if they do not sell because I don't want my inventory sitting around."

Do you sell via the Internet or from a website?

"I have just begun to sell this way and find it has already given me credibility and a different perspective as people from outside my little world comment on and appreciate my work. I see that I can reach specific customers through the use of search engines and plan to explore that more."

To close, Tori offers a specific formula when she designs, makes and paints a hard-cover book with blank pages others use as a gift or a standard journal. If a customer wants more pages, she just adds the cost of the paper and the time it takes to bind more pages.

Canvas (for cover)	.50
Paper filler	$1.00
Thread and beads	$.50
Labor/profit	$12.00
Wholesale price	$14.00
Retail price	$28.00

QUICK REVIEW of PRICING METHODS IN THIS CHAPTER

X   Consider a firm Pricing Template when painting on nearly identical items and/or surfaces. Include the price of the item on which you will paint, paint, wear and tear on brushes.

X   Work assembly line methods when filling large orders which cuts painting time in half.

X   When painting/refinishing antique furniture, charge 10-15 times what it costs to buy the piece itself plus all the materials, supplies and paint to refinish.

X   When painting murals and portraits, the over-all size is critical. Measure accurately since errors affect the cost of paints and materials critically.

X   Think about the media you will use: Oil on glass, temporary paint to wash off, copy or lettering included?

X   Labor based on many hours or days is quite different than pricing labor on small items.

X   Painting large murals and windows bring different considerations to the equation. You cannot work privately at home and must work visibly on someone else's property.

X   Using an option described in my first book, *Crafting for Dollars,* use the 1/3, 1/3, 1/3, system when estimating large, commissioned work. Divide your final price into three even parts—the first paid before the work begins, the second, midway through the work and full payment when you complete the work. If customer backs out, you have at least recovered the cost of raw materials.

X   If a shop features your work and charges you rent plus commission, do not pay the shop owner more than 20% of the retail price. Instead, divide what you want for an item by the remaining percentage.

X   If supplies cost $5 to make + $3.00 labor, total to $8.00. Double this for final retail price of $16.00 + tax.

CONTRIBUTORS TO THIS CHAPTER

Marlene Watson
Marlene's Craft and Design Studio
1278 Via Del Carmel
Santa Maria, Ca. 93455
Phone/fax 805-937-6415
E-mail: MR3653@AOL.com
http://www.craftplanet.com/MWD

Monica Obenchain-Janis
changing her address during preparation of this chapter.
E-mail: souljanis@aol.com

Steve Matosich
305 Ilo Lane
Danville, CA 94526
Phone: 925-827-0641

Kathy Anderson
20533 SE 272nd Street
Kent, WA 98042
Phone & Fax: 425/413-1267
E-mail: KMA205@aol.com
http://members.aol.com/kdesigns.htm

Melissa Seigfried
Lazy Day Creations
RD #l. Box 1098
Orwigsburg, PA 17961
Phone: 570-943-7666
E-mail: lazyday@pottsville.infi.net
Fax: (415) 863-4546

Susan Young,
227 Usher Road
Madison, AL 35757-8010
Phone: (256)895-0656
E-mail: dgyshy@aol.com
Website: http://www.craftmallweb.com/peachkitty

Tori Hoggard
3804 S 300 E
Salt Lake City, UT 84115
Phone: 801-263-0329
Fax: 801-263-0329
E-mail harmonyart@aol.com
Website:
http://www.freeyellow.com/members6/harmony88/index.html

Chapter 13

Ceramics, Sculpture & Glass

Pricing Template: Judy Sims
In Depth Interview: Robert Houghtaling

Frequently, a new product can set the craft industry on its ear. Such was the case when the polymer clay, *Fimo®*, reached the market. Not only sculptors and ceramists took to this product; the most popular craft classes offered at the annual seminar of The Society of Craft Designers, were those introducing the *Fimo®* to crafters of other persuasions. Donna Cato vending at this seminar, who has helped popularize this product, found her booth continually surrounded by professional crafters who could not wait to buy her unusual necklaces. They did not look like marble, glass or clay yet, seemed like all of these.

Creative crafters, including me, thronged to buy old and new pasta makers. No, not to make pasta but to roll *Fimo®* clay into figures, buttons to match handmade clothing and of course, jewelry. E-Bay, the Internet online auction site now has eager buyers for old pasta makers as craft tools. An enterprising artist recently put up a Website just to make custom *Fimo®* buttons for knitters, crocheters and garment makers across the country. In this chapter, you will meet artisans who may not have quite grown up—they still play with clay, including *Fimo®*.

*   *   *

Judy Sims, of *WildCat Molds*, provides bisque and green-ware, (basic clay before it's worked and finished) plus occasional custom molds for sculptors and ceramists. Her customers are crafters who work in ceramics, resin ware, plaster ware, bisque and clay in various stages of growth with their own products and media.

WildCat Molds, a full service ceramics and designing workshop, also designs for the public and provides created molds. "We provide for others who are in business, producing gift items in ceramic, plaster or resins (plastic). We make molds for ceramics, plaster ware and resins; production of a master block for subsequent molds; mass production of green-ware, bisque and will even finish items for others," Judy says. Her company aims to help with whatever a customer needs in this field. Recently, Judy added *Castle Creations,* a new line of architectural tile works, in the form of 3-D wall sculptures and tiles anywhere from 7/8" thick up to 5" thick, but poured hollow to keep them lightweight.

Customers come to Judy's factory and produce a limited number of new items to their line to test them in the market or even mass produce, using Judy's facilities and services. Artisans need not invest in their own workshop space until they know for sure that their latest creation will sell. As each individual client using Judy's business services grows, they soon outgrow *WildCat Molds* though a few continue to share her company's space.

Judy's principal resource is "Clay slip," delivered by truck in quantities of 100 gallons at a time, as often as needed. She has been in love with clay and pottery since she discovered the work of the Pueblo Indians when she was eight years old. She continued working with clay but admits she was 40 years old before she had the opportunity to see one of her creations fired and finished. Judy began to see the need for a facility for firing ceramics, mold making, pouring and finishing.

"When I began working from my kitchen table," says Judy, "I thought that setting prices would be easy. I totaled rent + utilities and divided by the square footage used. But in a workshop, things changed. Now I go strictly by square footage even to determine overhead per piece. In my particular workshop, I divide the work areas according to the process currently underway. In other words, everything being painted has to come from the pouring area. Since we use about 1/3 of the shop space for pouring green-ware, everything we touch is created there. Our pouring area supports the entire shop," she explains.

When figuring product cost Judy counts everything, however small. Since she uses her pouring area as her basis for profit, she divides the square footage into the total of her fixed expenses. "Within that square footage," Judy explains, "I have five pouring tables, each surface measuring 2 feet by 8 feet. To figure the cost for an item requiring a mold measuring one foot square, I fit 16 molds onto one table and pour twice per day." She explains her formula below which leads to her Pricing Template to follow:

5 tables x 16 molds x 2 pours per day = one day's pour.

Multiply by 20 days per month = monthly production cost of that particular item.

"Sometimes, I produce nothing but one item for a solid month and I use every pouring table," she explains. In that case, she expands her formula to: 5 tables x 16 molds x 2 pours x 20 days = 3200 pieces poured per month.

Judy continues. "If my rent is $600 and my utilities and taxes total $400, my overhead is $1000. Divide $1000 by 3200 pieces = $.3125 rounded up and I charge 32 cents each," Judy says. "It takes two workers to pour and pull that many molds in one day," she adds. Using an example of $5 per hour, she provides a complete Pricing Template for pouring and manufacturing a single mold shape:

$5 x 2 workers =	$10 per hour
8 hours per day =	$80
$80 per day x 20 days per month =	$1600
$1600 x 3200 pieces =	$.50 each.

Judy explains it will take just as many man hours to clean, paint, fire, glaze and pack the product so she doubles the amount for labor which results in a final price of $1 per piece.

Materials costs: slip clay, about 1/8 of a gallon at $1.25 = $.16

Glaze: about 2 ounces at $.40 per ounce = $.80 to total $.96

She totals all costs:

Overhead =	$ .32
Labor =	$1.00
Materials =	$.96
Total	$2.28

Next, Judy compares her product with similar items in the marketplace. "I know this product will sell easily at $30 retail," she says "but I don't want to ruin the market by selling too cheap or I will flood it resulting in a lowered market demand defeating my own purpose. If the perceived value ranges about $30, I want to keep the perceived value as high as possible," she adds.

"Wholesale prices are 50% of retail so I can sell this particular product for $15 but since I prefer not to damage the market, I settle for $12.50," she explains. "If I go through a distributor or sales rep, I expect to pay anywhere from 15% to 30% of my wholesale price. Taking the higher cut, I subtract that from my wholesale price," she says.

Wholesale price =	$12.50
Commission/cut	3.75 30%
	$8.75 remains.
Minus costs	$ 2.28
Balance:	$ 6.47

$6.47 divided by $8.75 = 74% profit, a satisfactory one for Judy who points out that not every product will produce this high a profit, so after figuring costs on each product you make, you should add them together then divide by the number of products to see what profit margin you can maintain. She acknowledges that some of her items yield a 10% profit while others bring in 30% profit and a very few as high as 200% profit. "Some products sell faster than others so consider all these factors to know if you are actually making a profit," she concludes.

*   *   *

Arles Mitchell-Price of *N2 Crafts* began her ceramics business in 1996 and works at her ceramics business full-time. She works about 14-20 hours per week producing items to sell and uses the remaining time shopping for slip, molds, glazes and green-ware—her raw materials. She takes advantage of the sales her supplier offers throughout the year by trying to purchase in quantity.

Preferring to sell at retail she offers her goods to craft shops on a consignment basis, Arles aims to find more shops that will take her products to increase profits. She chose consignment rather than pay high rent and commissions to craft-malls. She finds she can place her items in more shops if she can pay modest fees for consignment only.

Like several other artisans in this book, Arles has not had a good experience selling in craft malls. She advises crafters, as do I, to thoroughly check the references from a craft mall before leaving items. Some craft malls charge high rents to each crafter but do not always have the crafter's interest at heart. Since they make most of their profit from renting space whether or not buyers come to buy or browse, their profit is secured. Check to see that craft malls you are considering do not display and sell cheaper imported items to compete against your hand-crafted products.

Arles sells directly to customers via craft shows from her home two to three times a year She invites friends and family and offers an incentive of 50% off total purchases if they bring another guest along. She chooses not to advertise publicly to avoid strangers in her home. Her invitational shows have proven successful for her. Friends visit with one another so she offers refreshments and provides a 30-day lay-away plan. Due to the selectivity of her guests, Arles has never received bad checks or had a customer not follow up on lay-away items.

Purchasing craft supplies from catalogs works well for Arles but she purchases ceramic supplies locally through a dealer/distributor or from a ceramic studio where she maintains a dealer's account status. Arles checks websites of other ceramic manufacturers to observe popular molds and colors. Though a few ceramic manufacturers sell molds directly, Arles finds it cheaper to pick up her molds from a dealer rather than to pay the high shipping costs of ceramic materials that can weigh up to seventy pounds.

Arles says that numerous online craft e-mail groups on the Internet have provided a rich source of information to her. She explains, "Joining e-mail lists provides valuable information on supplies and what is currently selling well at big craft shows," she says. "The greatest advantage is that since the lists are made up of crafters (both professional and hobbyists), it's a great way to share information about suppliers and products. This was a great help to me when I started my business and my online friends still help me today. I cherish these relationships as we support one another personally and professionally," she says.

Arles worked out a good system to buy raw materials at dealers' cost. She has a retailer's tax number which allows her to buy at a dealer's cost which is more than wholesale but less than retail. For example she buys ceramic supplies from 10-20% off and brushes and paints for 30-40% off. She stresses that by establishing herself legally, obtaining proper licenses and permits, she gains more respect from suppliers who view her as a businesswoman rather than a hobbyist.

Looking to lower prices for raw materials, Arles shares data about what she achieved even without buying wholesale. "The distributor from whom I buy molds held a sale recently on overstocked molds at 70% off. I purchased 35 molds, at tremendous savings. He also has various sales throughout the year, such as 40% off purchases of 24 or more cans of glazes, stains, 40% off sale on purchase of stilts when buying 12 or more and music boxes. I take advantage of these sales and purchase supplies I may not use until the next season when I may not find prices as good as these," she explains.

In 1998, the ceramics studio from which Arles had been buying green-ware, glazes and other supplies closed its doors. Arles' husband commented on the time she spent hauling green-ware back and forth to the studios for firings and suggested that she consider purchasing her own kiln. She took his advice and purchased it 1998. They felt their money was well spent if she selected one that was fully automatic, requiring no monitoring or manual temperature control. Today both agree that is the best investment ever made for the business. Says Arles, "Though our electric bill is a bit higher than before, we have saved a lot of time and money. The distributor from which I purchased the kiln encouraged me to pour my own molds—something I had never done before. At one of their sales in 1998, the company gave away a free mold with a $100 purchase of supplies. From that free mold and a 2-gallon bucket of slip, my pouring days began. It was trial and error but the distributor was helpful and many of my ceramic friends online helped as well. Since I pour most of my own pieces, I use the same Pricing Template as if I were purchasing actual green-ware and paying to have it fired in a studio."

Arles comments about labor for ceramists. "I account for labor in my pricing to a certain degree but realistically, with competition from foreign imports, customers will only pay so much for an item. If they can buy what they perceive as the same item from an importer more cheaply, they do. Crafters who take pride in their work must contend with consumers who want to make a 'deal', want to bargain or do not recognize the difference in quality, handcrafted items compared to imports. Many of us do not cover our labor at times but, under no circumstances will I devalue my work to make a sale. I build my profit margin into each piece, ranging from 100% to 200% of the cost of green-ware," she adds. Planning for the new century, Arles is considering vending at larger craft shows to expand her business.

*   *   *

Michael R. Harvey owner of *Visual Energy Studio* began his business 1987 but has been selling his crafts since he was twelve. Michael, a talented sculptor, makes contemporary designs ranging from jewelry to fine sculpture. He makes stone and metal sculpture, recycled metal planters, stone and metal fountains, fossil ivory and shell and wood jewelry. Working as long as twelve hours per day, Michael estimates that he spends about half his time producing his craft and the remainder on errands, administration, marketing and maintenance.

Though he sells at both retail and wholesale, some of his designs are so labor intensive he feels he must offer them at craft shows directly to consumers as his final price does not allow him to sell at wholesale. Such a markup would price him out of the market. He says selling at craft shows provides observance of current craft trends and he finds more profit in selling at full retail than wholesale.

Selling on consignment at a gallery, Michael says he simply looks at other art offered in that and similar galleries, factors in how well known he has become compared to other artists in these galleries and then arrives at his retail price. He then subtracts the gallery commission and compares it to the labor it took him to produce a particular piece. "If I feel good about the end result, I use that price," he says. "If not, I raise the price until I am happy with it and hope for the best. Keep in mind," he advises, "that in the world of fine art, a piece priced too low can do more to harm the sale and your reputation than one that is too high."

Michael buys the raw materials he needs from local stores but much of what he uses he finds at no cost. He looks through abandoned rock quarries, construction sites and at materials that stone and metal contractors consider as waste.

Lowering prices comes about for Michael in a rather unusual way. Whenever possible, he changes his crafting procedures and material sources. "Cutting production time or finding cheaper and/or free material has a great impact on my ability to reduce prices which encourage more sales," Michael says. "Some items sell at a higher, price but I can sell more when I lower the price." He explains: "For example, if you can sell 100 units of an item per month at a profit of $10.00 you would make $1000.00 profit per month. If you can sell 200 units per month at $6.00 profit you would make $1200.00 per month."

Michael describes his Pricing Template. "As a general rule, I start with the minimum wage I am willing to accept per hour and multiply by the time taken to make an item using production procedures (it takes less time per unit to make several of something than to make just one). I triple this total to account for administration, errands, advertising show expenses, etc. Next, I add the cost of raw materials and consider one of the formulae below:"

Formula #1: wagesx3 + raw materials = wholesale.

SCENARIO ONE

"If half of the average price of these products (the store's wholesale price) rises above the result of my formula, I discard the idea and sell what I have made for the best price I can and wholesale it if necessary. I then look for another, more profitable product," he acknowledges.

SCENARIO TWO

"If half of the average price of these products (the store's wholesale price) is the same as the result of my formula, I begin production and sale of the item. During the next few weeks I look around for a cheaper supply of materials, modifying my product if needed. At the same time I begin adjusting my production procedures to reduce time. After I feel satisfied that I have the best material price and best production time, I attempt the next formula: Wagexlaborx4 + raw materials = wholesale," he explains. "If I arrive at a store's wholesale price or below, I feel satisfied and continue making the product. If not, I sell what I have and start looking for a new project idea," he says.

SCENARIO THREE

"If half of the average price of these products (the store's wholesale price) is less than the result of Formula #1, I proceed as in SCENARIO 2 but with more excitement," he adds. "Pricing to sell at craft shows is different, but simple," Michael says. "Most people who shop at craft shows expect to get a good deal and expect the crafter or artist to work for $2.00 per hour. Keeping in mind that you can't live on $2.00 per hour, you must compromise so I take my calculated wholesale price described above and multiply by 1½. While not a true retail price, this satisfies the customer looking for a good deal and covers your table fee and time at the booth," he adds.

Michael uses the Internet to his advantage but says that while having a Website is almost essential; it's only useful when used in conjunction with other advertising. Summarizing his pricing philosophy Michael concludes, "My formulae allow me to sell as much as I can produce, provides a comfortable wage, covers all business expenses, pays for holidays and allows me to save some—I make a comfortable profit," he concludes.

*   *   *

Genie Gnagi, owner of *Mrs. Pots,* hand-paints floral designs on 4", 6"& 8" terra cotta pots with saucers, glass pasta and cookie jars, birdhouses and mailboxes. Working about 25 hours per week, Genie spends about 70% of her time producing her items and the remaining 30% on bookkeeping, correspondence and looking for supplies.

She sells in consignment stores and at about seven craft fairs per year—the best method for her. She receives exposure at her booth at Coomer's Craft Mall and has developed a customer base. She schedules crafts shows two months apart so she has time to produce before each. "I am a stay-at-home mother," Genie explains, "so I only work on my crafting business part-time. Craft shows allow me to produce and stock inventory and then sell a majority of my stock in one weekend. I enjoy craft shows and the exposure I receive. I like hearing the public respond to my work and the public enjoys meeting artisans and asking questions. Shows also provide me with 'adult time' I need staying home with small children all day," she adds.

Genie buys raw materials come from craft supply catalogs, craft chain stores and a few manufacturers. She began purchasing terra cotta pots from a wholesaler for the first time last year. At first she found that the company was a bit difficult to work with because she worked from home but later, they became more cooperative when they saw the size of her orders. She picks up the pots herself from a Kansas City warehouse but is unable to inspect prepackaged merchandise. Buyers are responsible for breakage once they leave the warehouse. "Some pots come broken but others are of high quality," Genie says, "and I continue to finds this issue a tough one," she adds.

Genie also must buy jars, paints, brushes, birdhouses and other supplies for finishing from wholesale craft supply catalogs. The base-coat paint and acrylic sealer used on pots comes from a home improvement store using a tax-exempt number. When Genie contacted the manufacturer directly to purchase these products, she learned that shops nearby were already selling it for as low a price as possible so she decided to buy these products locally.

However, Genie felt happier with a glass company that required an initial order of $250.00 with a $50 minimum order thereafter. Glass jars for painting are heavy and difficult to find without ripples, indentations or decorations on them. "At Provo Craft, if I order a minimum of $200, they ship free *and* give a 1% discount," says Genie. "With glass being so heavy, this is a good savings for me and they set reasonable amounts for minimum quantities," Genie explains.

Genie is relentless searching for new suppliers with better products or prices. She explains how she manages. "A crafter's job is never done. I always look for lower prices and new products to expand my lines. When I see a product in a craft store I might want to try, I purchase one and experiment. If I like it, I call the manufacturer to see if I can buy in quantity at wholesale prices. So far," she says, "most companies have accepted my business," she adds.

It took Genie about a year to develop the painting technique she now uses. It also took time to find the right materials and the best possible products. She practiced her methods on paper, later on pots, giving products away until she refined her technique. "The first craft fair where I vended was local," she explains. "I shared a booth with two other people to split the $40 entrance fee. I was ecstatic when I sold more than $300! That made me decide to start my own business," she exclaims.

Lowering prices has not worked well for Genie. Once, she decided to make birdhouse clocks thinking they would be a hit. She priced them at $32.95 because she thought they would be popular and expected a high profit margin because she found them easy to produce. They didn't sell at two craft shows so Genie lowered the price to $22.95. "They still haven't sold," she says, "so even at minimum price they're not worth producing. I won't go below my minimum profit margin or below costs. If they don't sell at the lowest price I can afford, I give them away as gifts and stop producing them," she explains.

However, Genie has raised prices when she could not keep an item in stock. "If some of my products sell faster than I can produce them," she says, "I raise my price. My four inch pots and jars in wild-flower designs sell like that," she says. "I can't produce them fast enough or keep them in stock at shows so I raised the price from $7.95 to $9.95 about two years ago. This has worked well but if I sell out at a show, at least I'm still selling them at a higher price. My pricing strategy for products that sell too quickly is to raise the price $2.00 at a time. This way, I sell them at a rate where I can keep up with productions and still make the maximum profit," she adds. Genie's Pricing Template appears below.

Hand-painted, 4" terra cotta pots with saucers
Retail: $10.00 each Formula: Price = (Costsx2) + Overhead + Labor + Profit
Total Costs to make: $.88 each.

To determine overhead, Genie totals the bills from the previous year that didn't include cost of goods sold (i.e., paint brushes, craft fair fees, traveling expenses, office supplies) and divides by total sales for the year. This is usually about 30% so her overhead for this item is $10.00x30%, or $3.00.

Genie pays herself $10.00 per hour for labor. She produces four pots per hours.

Divide $10 per hour by four pots which equals $2.50 labor per pot. To determine profit, Genie multiplies the selling price by 10%: $10.00x20% = $2.00. A final example of Genie's formula using this method:

Price   = Cost of Goods Sold each x 2 + Price x 30% + $10.00/hour x 25 + Price x 20%

$10.00   = ($.88 x 2) + ($10.00 x 30%) + ($2.50) + ($10.00 x 20%)

$10.00   = ($1.76) + ($3.00) + ($2.50) + ($2.00)

$10.00   = $9.26 + a little extra ($.74) to round off selling price.

Genie compares her sales at craft malls and consignment. "I do well in Coomer's, though I pay a high monthly premium for a prime location (the front window of the store), but this location has doubled my sales from another area *inside* the store," she explains. "Craft malls require high-maintenance and a lot of bookkeeping but a well-stocked, neat booth is the key to success," she adds.

"I've had bad experience with a small consignment store where the owner of the store realized the potential of my sales and began to copy my products. Though it was her store, contracts forbid this behavior," Genie explains.

"I sell on consignment in two small stores in my husband's hometown. One of the stores is a hospital gift shop; the other, a small gift boutique shop. I sell for 20% consignment fee and receive a monthly check for products sold during the period. I like this method of selling because the percentage to these retailers is smaller and I control my inventory keeping as much or as little in the stores as I wish. I look forward to setting up my own Website very soon," she concludes.

*   *   *

Constance Gunderson began her business, *Glass Cellar* 1978. A stained glass artist, she also creates original fused and slumped art work. She began working with stained glass but over the last eight years she has learned to work with compatible glass, manipulating it in a kiln. Constance makes traditional items such as windows, window hangings and an occasional sun-catcher, but enjoys making lampshades, kaleidoscopes and boxes most.

"Fused glass is more to my liking," she says. "It gives me a certain freedom from the lines of stained glass that I consider important design elements. I can take colorful pieces of glass, cut and place the pieces carefully and create wonderful, whimsical masks-on-a-stick. I also make turtles that stand on their own four feet, vessels of various shapes and sizes, platters, plates and little bowls. Most of my work is sculptural in nature and stands on its own as displayed art," she explains. Lately, Constance has been fusing layers of clear glass with colors between, some in shapes of human or animal figures and others as abstract designs. She is also working on a line of liturgical art.

Constance does not work on a fixed schedule. She prefers to work on glass each day, but if she has a specific show or commission coming up, she will work to finish a design, ever anxious to see the completed project. She manages her own publicity using her computer, scanner and colored printer enabling her to print her brochures, show announcements, flyers, and art work postcards which she sends to her clients to stay in touch.

Galleries are Constance's preferred way to sell. Clients look for her work through word of mouth and occasional art and craft shows where she vends. Since her pieces are one-of-a-kind, she does not believe wholesale would suit her. Like other crafters in this book who work this way, (including this author), the idea of making the same item repeatedly does not appeal to her.

Constance buys her raw materials through catalogs which she found necessary when living in a rural area. Now she has moved to an urban area where she can hunt in salvage stores and discount hardware stores. Many shops, if asked will give some sort of discount when they know one is an artist in possession of a tax number. Buying from manufacturers at wholesale does not work for Constance as their minimum orders are too high and she cannot store large quantities of glass.

Constance worked with glass only for two weeks and knew she was hooked. Wanting to earn money so she could invest in tools of the trade, she designed a flying seagull window hanger which she sold to friends and family and neighbors for $10.00. With that money in hand, she purchased a glass grinder and more glass. "One thing led to another," she says. "I was still learning about the craft when I began designing my own patterns. My sister, a teacher, took boxes full of my Christmas stained glass, window hangers and small candle holders to school for me. Selling out the first day, she took requests for more. I felt thrilled to earn money from something I really enjoyed doing," Constance exclaims.

Constance has lowered her prices at times, explaining, "When I lower a price, it is to move an item after it has been in the gallery for a number of years. Galleries allow me to have annual "dent and scratch sales" to help move products, often for just a few dollars less than retail. It amazes me to see what people will buy at an event like this."

Raising prices is another matter for Constance. When planning to raise the price of an item in her line, she will not display new ones until the last has been sold. Then she raises the price on the new batch. She prefers not to do this but must when her suppliers have raised prices of her raw materials.

Constance says her method of setting prices is simple. She figures the cost of the materials, and multiplies by 5 to arrive at her retail price. She feels well paid and always makes time to research other glass objects similar to hers to make sure of her market price. "When I started 20 years ago, I only doubled the cost of materials," Constance explains. "Since then, my skill has grown, material prices have increased and I have more outside costs. All of these factors contribute to my pricing," she adds.

"I feel comfortable with the way I price my items," she continues. "I price so I know the item goes to a good home and that the buyer will enjoy looking at the piece which is most important to me. However, I do not use this pricing method when working on commission. I charge a design fee up front with no refunds. Then, depending on the size of the piece and its complexity, I work out a price charging by the square foot after researching the cost of glass, solder and other supplies. Clients must pay the full cost of materials," she adds.

"I add at least 45% for labor but often wonder if I am charging enough. I dislike commission work because many clients don't know exactly what they want," Constance continues. "Some clients only want to match the sofa which is not easy for me as I must spend a lot of time with such a client in tedious, less profitable decision-making, " she explains.

Constance recommends that other glass artists ask commission clients to do their own research and request that they bring pictures of what they like, such as flowers, landscapes, etc. Best for Constance—when customers have a picture of a piece of glass they like and can explain what they like and dislike about it.

"To determine profit when I consign to a gallery, I simply take the price of the object and add the percentage the gallery will take, rounding off to the higher dollar amount," Constance says. "This way I still receive the price I had originally set for the item. I sell at art and craft shows and retail shops and on commission at times." Constance has been a part of a cooperative gallery for ten years and has had one-person shows in local hospital art galleries and participated for two years in an art show at a college.

Constance does not employ a sales representative because adding their commission to her prices would price her out of the market. "Glass artists have not reached the status that other artists have to justify large price tags unless they are glass blowers, she says. "Part of my job as a glass artist is to educate clients so they appreciate the design and the time it took to finish a work of art they wish to take home." she concludes.

In-depth Interview:

Robert Houghtaling, of Houghtaling Sculpture and Design started his present business in 1992 and has been sculpting nearly all his life. He describes his work this way. "Collectibles are the largest part of my business. I sculpt the masters for many companies and/or their licensees. My clients include Disney and Warner Brothers and their licensees, The Hamilton Collection and The Bradford Exchange. For example, I sculpted the "Young Smokey" copyrighted by The Hamilton Collection which owns all rights. I also sculpted "Young Smokey" as a line of collectibles by The Hamilton Collection. It depicts a younger 'Smokey the Bear' interacting with his forest friends. Ads for this have appeared in *T.V. Guide* and other magazines and newspapers.

Describing his business, Robert says, "When you love your work as I do, 30 plus years fly by without feeling like a long time. I have worked in and taught most phases of sculpture and jewelry making. I enjoy sharing my knowledge and experience with students showing them the importance of art in the world and explaining to them the possibilities of making a living with their art. Besides the animation characters, I do realistic human and animal sculpts as well as technical pieces such as the Borg ship from Star Trek. My work includes full round figures, relief sculpts for plates, mugs etc. and almost any kind of three-dimensional work," he adds.

Though I am well versed in all sculpture techniques and reproduction methods, I prefer to work in polymer clay to make my originals. Presently I make most of my work with Super Sculpey, leached out to make it firmer. At times, I combine polymer clays to provide the feel I need for whatever part of a sculpting project on which I am working," he explains.

How much time do you devote to your business?

Robert works long hours—about 72 hours per week. "I begin my day at 9:30 a.m. and work until about 10:00 p.m. to 2:00 a.m. the next morning. I stop to cook and eat dinner with my wife, then continue sculpting or doing business related computer work while we watch television."

How much of your time do you devote to producing something to sell?

"I spend about 85% of my time directly producing sculptures and the remainder soliciting new jobs, keeping records and doing market research."

Do you sell both at retail and wholesale or just to the ultimate consumer?

"A large part of my work consists of commissioned pieces for the collectible market but I also market my own line on the Internet from my personal Website."

Where do you purchase supplies?

"I use catalogs, local shops, manufacturers plus resources on the Internet.

Do you buy raw materials at retail prices, "on-sale" or at wholesale?

"I buy at wholesale whenever possible."

How long had you been crafting before you began to sell what you made?

"I have been able to sell my artwork since I was a kid. I used to paint store windows and make signs if nothing else. Later, I made greeting cards to sell at school."

Have you ever lowered prices because you found they were too high?

"Not very often but it can be a useful technique when you are trying to find your market."

Have you ever raised your prices? If so, Why?

"Of course. I adjust prices as the market dictates. As one's reputation and skill increases, I believe you should raise your prices. If you find that you are pricing yourself out of your market you adjust and lower prices."

Do you have a system for pricing your items? Please describe.

"Over the years I have slowly increased my prices. If demand for my work continues to increase, I may have to increase them again. However, if my market slows and jobs become scarce, I will have to re-evaluate my system."

Do you consider labor when you set your prices?

"I base my prices for commission work primarily on my labor. I consider design time sometimes factoring it into the overall contract. Other times, I list it as a "per finished concept drawing." At times, I am asked to do color rendering which is of course, more expensive than black and white."

Do you consider raw materials when you set your prices?

"When I set prices for commission work, raw materials are a small part of the final fee. Graphic materials for design work do not amount to much nor do bits of wire and clay for my sculpts. Most of my fee is based on the time involved. If a contract requires molds and castings, however, I must charge the customer extra to cover my costs to the mold maker and include the time I spend working with him. When I design my own collectible pieces, raw materials go up as I must cover mold costs and the costs of resin and other materials."

How do you determine overhead?

"I keep track of all my time and expenses not directly involved in production.

How do you determine profit?

"Most artists and crafters feel that anything over and above their actual material costs becomes profit. This way of thinking can spell disaster for your business. You must also consider your time and this should include not only the time it takes to make a single item but also the time you spend running vital business errands such as the bank and post-office and time spent shopping in art shops. Discussion time at galleries that exhibit your work, the time you spend making contacts and showing your work to potential clients must also be considered," Robert advises.

"If you vend at arts and craft shows, you must consider not only the time actually spent selling from your booth, but travel time as well. There are so many other detailed costs to consider that I recommend that newer crafters read many books on small business management to assure themselves that they are consistently profitable," Robert stresses.

How do you determine the value of your time?

"I bid a job based on a time estimate and base my rates on the factors mentioned above. For example, when you take your car in for repairs and see a sign that says, 'Shop Rate: $40.00 per hour', the individual technician is not earning $40.00 himself. The shop owner has figured his total costs based on all the same factors I mentioned. And, most of us who consider ourselves as artists and crafters must do likewise. Never stop researching your market and checking prices for similar work. You cannot merely decide that your time and the quality of your art are worth a specific price and ignore what others who do similar work earn. To arrive at a price for a finished piece of work, you must have all possible information before you begin," Robert believes.

Continuing, Robert shares his rich experiences. "Commission work requires you to rely on your past experience to arrive at reasonable estimates. If every detail goes as expected, be satisfied but sometimes you may find problems you didn't anticipate and you cannot expect customers to pay for your problems. At times, this may mean that you will not earn as much as you expected to. To minimize this, try to figure problems or delays into your estimate but don't try to cover yourself to the extent that you price yourself out of the market," he adds.

Do you sell on commission?

"Except for my own line of collectibles, most of my work *is* commission selling but I do not work like other painters or sculptors. Their commissioned work becomes their final product but my finished commission piece is not the final product but a master which will be used by others to manufacture and mass produce the idea. Often, I am asked to design the piece but I also work from drawings supplied by product development people. Sometimes I make original sculpted items and other times, I supply the molds and castings for the production masters. At times I make painted master castings for the manufacturer to follow and/or use for product photo shoots. I consider all these issues in addition to the size and complexity of the project to determine my price, which challenges me most. If you get all the details just right and don't run into any difficulties you can earn a good profit. Now, I am designing and sculpting a line of collectibles based on the Lone Ranger for a Florida company. It's great fun and I got to meet the actor who played The Lone Ranger which was quite a thrill for a kid who never grew up like me."

Do you employ a sales representative to sell for you?

"I don't use a sales rep but on occasion, have used an agent but I don't really care for either of these. It just adds one more person to the equation. I prefer to be in direct contact with my customer and that the farther from the source you get—the more mistakes can happen. Mistakes cost both time and money."

Do you sell via the Internet or from a Website? If yes, did this increase the business you were doing before?

"Yes, I sell from The Internet quite a bit. It did not help me find new commercial commissions but has been most helpful in a way I did not expect. Now, I use e-mail to pass information and pictures back and forth with my customers which helps eliminate miscommunication and often takes the place of face-to-face meetings. All my commission projects are one-of-a-kinds and distinctly different from one another so using a consistent Pricing Template does not apply to me," Robert explains.

"Selling my line of collectibles from my Website in addition to online auctions has increased my business. I completed the first items for the premier offering of my line—ornaments and figurines based on humorous frogs which have been an important part of my work over the years. I named my site, Figgy Mountain Frogery after the Figueroa Mountain where my studio is located. I believe selling via the Internet deserves a very broad look as increasing numbers of artists and crafters move to Website sales."

Please tell readers more about the surroundings of your mountain-home studio and if you ever make use of the wild life you see from your studio in your work?

"Yes, I love to make my animals as realistic as possible in my work and have always done so. I also refer to my collection of *National Geographic* Magazines to get ideas for my sculpted wildlife animals which I often sculpt in bronze," he replies.

"I live in an "A" frame house in the mountains north of Santa Barbara, CA with my wonderful wife and helpmate Denise, the CFIC (Chief Frog In Charge) of the Figgy Mountain Frogery. We overlook the beautiful Santa Ynez Valley from an elevation of 3300 feet where we get a dusting of snow now and then. We live thirty minutes from the nearest village and are surrounded by national forest," he relates.

"I keep in touch with friends and customers by computer. I take pictures of my work as it develops with a video camera connected to my computer then e-mail the resulting pictures to my customers. We then confer in real time as to the progression of the work. I also use this technology to capture pictures of my Frog collectibles for my Website," Robert says.

Robert's studio sounded so interesting to me that I asked him to describe it in great detail. Happily, he obliged. "My studio is a glassed in deck with an 180° beautiful view that sometimes it can be hard to concentrate but I find it always inspiring. Wildlife such as mountain lions and bears are abundant but I have never seen tigers. Since I sculpt many of my designs from animals in the wild, I have subject matter everywhere I look. Once, a large bear tried to come through my screen door interrupting me while I was working," Robert began.

Most crafters comment on their frustrations with telephones interruptions but none have related being interrupted by a bear. Please don't keep us in suspense. Tell us what happened after the bear came to your screen door?

"My computer work station lies between my kitchen and living room so I can spend time with my wife while working. When I first heard tapping at the screen door, I thought it was the cat wanting in. I turned and was amazed to see a huge, black bear sitting outside the door only 25 feet away looking at me quizzically with his head to one side. I quietly rose and moved slowly moving about 8 feet from him in order to reach my camera in the hallway, off the kitchen. Holding my camera, he came right up to the door so I took pictures as he began to claw the screen door. I wagged my finger at him and said, 'No, you don't want to do that.' He looked me in the eye then took off, scooting off the porch and ran up a nearby tree," Robert concludes rather calmly after relating this experience to me.

BRIEF SUMMARY OF PRICING METHODS IN THIS CHAPTER

X   Determine overhead to set prices when operating from a shop rather than from a home studio can be easy. Rent + utilities divided by square footage times the amount of square footage used. The square footage system can also be applied to figure overhead costs on per-item small pieces.

X   A formal Pricing Template is invaluable when turning out dozens of items per day. Determine how much green ware you can pour in one day. Example: 5 tables x 16 molds x 2 pours per day = one day's pour. Multiply by 20 days per month to determine monthly production cost of a particular item. During heavy manufacturing periods, expand the basic Template this way: 5 tables x 16 molds x 2 pours x 20 days = 3200 pieces poured per month. If your rent is $600 and utilities and taxes total $400, your overhead is $1000. Divide $1000 by 3200 pieces = $.3125 rounded up to 32 cents each. Using this Template and two workers to pour and pull that many molds in a day, paying $5 per hour for labor, a new Pricing Template emerges just for pouring and manufacturing a single mold shape:
$5 x 2 workers = $10 per hour
8 hours per day = $80
$80 per day x 20 days per month = $1600
$1600 x 3200 pieces = $.50 each.

X   Consider selling at home-based craft shows 2-3 times a year inviting friends and family. Offer an incentive of 50% off total purchases if they bring another guest along.

X   When selling on consignment at a gallery, consider monitoring other art on exhibit to arrive at a tentative retail price. Then, subtract the gallery commission and compare it to the labor it takes to produce the piece. If this satisfies you, stay with the price. If not, raise the price until a profit is assured while staying within your market.

X   You may sell a few products at a higher price but perhaps you may earn more if you lower the price. For example: if you can sell 100 units of an item per month at a profit of $10.00 you would make $1000.00 profit per month. If you can sell 200 units per month at $6.00 profit you would make $1200.00 per month."

X   Formula #1: wages x 3 + raw materials = wholesale.

X   Formula # 2: wagextime x 4) + raw materials = wholesale

X   Formula #3: to retail @ $10.00 each,
     Price = (Costs x 2) + Overhead + Labor + Profit
     Total Costs to make: $.88 each.

X   If you pay yourself $10.00 per hour and can produce four items in that hour, try this formula: Divide $10 per hour by 4 = $2.50 for labor per item. To determine profit, multiply the selling price by 10%: $10.00 x 20% = $2.00. An example using this formula:

Price = Cost of Goods Sold per item x 2 + Pricc x 30% +

$10.00/hour x 25 + Price x 20%, $10.00 = ($.88 x 2) + ($10.00 x 30%) + ($2.50) + ($10.00 x 20%)

10.00 = ($1.76) + ($3.00) + ($2.50) + ($2.00)

10.00 = $9.26 + a little extra ($.74) to round off selling price.

X   A simple method for pricing is multiplying the cost of materials by five to arrive at the retail price.

X   When working on commission, determine the size of the piece and its complexity and charge by the square foot. Clients must pay the full cost of materials + 45% of materials for labor.

CONTRIBUTORS TO THIS CHAPTER:

Judy Sims
WildCat Molds & Castle Creations
4514 4th St. NW
Albuquerque, NM 87107
Phone:505-344-8086
Fax:505-344-1740
E-mail: Red46@aol.com
http://www.angelfire.com/biz2/craftsnetworkguild/WildCat.html
http://red46.hypermart.net/index.html

Arles Mitchell
12343 South Ada
Calumet Park, Illinois 60827-5823
Phone: 708-388-7567
Fax: 708-388-8849
E-mail: Introcrafts@aol.com

Michael Harvey
11 Middlebranch Lane, RR 11
Brewster, NY, 10509
Phone: 914-279-8295
Fax: 603-462-2010
E-mail: sculptor@rcn.com

Genie Gnagi
Mrs. Pots
7426 SW 24TH St.
Topeka, KS 66614
Phone: (785) 478-1287
E-mail: gnagic@email.msn.com

Constance Gunderson
Glass Cellar
5479 River Wood Dr
Savage, MN 55378-4638
Phone: (612)447-4696
E-mail:Glasscelr@aol.com

Robert Houghtaling
Sculpture and Design
P.O. Box 256
Los Olivos, CA 93441
Phone: 1-888-550-FROG
Fax: (805) 688-0341
E-mail for The Figgy Mountain Frogery: (his whimsical Website)
rhought@silcom.com (his serious Website)
http://www.silcom.com/~rhought/

Chapter 14

Basketry, Florals & Misc. Crafts

Pricing Template: Amanda Popelka
In-Depth Interview: Tonya Caudle

Baskets, one of the earliest containers known to humans may be one of our oldest crafts as well. Egyptian and Mayan tombs contained hand-crafted baskets and the skill required continues to fascinate artisans today. From coil baskets from Africa and the U.S. Appalachians, baskets represent the artist's skill as both designer and technician.

Pounding to soften ash wood to separate natural grain lines into pliable splints sounds like hard work. So does collecting pine needles, sweet-grasses, Danish cord, hemp, sea grass, grapevines, rattan and bamboo. Yet today, basket makers seek, collect and process all of these fibers and more in the name of creative basket-making. Brown ash wood, essential in the crafting of Shaker baskets requires skilled woodworking to make the forms as well. Basket makers must learn to shape and bend basket rims and handles from the green wood of birch, cherry and ash in the same manner as the early Shakers did.

Today's baskets can be made from paper maché, cords, yarns and even fabric strips along with the traditional, natural materials. Crafters not only make them but paint, shape, line and cover them adding elaborate handles at times. Baskets are an art form in themselves but from a practical point of view, where would modern crafters be without countless baskets serving as containers to store craft supplies, yarns and threads?

*   *   *

Amanda Popelka, owner of *Mandy's Hopechest* started her basketry business in 1996. "I started basket weaving one year before I started selling baskets but had been crafting in other media since childhood. Basketry came very natural to me," begins Amanda. Working about thirty hours weaving baskets or preparing materials such as dying reeds for them, Mandy also does two home shows per month. Home shows require different pricing than others in this book. Mandy totals materials and labor then doubles the total, adding 10% to cover office supplies and allows 10% more to the hostess who offers her home for the show.

Mandy spends three hours a week updating her website and responding to e-mail from her retail customers. Though she considered selling at wholesale, she finds it impossible to compete with imported baskets sold in discount stores. Strangely enough, she finds that such shops are usually not interested in American-made baskets. She buys her raw materials at wholesale so she can create her baskets without having to charge too much. She offers her thoughts about lowering prices. "I never lower my prices except when a wholesaler lowers prices for raw materials. I think businesses should lower their prices if possible and pass the savings to consumers instead of pocketing the extra profit," she says earnestly.

Mandy had to raise her prices, however, when her husband noted she was selling them for just above cost. "We came up with a formula that covers expenses yet allows me to make a profit. I take materials cost and add in my labor at $5 per hour. This may seem low but baskets can take up to ten hours to make. Next, I double this total and add an extra 10% to cover miscellaneous costs."

Determining overhead methods works well for Mandy. She bases overhead totals on a full year's cost for everything from printing business cards and stationery, a computer, phone and adds $200 for household utilities for her home-studio. Dividing this total over twelve months, and based on selling 25 baskets a month, overhead always totals about 10% of each basket's cost.

Mandy finds that baskets do not sell well at craft shows as consumers come looking for items priced at less than $10. "I placed my work in a craft mall for one year," says Mandy, But it was an awful experience. I ended up paying the store rent for the rest of the year, and sold nothing." Interior designers often order Mandy's baskets when they decorate rooms for their customers. Selling from her Internet Website has increased Mandy's business. While she was sharing space with others at a free Website, sales were low but once Mandy created her own web page using her domain name, sales picked up and she made better contacts.

"Basket makers will find it helpful to base their fees based upon 1 pound of coil," says Mandy. She provides an example. "Let's say I pay $6.00 a coil. The first time I make a basket I use a new coil for each size so I know it will weigh a pound. I weave the basket and then take the coils with the unused reed and weigh each. I figure how much I used and how many baskets I could make with that coil. If I can make two more baskets with the leftover reed, I plan to make three baskets from one $6.00 coil or $2.00 per basket. I do this with each size reed I use and add $3.00 to each basket for stain, rims and twining the base," she explains.

"If I use three different sizes of reeds and determine that each basket cost $6.00 in reed and $3.00 for the rim and extras; the total material cost comes to $9.00. If the basket takes four hours to weave, I add $5.00 per hour or $20.00 to bring the final price to $29.00," Mandy says. Adding embellishments to a basket may mean $5.00 or $34.00. Mandy doubles the total costs for embellishments then adds 10% to cover overhead. Such a basket would sell for $75.00 at retail. If shops buy Mandy's baskets to resell, she offers a 25% discount from her retail price. Mandy shares her Pricing Template:

One Basket:

Raw materials:	$ 6.00
Four hours of labor: ($5 per hour)	$20.00
Stain & Rim:	$ 3.00
Embellishments	$ 5.00
Wholesale price	$34.00
X 2 = Retail Price	$68.00
10% of total cost	$ 7.00
Final Retail price	$ 75.00

If a customer requests a basket not in stock and requires Mandy to design a pattern, she adds an additional $25 to the cost. As this book goes to press, Mandy is preparing to open her first shop in Hinckley, Illinois. She wants a craft shop with a homey feeling that will accept consignment work from artisans from all over the country.

Illustrating the importance of the Internet, 30 of the artisans who are consigning hand-crafts to her shop come from online craft groups to which she belongs. She has never met any of them personally.

*   *   *

Lori Ann Scianna, of *Capri Crafts & Collectibles*, admits she works 75 hours per week on her business, started in 1993. Of those 75 weekly hours, she devotes about 55% of her time producing handmade soap, candles, toiletries and aroma therapy products, cloth dolls and doll clothes. Having sensitive skin herself, Lori uses natural and alternative treatments as much as possible.

Lori sells primarily at retail though she is just beginning to add wholesale accounts as well. Due to her pressing work schedule she finds it easiest to buy raw materials by catalog or from the Internet buying at wholesale whenever possible.

Lowering her prices only occurs if an item does not sell at a show. Lori lowers it a bit for the next show. However, like many crafters in this book she has raised her prices for altruistic reasons. "After joining an online crafter's group," says Lori, "I learned about undervaluing your work and the effect it has on other crafters. I have also found that if I set prices too low on hand crafted items, customers assume mine is not quality work," she adds.

Lori offers her Pricing Template for a rather unusual product she manufacturers herself. She makes two types of bath salts. First, her regular blend of sea salts. Second, a blend of Dead Sea Salts. Starting with the latter, Lori explains:

She takes the total cost of all her salts, usually $13.82

She figures her cost of the salts per oz. ($ .08)

The cost of the jar in which they will be packaged, 9 oz jar = $.62

To produce a 9-oz. jar of Dead sea salts, Total Cost: 9 x $.08 = $.72 + $.62 = $1.34

15% for labor & overhead brings the total to $1.34 + $.20 = $1.54

To arrive at a wholesale price, she doubles this: $1.54 = $3.08.

Doubling again = Retail price. $6.16 for plain, unscented salts.

If Lori adds essential oils, fragrance oils and coloring she adds these to the retail price which brings her scented Dead Sea Salts to a retail price of $6.50 for a 9-oz. jar. Her chart appears below:

Unscented Dead Sea salts	Cost	Wholesale	Retail
Total Salts	$13.82	$27.64	$55.28
per oz	$0.08	$0.16	$0.32
9 oz jar	$0.62	$1.24	$2.48
9 oz salts	$0.71	$1.44	$2.88
Subtotal	$1.33	$2.68	$5.36
15% labor/overhead	$0.20	$0.40	$0.80
Total	$1.53	$3.08	$6.16
12 oz jar	$0.69	$1.38	$2.76

12 oz salts	$0.94	$1.92	$3.84
Subtotal	$1.63	$3.30	$6.60
15% labor/overhead	$0.24	$0.50	$0.99
Total	$1.88	$3.80	$7.59

Lori says that her Website is her regular base of operation but also sells her work at a small shop. She works six regular craft shows a year and tries to explore new ones to decide if she should add it to her present show schedule.

Selling on consignment brings Lori the same cautionary thoughts as other contributors have expressed in this book. Says Lori, "I have sold on consignment but must raise my prices to make up for the percentage the shop will take. I only sell in one shop in my area but I realize that if crafters sell in a lot of different venues in one area, prices must remain comparable in each shop that sells your goods."

Internet sales have vastly increased Lori's profits though. She admits that though her site reaches a larger customer base, Internet selling is not easy. Setting up a Website, maintaining it, getting listed with good search engines so people know where to find me is hard work," she concludes.

*   *   *

Karen Barkley, of *Kraftabilities,* a very versatile crafter, sells her products primarily at retail. She paints wood products, paints floor-cloths and makes dried floral wreaths. Combining her floral wreaths with painted wood crafts and adding birchbark crafting, Karen produces charming, unique centerpieces.

"Since adding birchbark, floral birdhouses and utilizing nature's bounty of dried flowers in her back yard, Karen makes 2" plant-pokes, 4" shelf-sitters and 4" wind-chimes. Birdhouses bring her the greatest success as she sells them in Summer craft-malls in her region. "I use my knowledge of wreaths and florals making craft projects called, *Kraft With Me* on my Website," Karen says.

She also makes seasonal dried floral and wood centerpieces and places them in her sister's hair shop as decoration. Her sister refers clients to her if someone wants a custom piece. Karen says this works well allowing her to concentrate on making birdhouses, new designs and building her online craft business.

Expanding her craft projects, Karen uses dried florals combined with crochet projects and scroll-sawn projects. She works on these designs and incorporates them into her catalog. Karen also sells at *Minnesota Crafted*, a mall that offers free display space to artisans that utilize Minnesota's wood and natural resources.

To determine her labor costs, Karen jots down her starting and stopping time for each project to get an exact use of the time involved in creating a project. She concludes, "I try to use assembly line procedures when preparing for a show which is a true time-saver in labor when producing alike items keeping labor costs down."

*　　　　　*　　　　　*

Cathryn Peters, of *The Wicker Woman* in Zumbro Falls, Minnesota, specializes in wicker restoration, chair caning and basketry. She began the business of chair caning and other seat weaving in 1975, wanting to be a stay-at-home Mom yet wanting to earn her own income. Taking in chairs to repair at home suited her perfectly.

Chair caning, wicker repair and basket-making remained a hobby until 1991 when Cathryn opened her own retail shop, working at her craft full-time. Devoting 8-10 hours in a business a day, 5-6 days a week, Cathryn works hard restoring wicker furniture and making baskets for sale.

Cathryn tried selling her baskets to wholesale buyers but like many talented artisans in this book, found it did not suit her. She did want to do production work usually required when selling at wholesale.

Today, Cathryn works on her signature, original design—one-of-a-kind deer-antler basketry, selling them directly from her shop, craft shows and galleries. "I prefer to keep all the profit generated from my designs and do not want to share a part of it with shops that buy at wholesale," she says honestly.

Though Cathryn began wicker restoration and chair caning repair in 1975, she began to make traditional baskets in 1984 as an entry into craft shows. She demonstrated chair caning in her booth which not only drew attention to her space but also drew customers to buy her baskets and request services to repair their wicker and cane furniture. Demonstrating chair caning or basket weaving remains an important selling tool for her today.

Cathryn generates a profit and loss statement at the end of each year to determine and evaluate what items sold, what did not and to make sure she earns enough to keep the business going. Cathyrn explains that she values her time and hard learned skills and frequently raises prices to meet demands, increased raw material costs and the cost of living.

Wicker Woman has so many different facets that Cathryn has devised several different pricing strategies. Before she began her chair caning and wicker restoration business, she researched first. She called others in her field to check prices. She consulted with suppliers and then figured a pricing schedule to maintain a business including fixed and variable costs. Through the years, she has adjusted her pricing based on the cost of living and supplier increases. She also considers her growing ability level and the scarcity of experts in her field. "I am one of only a handful of wicker restoration specialists in Minnesota," she explains.

Wicker furniture restoration costs are by the shop hour plus raw materials. For cane seat weaving, Cathyrn calculates her labor according to the number of holes drilled in the seat for strand caning or by the frontal inch for pressed cane. Most other types of seat weaving are charged by the longest rail according to Cathyrn.

"Labor costs vary around the nation, but range from .60 to $1.75 per drilled hole for caning, $2.35-3.50 per inch for pressed cane, $2.00-4.00 an inch for paper fiber rush, $5.00-20.00 for natural cattail rush, $2.00-$5.00 for splint or porch cane weaving," she explains. "Material costs are separate from labor costs and usually fall into the $10-80 range," says Cathyrn, She advises crafters to double their wholesale raw material costs and to sell to their customers at retail in order to make a profit.

Wicker restoration is a rare specialty without many experts around, so Cathryn can charge whatever the market will bear. She calculated overhead costs, her years of experience and education and settled upon $40.00 as her per hour labor price in addition to the retail price of needed materials. Pieces that she finds exceptionally difficult to repair also require price adjustments so Cathryn must estimate the time needed for extensive repairs carefully. To charge consistently, she works to provide accurate time estimates so she does not vary more or less than a 10% margin on the actual work order receipt.

"I price my one-of-a-kind deer antler baskets differently," she says. "I figure my time at about $25-40 an hour, my wholesale raw material costs and consider that each is unique whether or not it is a commissioned piece. Finally, I must consider what the market will bear."

Deer antler baskets range from $85-$2,000, a far cry from the $25-50 when I first started!" she exclaims.

"Traditional basket prices range from $25-$100. To determine price, I use the same calculations as for the antler baskets but since they are more traditional and less unique, my hourly wage is lower. I make traditional baskets commercially and to give as gifts," Cathyrn says, "but since I concentrate heavily on furniture repair, teaching and making antler baskets, I don't have the time I need to make more traditional baskets."

Overhead for a retail store like Cathyrn's differs greatly from a home-based business While working from home, Cathyrn had few overhead expenses and deducted a portion of her mortgage and utilities as allowed by The IRS's *The Home Office Deduction*. Moving her business to a storefront location increased overhead expenses to include a monthly lease. After buying the century-old building and choosing to live in an upstairs apartment, she now divides the mortgage payment and utilities between the apartment and the shop equally each month.

To determine restoration labor pricing, retail prices on basketry and wicker furniture and other items for resale in the store, she must work with a new equation.

X   Electricity,

X   Water,

X   Fuel/heat,

X   Telephone,

X   Health and business insurance

X   Freight,

X   Packing materials,

X   Office equipment and supplies,

X   Show and sales costs,

X   Nonproductive time like billing, shipping, running errands, cleaning, bookkeeping

X   Permits and taxes, city and state.

X   Education costs, books, periodicals

X   Tools

X   Dues for business organizations

X   Taxes

To calculate her net profit, Cathryn figures all operating expenses—fixed and variable, then subtracts gross sales. She works to determine profit on each item to see if she should continue to make a particular item or drop it. "Whenever my profit is not enough," she says, "I consider:

X   Raising prices,

X   Cutting back on advertising,

X   Dropping the least profitable shows,

X   Dropping least profitable retail items,

X   Finding a better or cheaper supplier,

X   Reduce inventory purchases,

X   Make more products,

X   Focus on working smarter and more efficiently

X   Teach more classes,

X   Write more about my craft.

A new alternative has gotten Cathryn's attention—the Internet. Her five websites are informational at this point but do not cost her anything. "There are plenty of web sites that offer this service," she says. "All you need do to set up your page is to sign up. She purchased the domain rights to: www.wickerwoman.com. Her sites remain "under construction" until she decides how best to utilize them.

*   *   *

Melissa Woodburn makes one-of-a-kind pine needle baskets. She began making baskets in 1996 when she and her family lived under several long-needle pine trees that shed huge amounts of pine needles. As she began to think about a creative way to use them, she received a catalog of craft books, one of which was a how-to book for making pine needle baskets. Melissa sent for the book, taught herself the needed technique and began making baskets.

Spending three or four days a week in her home studio, she creates to sell at specific events. Other times Melissa creates a basket on a specific topic for a juried art show that piques her interest especially if she believes it may stretch her abilities. She says, "I prefer to just create freely and then gather my creations together for a show or sale."

Melissa prefers selling directly to the consumer but when she began her business, she placed her baskets in a gallery on consignment. "I priced them ridiculously low figuring it was better to sell them, but they didn't sell anyway." Next, she tried consignment in a local gallery with the same results. Through trial and error, Melissa found that people notice and appreciate her baskets more as works of art if they are priced between $275 and $450. Customers overlook her work if she prices it too low.

Melissa uses many found objects for her baskets and gathers dry pine needles locally. She acknowledges that she even has favorite trees. She adds items she finds such as driftwood bits of fur, shells and feathers. She buys waxed linen, raffia or yarns used to stitch the baskets together. She does not concern herself about buying supplies wholesale because her principal supply items —pine needles are free.

"Pricing for me is intuitive," Melissa explains. "I have a couple benchmark baskets that I feel are grounded in the price. If I create a bigger or especially, wider baskets or add some one-of-a-kind item such as vintage fur, or if it is particularly beautiful when completed, I raise my price. Raw materials are not pricey, so labor, beauty or uniqueness of the finished basket become my criteria in pricing," she admits.

"Presence" is Melissa's original term, being synonymous with "noticeability," she explains. "Presence means a basket with such allure that your eye keeps going back to it. This does not correlate with cubic inches but relates more with height and width," she adds. "At first, I priced by the volume the basket would hold but it didn't quite translate," she continues. "More than strict volume (lengthxheightxdepth) my price must relate to the 'presence' of the basket, which is more functional than just thinking of widthxheight. I still work with my benchmark basket 'Ceremonial Offering' which measures10"widex10"deepx9" high. My price is $450, 10x9 = 90 to arrive at my 'presence' factor," she says.

"Now I use that multiplier with the presence factor to compute a price for any other basket," she explains. "For example, another basket she calls 'Elegant Rags' measures 8" widex8" deepx11" high. Its presence factor comes to 88 so I multiply 5x88 = $440."

Melissa continues, "In cases of exemplary design, one-of-a-kind materials or fitted lids, I increase my multiplier to 5.5. In fact, for 'Elegant Rags', which I consider to be my best design, I use 5.5 to bring the total to $484. In the case of small baskets, with a presence factor of less than 21, my minimum price is $125," Melissa explains.

When Melissa places her baskets on consignment, she increases the basic price by 20%, not enough to cover the entire commission percentage but a price she describes as "comfortable." As her reputation as an artist grows, Melissa plans to increase the multiplier which will still allow her to work with her present pricing structure.

In Depth Interview: Tonya Caudle

Tonya Caudle, owner of *Inspirations,* whom you met in Chapter 7, describing her crocheted rag baskets uses other materials for basket-making in addition to fabric strips. She also works with dried apple, wood, and woven materials. Additionally she creates potpourri, inspirational gifts, note cards, wooden and wall hangings, soap gift sets and of course, baskets.

How much time do you devote to your business?

"I work full-time, 40 hours per week and spend 20 of these hours making products for sale. I devote the other 20 hours to office work, product and materials research, designing new products, evaluating old products, making new contacts with potential buyers and maintaining, evaluating, and working on my Website," she says.

"Sometimes, I spend a week of brainstorming to decide how to sell my products, how to make them more marketable and researching existing markets. When I begin this way, I remain focused on the product as a whole," she adds.

Do you sell both retail and wholesale or just directly to the ultimate consumer?

"I sell both at retail and wholesale through my Website almost exclusively. I found that when I limited myself to selling only at retail, I missed many potential customers. Selling at retail limits your products' exposure. Better, is receiving orders from customers who bought one of my products from a boutique or specialty shop where I sold it at wholesale. Customers find me from my hang-tags attached to each product. I have also received wholesale inquiries through retail sales. It's a small world out there and you never know who your customer knows so why limit yourself to whom you sell?"

Where do you purchase raw materials and supplies?

"I buy from many catalogs such as Craft King and from local shops such as Hancock's, Walmart and Michael's. I also deal with manufacturers directly such as, Sweetcakes, Monterey Bay Spice Company, BagsPlus, Walnut Hollow and Wood 'n Crafts," she replies.

"Though I purchase most of my supplies from manufacturers and catalogs, when I'm designing, I buy from local shops. I found that this is a good way to bounce ideas off the employees and only buying as much as you need to try a design. This practice keeps my costs down if a particular idea flops!" she adds. "I find most of my suppliers through the Internet, *The Crafts Supply Sourcebook,* listings in craft books and from consumer magazines such as *Painting, Crafts N Things,* and *The Crafts Report,*" says Tonya.

Do you buy raw materials at retail prices, on-sale, or at wholesale?

"I purchase most of my supplies at wholesale or discounted prices. When buying fabric, I buy on sale or retail in a pinch. Most of my wood products I cut from lumber bought at retail prices. I charge wholesale + 10% for finished wood products. When I began making crafts professionally, I did not consider supplies if I got them free, from a relative or a friend. If a neighbor cuts wood for me and I may make him a pie in payment, I still include their labor in my price as they helped prepare the unfinished piece for me. Don't leave out the full price of raw materials just because you happen on a good deal! It may not be there when you need more supplies!" she adds firmly.

How long had you been crafting before you began to sell what you made?

"I have been crafting for 18 years. As a youngster, I used to make friendship bracelets and pins and sell them on the playground in elementary school. I assisted my church and a local craft shop by coming up with original craft ideas for Sunday School and Vacation Bible School. Coming from a long line of craftsmen gave me the chance to see and experience various arts and crafts and the influence they had in my early life," she explains.

Have you ever lowered prices because you found they were too high?

"I have lowered prices but I always build a cushion into my original price. I figure my cost-sx2 to arrive at my wholesale price andx3 to arrive at a final retail price. Sometimes, I lower my price by a dollar or two if I can still make a fair profit. This creates good will if customers deserve a discount (military, orders a lot or is a very regular customer). I like to show my good customers that I appreciate them. Snipping a little off the price also pays off if you plan to have an item on sale for whatever reason. It may appear to be 'on sale' because I lowered the price but lowering the final price does not cut into my profit as it would have without that extra 'cushion' built into my prices," says Tonya.

Have you ever raised prices? If so, Why?

"I raise my prices due to any of the following factors:

X   Inflation,

X   Increased prices of raw materials,

X   Increased demand. I raise prices on high-end items when they sell well but I can't meet customer demands due to limits on my production time," she explains.

Do you have a system for pricing your items? Please describe.

"My system for pricing follows:
Cost of materials (including shipping costs, if applicable)
I multiply by two to arrive at my wholesale price and by three for retail.
Sometimes I add the 'cushion' of .50-$2.00 so I can lower prices if necessary to remain competitive with similar products," Tonya explains.

Do you consider labor when you set your prices?

"Yes, I always consider labor and charge $5 per hour to make most of my items. For custom orders, I charge $20 per hour. On lower priced items, those that don't take much time or can be mass produced (potpourri and note cards), I add overhead, including estimated labor to the final price."

Do you consider raw materials when you set your prices?

"I not only consider the cost of raw materials but the shipping/drive time it takes to get the materials to my studio," says Tonya.

How do you determine overhead?

"Fortunately, I discovered *QuickBooks,* a great accounting program. I look at my expense chart and add the expenses I consider overhead such as:

X   Booth rentals,

X   Commissions to sales reps,

X   Bank and credit card fees,

X   Interest fees on loans and credit cards,

X   Postage and freight,

X   Advertising,

X   Packaging and shipping materials,

X   Dues to business organizations,

X   Subscriptions to trade journals and publications."

Tonya continues, "I determine overhead by adding the total number of items that accounted for my expenses. Next I total the number of expenses and divide it into the total percentage value of those expenses. This total provided my average overhead. For example:

Bank fees: 2.10%,

Credit card fees: 2%,

Rent 20%,

Advertising 25%,

Total percentage 85.01%,

Total items: 4

4/85.01 = 22.21% average overhead."

Tonya advises others that if they want their business to grow, they should look to their business plan for the percentages needed to adjust prices for the upcoming year. "However," she continues, "sometimes my overhead costs increase my product's value to where I feel an item will not sell at the new, projected price. This formula is only my starting point in setting my prices," she adds.

How do you determine profit?

"Profit for me results from totaling raw material costs, labor and overhead multiplied by two to arrive at the wholesale price and by three to arrive at the retail price. I choose my final price based on the total sum. Here is an example for making a small item:

$12.35 for cost, labor and overhead totalx3 = $37.05, Less $12.35 = a profit of $14.70," Tonya explains.

"One way for me to keep track and not use my calculator constantly is my use of *Excel*," says Tonya. " This software allows me to look at costs, selling price and profit at a glance. The program makes it easier to add in new products as I design them. I use an *Excel* spreadsheet to determine overhead on a quarterly basis when new products or costs have appeared consistently," she concludes.

How do you determine the value of your time?

"I determine the value of my time by the product I make. If it involves very little time or I can mass-produce a small item to where the time on each is minuscule, I don't fool with it. I just raise my overhead percentage. On other products I add $5 per hour. Since I'm just starting my new venture, I pay myself a minimum wage but as my business, knowledge and experience increase, I plan to raise my hourly rate," she acknowledges.

Do you sell at Craft Shows and Craft Malls?

"I sell at few craft shows but do it more for exposure and to promote my home shows. I have sold in craft malls but found very little profit there for high end items. I may try it again for low end products but I still find it hard to make a profit in craft malls as it increases my overhead considerably. When considering a mall, I figured the rent, shipping costs, time in phone conversations with the manager to check stock, etc. I find it too time consuming to be really profitable for me," she admits.

Do you sell at retail and specialty shops?

"Retail shops and specialty shops to whom I sell at wholesale have been wonderful to me. When wholesalers buy from me, they become responsible for selling the product—not me. I thought at first that I would never work on consignment but now that I have higher end products, I may try again. I don't think that this is a good idea for low-end products because the consignor doesn't make much from selling each product for you," says Tonya.

Do you use Sales Reps?

"I am pursuing that right now. I have been asked to send samples to a customer who runs a marketing firm using numerous sales reps," she replies.

Do you sell via The Internet?

"Yes, I sell from my Website and have made more sales, wholesale and retail, than any other method I tried. It's an inexpensive way to operate my business because I have complete control over marketing, how my products look and how I represent myself. It also provides customers an inexpensive way to order at their leisure, 24 hours per day, 7 days a week. I plan to expand and remain focused on my Website in the future. It works perfectly for me!"

BRIEF SUMMARY OF PRICING METHODS IN THIS CHAPTER

X   Again, a formal Pricing Template is useful for producing sea-salt products.

X   Consider totaling raw materials cost and adding labor at $5 per hour. Though this may seem low, baskets can take up to ten hours to make. Double the total and add 10% to cover miscellaneous costs.

X   Determine overhead based on totals for a full year. Consider everything from printing business cards and stationery to computer costs and phone calls.

X   Add $200 for household utilities when working from a home-studio. Spread this total over twelve months and based on selling 25 baskets a month, overhead will total about 10% of each basket's cost.

X   Basket makers may find it helpful to base their fees based upon 1 pound of coil. Example: If you pay $6.00 a coil, when you make a new basket, use a new coil for each size so it weighs a pound. Weave the basket and take the coils with the unused reed and weigh each. Determine how much you used and how many baskets you can make with 1 pound. If you can make two more baskets with the leftover reed, plan to make three baskets from one $6.00 coil or $2.00 per basket. Do this with each size reed used and add $3.00 to each basket for stain, rims and twining the base.

X   If you use three different sizes of reeds and determine that each basket cost $6.00 in reed and $3.00 for the rim and extras; the total material cost comes to $9.00. If the basket takes four hours to weave add $5.00 per hour, $20.00, bringing the basket cost to $29.00. Embellishing a basket may mean $ 5.00, or $34.00 so double total costs and add 10% to cover overhead. Such a basket would sell for $75.00 at retail.

X   Check the starting and stopping time for each project to get a realistic sense of how much labor it takes to create a project. Then, place a value on your time.

X   Do your market research before you start your business. Call others in your field to check prices, consult with suppliers and figure a pricing schedule to maintain a business including fixed and variable costs.

X   Adjust pricing based on the cost of living and supplier increases along with your growing expertise and experience.

X   Labor costs vary around the nation, but for wicker restoration, they fall somewhere in the range of .60-1.75 per drilled hole for caning, $2.35-3.50 per inch for pressed cane, $2.00-4.00 an inch for paper fiber rush, $5.00-20.00 for natural cattail rush, $2.00-$5.00 for splint or porch cane weaving.

X   To calculate net profit, total all operating expenses—fixed and variable then subtract gross sales. When profits are enough, consider:

X   Raising prices,

X   Cutting back on advertising,

X   Dropping the least profitable shows,

X   Dropping least profitable retail items,

X   Finding a better or cheaper supplier,

X   Reduce inventory purchases,

X   Make more products,

X   Focus on working smarter and more efficiently

X   Teach more classes,

X   Write more about your craft.

X   One pricing system to consider:
Cost of materials (including shipping costs, if applicable), multiply by two to arrive at wholesale price and by three to determine retail price. Add a 'cushion' of .50-$2.00 so you can lower prices if necessary to keep them competitive with similar products.

CONTRIBUTORS TO THIS CHAPTER

Amanda Popelka
Mandy's Hopechest
660 Coster Court
Hinckley, IL, 60520
Phone: 815-286-3975
Fax: 815-286-7172
E-mail: mandy@mandyshopechest.com and mandy@hinckleynet.com
http://www.geocities.com/SouthBeach/Lights/7358

Karen Barkley
420 Montcalm St W
Ticonderga, NY 12883
Phone: (518)585-3373
E-mail: Kraftabilities@webtv.net
http://www.angelfire.com/mn/Kraftabilities**Lori Ann Sciana**

Lori Ann Sciana
Capri Crafts & Collectibles
43 Courtland Lane
Matawan NJ 07747
Phone: 732-583-4330
E-mail Owner@CapriCrafts.com or Capri@CapriCrafts.com
http://www.CapriCrafts.com

Cathryn Peters
Wicker Woman
531 Main Street
PO Box 61
Phone: 507-753-2006 Toll-free: 1-888-WICK-R-WN
Zumbro Falls, MN 55991-0061
E-mail: Wickrwoman@aol.com
http://www.members.about.com/Wickerwoman
http://hometown.aol.com/wickrwoman/myhomepage/index.html

Melissa Woodburn
7 Mt. Burney Court
San Rafael, California 94903
Phone: 415 / 499 / 1655
MKWFineArt @ aol.com

Tonya Caudle
Unique baskets, Gifts & Inspirations
7026 Velvet Antler Drive
Midlothian, VA 23112
Fax: 804-739-7007
E-mail: tlc@inspiredgifts.com
http://www.inspiredgifts.com
http://www/ctsi.net/addedtouch

Chapter 15

Setting Prices When You Teach

Contract: Sylvia Ann Landman
In-Depth Interview: Claudia Chase

I began my career in fiber arts as a dressmaker and a designer of custom knitting, crochet and embroidery working from my home studio. Not long afterwards, it became a teaching studio where students came to learn and share skills. I began teaching classes in needlework, quilting, sewing, fiber arts and color and design for California Community Colleges in 1962. Students from these classes were increasingly curious as to how I made my livelihood in the creative arts believing it was impossible. Due to their requests, the college asked me to add business and entrepreneurial classes to my teaching schedule to show students they could do it too! I added seven business classes and continue to teach them today.

X   Your Arts in the Marketplace,

X   How to Start a Mail Order Business,

X   Writing for The Crafts Market,

X   Couples and Families in Business,

X   Time Management & Organization,

X   How to Operate a Small Business,

X   How to Start Your Own Teaching Studio.

I have drawn from my teaching experiences to write this book and this chapter particularly. Today, I design crafts part-time and write about the business side of crafts for many publications and books full-time. I still teach for local Community colleges and travel throughout the U.S. giving workshops and lectures at regional and national guilds and seminars. I serve as judge in the fields of sewing, knitting, crochet, quilting, color and design but I often admit that my favorite classroom over the years was aboard Holland America Cruise Lines sailing as their arts and crafts instructor.

Providing a pricing template for craft teachers does not seem appropriate for this chapter.

Instead, I am sharing with you a copy of my teaching contract—the very one I send to groups, guilds, shops, schools and organizations who want to hire me as a teacher. The only time I do not use my own contract is when the group who wants to hire me has their own contract, *and* their version includes *all* of the concerns listed in my contract below:

CONTRACT FORM

This contract confirms the understanding between teacher/speaker, Sylvia Landman and _____ . I understand I am being hired as an independent contractor, and solely responsible for payment of taxes from my earnings.

Date of Program:
Hours of Program:
Location of Program:
Subject of Program/workshop:
Required Materials: to be provided by each participant:
Cost of materials provided to each participant by teacher:
Contents of kit or Total Number of Handouts
Maximum number of participants attending _____**Minimum number**_____
Deadline for group to cancel without penalty: 10 days before presentation
Penalty if canceling in less then 10 days: Cost of materials and copy costs of printed literature.
Travel by Car: IRS allowance, per mile as stated for each year.
Bridge or Parking Tolls:
By Air: Airline ticket + ground travel to and from airports:
Meals & Lodging: provided by group from: to:
Fee per Day: $325 for full-day program; $175 for partial day or evenings (2½ hrs. or less)
Fees and Expenses: due and payable upon receipt, following presentation.

Non-smoking home-stays: acceptable with private bedroom

Sylvia Landman, Teacher/Speaker   Group Representative

_____   _____

TEACHING FROM HOME

Teaching from home provides additional income to your craft business. Though you may also teach from a shop, Community Colleges, Park and Recreation programs or other community centers, teaching from a home-based studio provides many advantages:

1 You have fewer expenses than teaching for a shop, school or other agency.
2 You have fewer federal, state or local regulations than teaching anywhere else.
3 You can teach weekdays, evenings or weekends setting your own pace.
4 You do not have to incur child-care, commuting, clothing expenses.

SETTING FEES

Everyone wants to know what they should charge. Unfortunately, no rule exists suitable for every teacher across the country. Teachers must set their own fees taking several factors into consideration. Think about:

X   The degree of expertise and experience you have in your craft,

X   Credentials or other certification you may have,

X   Years and training of teaching experience,

X   The geographical area where you live,

X   Current trends in style, color and craft techniques,

X   What other teachers charge locally, regionally and nationally.

X   If you will accept a flat fee offered by a specific organization for teaching.

At times, large seminars and conferences want to be fair and pay each teacher the same amount. Teachers with experience may have to settle for less than their usual fee. Newer teachers may be delighted with a higher fee than usual but may be unable to demand this amount when they return home.

I researched my market many years ago to learn which classes were popular, in demand and well-attended. You must do this too. How much do classes cost where you live? Visit local shops. Inquire if they give classes and what they charge. Call your local community college, adult school or city sponsored recreational classes. Check out their fees. Last, determine the minimum amount per hour that would satisfy you.

Let us say that a shop you visit charges $20 per student for four classes of one hour each. Let's further assume the adult school or community college offers classes for $15 for ten weeks of two-hour classes with 20 students per class. When you call the city recreation program, you learn that the fee is $25 for six two-hour private classes.

Call a few private teachers who advertise in the phone directory. Ask their fees for individual lessons. Now, sit down and do a little figuring to arrive at a sensible fee for you and your students that fits in with your community.

Analyzing the data above, reveals that the highest amount student pay is $20 for four lessons of one hour each or $5 per hour. The lowest they would pay is $15 for ten classes of two hours each or 75¢ per hour. The median is $25 for six two-hour lessons or $2.50 per hour.

The highest hourly payment from each student is for private, individualized instruction. The lowest is for large classes where individualized instruction is minimal. Now, you have an idea of what the traffic will bear. Translate this information into setting your tuition fees for classes of two hours each.

Learn what craft instructors earn at your college or city program. Assume an art teacher with a college degree earns $20 per hour. If you do not have a degree, perhaps $20 is too high but minimum wage is too low. Try averaging. How about $15 per hour as your minimum? You can set the tuition high to attract a few students at a time and stress the individualized learning available to them. Or, lower student fees which means you must hold larger classes to reach the same base pay. How about a class for five weeks of two hours each? Four students paying $35 each would bring you a total of $135 per class, or $14 per hour. Such students would be paying $3.50 per each hour of instruction which is in line with the amounts we discovered were average in a given, local area. You also could charge each student $20, require at least seven per class and earn the same $140 or $14 per class. Remember that one day away from home when traveling out of state counts as three days lost from your regular work.

TEACHING CREDENTIALS AND QUALIFICATIONS

If you have a teaching credential, state it in your advertising, résumé and stationery. Teaching experience and/or credentials add credibility to your teaching status. If you want accreditation and are not a college graduate or have no specific teacher training, look to your State Community College system or University for help as rules vary from one state to another.

Look for courses to help inexperienced teachers who may know their field well yet need basic teaching education. Consider adult psychology courses at local community colleges. You will find them helpful in managing groups of students. Teaching from a home studio or near-by shop does not require teaching experience or credentials, but those who have them usually succeed more than those who do not.

Individual craft groups, guilds and associations often offer teacher certification programs. Contact a specific group for specialized programs or national craft groups such as HIA or SCD and industry specific associations for more information. (See end of this chapter these and other organizations that offer teaching certification programs.)

Trained teachers find it easier to inspire students to return repeatedly. Good teachers instill an appreciation for the subject and help students feel confident with their new skills. Craft teachers, particularly, must generate enough enthusiasm that students dispense that most valuable form of advertising: word-of-mouth.

TEACHING BY CORRESPONDENCE

People study by correspondence for many reasons. Perhaps they are home-bound with physical limitations, have small children, transportation problems or not enough time to travel to classes. Others just prefer to learn at their own pace. Whatever the reason, students who study at home, need instructors who teach from their homes and mail them the courses. Why not you? I have taught by correspondence three different ways:

X   I developed, marketed and sold my own courses through classified ads.

X   The community college where I teach offered students the option of taking my courses in person or by correspondence.

X   A national craft organization sponsored my courses.

Established teachers have the advantage of not needing much time to gather information to begin teaching by correspondence. They already have lesson plans for classes and workshops in place. Each time you sell your course to a new student, make copies for them and retain your masters. The real work comes with preparing the course the first time. It takes months to complete a correspondence course—it is not an over-night project. Profits begin with the second course you sell and every other one thereafter.

I cannot tell you what to charge for selling your correspondence courses. Much depends on how long it is, the market you approach and your degree of experience in teaching, crafting and writing.

To reassure potential students, I send a copy of my guarantee when they inquire about my courses. I promise I will *always* respond within 2 weeks—no delays! I learned that response delays from teachers was the most common complaint from students learning by correspondence. They expressed frustration with long delays from the time they returned a lesson for the teacher's comments and received the next lesson. I chose this as my niche in the teaching market place and I stand behind my promises.

TEACHING ON THE INTERNET

I have just begun offering classes from my Website but **Marty Donnellan**, owner of *ClothArt,* whom you met in Chapter Six, has experience teaching in this exploding arena. Marty shares her tips with readers as she has been teaching doll classes via the Internet for some time. Her class Website combines text, photos and illustrations similar to what one would find in a How-to Book, or manual. To achieve student/teacher interaction during her courses, Marty first experimented with a Bulletin Board from her site but found it cumbersome. With her students' approval, she scrapped the online Bulletin Board in favor of a Mailing List from "OneList", an online provider of specialized mailing lists for Internet users.

Marty explains her reactions to her success teaching online. "I've tried using a Bulletin Board on my Website and an online mailing list and prefer the latter. Bulletin Boards require you to go to the Website and hunt for new postings. Every type of information is posted at the same time. With mailing lists, new messages come in day by day via the students' e-mail programs. The class has a sense of connection, of sequential continuity and completing the project together which I found lacking in the Bulletin Board format. After we made the transition I began hearing from my students much more frequently as they posted to share their problems and successes. I feel that I am actually teaching now instead of twiddling my thumbs wondering why no one has posted to the Bulletin Board," Marty explains.

Marty offers details about how she set up her system. "In my dollmaking class, in addition to the downloadable lessons I offer students, I also put into place a sort of 'behind-the-scenes' script. At certain times, I introduce subjects gleaned from discussions from previous classes or from other sources to the present class via the list which keeps conversation going and helps generate new ideas," she says.

New teachers have asked Marty how to set up pass-word systems so that only paying students could access the online class. She replies, "The best web authoring software I know of is Microsoft FrontPage for PC users. It allows you to create any number of webs easily. My root web, the one I use for my business: is not password protected since I want the world to flock to it."

"The class website is contained within but is technically a brand new web. I simply enabled the option to add the new web to the root web. The new web is password protected. I created a universal User ID and password which any student can use. The class website: is a website within a web and password-protected. As far as I know there is no way to have one or more pages within a web password-protected. It must be a new website. Using FrontPage means that you do not need to know html codes. Primarily, you point and click," Marty adds.

Marty responded to my question asking how she encourages student participation in her online classes. She responds, "Student participation can be tricky in an online, life-enrichment, for-pay craft course without personal contact. My Twilight Fairie course has twenty-four students currently enrolled. Teachers in real classrooms can lecture, demonstrate, guide and inspect each student's work. Additionally, each student's work serves as a model on what or what not to do," she adds.

"In a virtual classroom, you may never hear from your best students," Marty says. Those who are adept at finding their own solutions, take the ball and run with it. You may also never hear from your worst students, those with the most questions, because they may be too shy or intimidated to post. Still others have no greater ambition than to download the class and hang onto it as reference material and may or may not make the doll at some later date. I define these as students who show up on the class roster but for all practical purposes, are not there," she explains. "Here are some approaches that work for me," she adds:

1   On the first day of class, take a "roll call." This gets students talking about who they are, what their strengths and weaknesses are as dollmakers may be and what they expect from the class. I feel humbled when I read some of these bios as many students are busy people with little spare time yet determined to complete the course.

2   At the end of each class section or lesson, I post a list of questions as you would find in a real textbook. My course lasts 5 weeks and at the end of each week, I ask many questions to stimulate their thinking.

3   Establish private e-mail support for the 'frankly terrified.' They won't talk to the class but they will talk to you. If their concerns are pertinent to the class, post them, without giving their identities.

4   Let students know at the beginning of class that you will e-mail them privately to find out how they are doing, then do it! You'll be amazed at the torrent of questions and concerns that issue forth.

5   Have a firm cutoff date for enrollment even though it may mean a little less money. Late enrollees distract everyone repeating what you have already covered.

6   Post pictures of completed dolls that student provide from your last class.

7   At the end of class, pass out a teacher evaluation form! These will help you learn how to do it even better next time," Marty concludes.

*   *   *

Joan Schrouder, a well-known knitting instructor travels all over the country presenting well-organized knitting workshops and lectures. She shares her thoughts about teaching on the local, regional and national level and divides her information that way. Joan explains:

Teaching Locally

"Park and Recreation Departments, Community Colleges, Adult Education programs and others follow a payment schedule that limits what teachers earn when teaching locally. Yarn shops nearby may also have a policy to pay teachers but that doesn't mean that a teacher can't negotiate. I suggest that someone starting out as a knitting or crafts teacher, call the other venues available in the area to learn the going rates for local teachers. If a shop's rates compare favorably with what you want to earn, agree to it but teachers with a lot of experience may ask for additional compensation," Joan advises.

"Shop owners may suggest an hourly wage while others prefer a percentage split from the total amount of student fees for a particular class," Joan finds. "A few shops where I have taught paid me the entire amount collected from students explaining that their compensation was the sale of supplies for the class, and hopefully, future sales," Joan adds, "but once I determine my minimum, hourly pay and knew how the shop owner prefers to pay, I calculate how many students must register to earn that amount. For example, if I set my minimum wage at $10 per hour and students pay $2 per hour to take the class, I need at least five students. Fewer sign-ups than this cause me to cancel the class," Joan explains.

"Local economies affect the rates one can charge. This is why it would be imprudent for me to suggest that all teachers should charge $20 per hour, for example," Joan adds. "However, I think it wise to gently increase your rate as your experience increases. Remember also, many hours go into developing class handouts and samples for which will not be paid. You may only bill actual hours taught," she says.

Teaching Nationally:

"National and regional conventions such as 'Stitches' or The Knitting Guild of America, (TKGA) have set rates for their teachers. In 1999, TKGA paid $220 for a 6 hour class, plus expenses (travel, hotel and meals). 'Stitches' on the other hand, pays an hourly rate based on the number of students: $60 for10-15 students, $70 for 16-20, $80 for 21-25 and $90 for 26 students or more. They offer a hotel allowance, but do not cover travel or meals," Joan explains.

"Teachers teaching at this level," she says, "often receive many requests to teach at local guilds/shops around the country resulting from their national exposure. The teacher can and should set up a contract spelling out rates and expenses and continue to charge comparably," she suggests.

Joan stays in touch with other teachers regarding their rates to remain competitive. She says that she has a sense of where she fits into the hierarchy of nationally known knitting teachers.

"Some command higher rates and others with less experience may receive less," Joan acknowledges. "I have gradually increase my fees about every two to three years knowing that many teachers in other crafts such as weaving and quilting receive more than knitting instructors. I take into account how much a local guild or shop must charge each student for a day's class to make sure I cover all expenses such as, my daily fee, travel, meals and hotel. I offer to stay in private homes to eliminate hotel fees when possible," Joan says. "In most cases this amounts to about half of what students would pay to take the same class at one of the national conventions so I feel comfortable that I'm not overcharging. I have no objection to letting your readers know that I charge $300 for a 6 hour class and $175 for 3 hrs or less. Next year, I plan to raise my rates $350/$200 next year," Joan concludes.

*   *   *

Patricia Hammond says that one of the hardest decisions she has had to make as a professional quilter is pricing her lectures and workshops. She admits it challenges her to consider the preparation time that goes into her programs. Many of her workshops contain a student "kit" of materials which add several hours more preparation time for a large workshop.

Patricia gathered information from other speakers and teachers concerning standard fees for teaching at quilt shops versus teaching at seminars and national shows. "How much experience matters," she asks? "Should you charge more if you have won awards? Should you base your fees on per-student cost or use an all-day flat fee?" she asks. Patricia finds that most shops pay $20-$30 per hour for instructors and some include mileage. Continuing, Patricia comments, "Most national seminars have a set budget and pay all instructors the same flat rate per workshop fee. For example, a half-day workshop may pay the instructor $175.00 plus travel expenses while an all-day workshop pays $250-$300 in addition to travel expenses and meals. A few national shows where I have taught pay whatever fee I asked in my fee schedule," she says. "Some instructors charge $450.00 for an all-day workshop while others charge $300 even though both perform the job, in the same place for the same number of students," she adds. "With so many variables in earning power, teachers must pay close attention to their contracts and marketing information," Patricia advises.

*   *   *

Markena Lanska, of *Daydream Creations,* teaches embroidery and surface design techniques. She describes three different ways in which she sets her fees:

1. Flat Rate. I set amount regardless of the number of students in a class. In addition to the flat rate, my sponsor also pays travel and kit expenses (if any). Flat rates range from $50-$380 dollars, for simple lectures to a small group, through all-day or two-day workshops. This arrangement works best for smaller groups who cosponsor a teacher and share her travel expenses. It also works well for local groups when the only transportation expense is mileage.

2. Per Student Rate: A per student rate is based on a minimum and maximum number of students with a minimum number of students required. If I do not incur travel expenses pr kit costs, I use a per student rate of $3-$10 per classroom unit. A classroom unit is equivalent to one teaching hour. Using this system, I charge $5-$7 per classroom unit for most 2-4 hour classes. Longer classes may have a lower per classroom unit charge because are more total units. The per unit rate is generally higher for more complex classes or very small classes. If a particular class determined to be a $6 classroom unit and lasts for 4 hours, the final per student cost would be $24. With 10 participants in the class, I charge $240. Some sponsoring shops will take up to 25% of the teacher's total fee for classroom space and publicity, particularly if the teacher does not provide supply lists and sells her own kits. Check this out before determining the minimum number of students you will accept to conduct the class. You may need to adjust your per student charge to remain competitive with other teachers' fees in your area.

3. Large Trade Show Rates are those which require extensive travel and kit expenses not covered by the show sponsors. I total all projected expenses for the trip including airfare, taxis, limos, meals, hotel, etc., and divide by the minimum number of class hours
   I will teach. Next, I divide the resulting total by the minimum number of students attending to arrive at the classroom unit charge. The minimum enrollment number becomes my break-even point. Enrollment beyond this point becomes 'profit.' Well known teachers use this formula at times but add the minimum amount they need to earn before they calculating the classroom unit charge. The final per student charge should be around $20 plus kit costs for a three to four hour class. Kits costs in this situation are calculated according to the teacher's actual costs for products and the retail

value of the written instructions and kit assembly. Some teachers develop corporate sponsorship so that needed supplies are donated to the teacher or at least, provided at deep discounts which should be passed along to the students. Markena provides an example:

"For a classroom unit of $6, a four-hour class and kit costs of $16, the per student charge would be $24 + $16 = $40. The show promoter adds in a charge to cover costs for classrooms, pre-show publicity, and other expenses. If the show promoter determines that a per student fee of $10 is adequate, final costs to each student come to $40 + $10 = $50 for a four-hour class. Lower kit costs will help offset fees added by the show promoter for higher teacher fees due to higher travel costs associated with staying at a host hotel," Markena explains.

"Classes requiring travel but not associated with large trade shows, cause me to calculate kit costs differently," Markena adds. "In this example, the event does not include product donation or discounts to the teacher by manufacturers. I offer another example: If a teacher drives to a meeting from another town and mileage is reimbursed at 30 cents per mile for 300 miles, a round trip would total $90. Eleven kits sold to the guild at $10 per kit total $110. The teacher receives $250. Out-of-pocket expenses: $15 for gasoline, $65 for kits total $80. The teacher in this example earned $170 after expenses. It is also possible for teachers already attending an event to give demonstrations while not actually teaching," Markena concludes. She has earned as much as $100 per day following this suggestion.

∗   ∗   ∗

Carol Heidenreich, of *Fun Fabrics* began her business in 1967. In 1988, she began teaching sewing classes for the Husqvarna Viking Sewing Machine Company. As a teacher, Carol offers seminars and software training to consumers, quilt shops and Viking dealers around the country. "A free lance teacher must investigate the market," says Carol. "She must also sell herself to potential shops, guilds and colleges by showing what she can do. Shop owners vary in the way they reimburse teachers so I prefer to have an agreement before teaching begins. Remember that when teaching in a shop, that your enthusiasm often generates increased sales for the shop owner," says Carol. She offers a few typical examples of shop/teacher agreements:

1 Shop determines the class price and pays a percentage to the teacher. (Often 80% of class fees collected).

2 Occasionally (though not often) the shop will collect and turn over all class fees to the teacher. The shop owner expects that the class will sell enough products to warrant offering the class.

3 Teacher sets a price for the amount of actual class teaching time. For example, a three-hour may cost $50. The shop owner expects this fee to cover:

X   Making sewing samples,

X   Preparing and printing class handouts

X   Set-up and clean-up time.

Carol suggests that new teachers entering this market concentrate on a special area of teaching such as serging, quilting, software for embroidery machines, heirloom sewing or applique, based on her main interest and expertise. She also suggests that you give your classes a catchy title since the shop/guild newsletter advertising your classes may be the only information your prospective pupil sees about you and your classes.

Describing the greatest challenge for hands-on classes, Carol explains that teachers must focus on keeping more advanced pupils moving at a good speed without losing the slower pupils.

"Good handouts and step-by-step examples are invaluable when facing students of mixed ability levels," she says. Carol concludes saying. "The popularity of your classes determine future wages. You will be invited back if your classes are well organized, warm, friendly and produce something useful and enjoyable."

*   *   *

In-Depth Interview

Claudia Chase, of *Mirrix Tapestry Studio Looms, Ltd. and Mirrix Tapestry Studio* began her business in 1990 and 1996, respectively. Expanding her teaching opportunities continually, she shares her philosophy about teaching when she says, "I think a good teacher must be able come up with new ideas constantly which become the basis for what they teach. A poor teacher becomes stagnant and does not come up with new concepts. You can teach someone everything you know technically but cannot teach them how to want to create new ideas and approaches for themselves. The greatest reward in teaching is when a student branches out in a totally new direction you never considered," she acknowledges.

"Many students initially 'copy' my work and this makes sense," Claudia says, "but, students must internalize what they've copied in order to make it their own. Eventually, they must find their own path. I have students who keep coming back to see my new work for inspiration as it is always evolving. This doesn't annoy me because I realize that the great joy I feel in creating something new cannot be taken from me."

How much time do you devote to your business?

"I devote forty to fifty hours a week to my loom business and twenty hours a week to my tapestry business."

Of the total time you spend on your business, how much do you devote to producing something to sell?

"I spend most of my time dealing directly with customers, researching and developing new equipment, expanding my markets and tending to the day-to-day details of running a business. The loom business is like a living thing. It keeps changing and so must my knowledge of the art if it is to contribute to the customers who purchase it. Most of my time with my tapestry business is spent researching and developing new ways to create tapestries entailing a detailed study of fiber processing, dyeing techniques and spinning for tapestry yarn. I used to spent more time marketing my tapestries and exhibiting them in galleries but since founding the loom company I devote my marketing efforts to that which contributed to my growth as a tapestry weaver. I am now relieved of the pressure of having to sell what I weave. Someday, I plan to resume marketing that business, but for now, I am doing a lot of weaving and research."

Do you sell both retail and wholesale or just directly to the ultimate consumer?

"I sell my looms through seventy retail outlets. I also have my tapestries in nine stores associated with the League of NH Craftsmen and in one lone gallery."

Where do you purchase supplies?

"My company provides my looms but I get my fiber from the sheep and goats next door. I buy various chemical dyes from many sources. I plan to learn about natural dyes and to collect my own dye stuffs but other supplies I need, I buy from catalogs. I have sold many looms from my Website but tapestries exist on the Website as a gallery of what can be produced on our looms," Claudia replies.

"I plan to revive the tapestry weaving business next year and to increase the number of workshops I teach since both inspire me. Teaching provided me needed income during my start-up years. I charge $50 an hour plus all expenses when I travel to teach a workshop. I prefer a class of ten students who pay between $10 and $12 to take the workshop plus materials fees. When teaching in my studio, I charge each student $25 per hour. I believe I get paid at the top of the pay scale for teaching tapestry. Why? Because I ask for it and my name has become well-known. I also give so much of myself when I teach that I feel I should ask for reasonable compensation. Many people in this field are afraid to ask for what they are worth in the same way that they are afraid to put a dollar value on the work they produce," she concludes.

TEACHER CERTIFICATION PROGRAMS:

American Needlepoint Guild
Box 241208
Memphis, TN 38124-1208
http://www.needlepoint.org

Craft Yarn Council of America
Box 9
800-662-9999
Gastonia, NC 28053-0009
http://www.craftyarncouncil.com

Embroiderer's Guild of America
335 W. Broadway, Suite 100
Louisville, KY 40202
egahq@aol.com

Hobby Industry Association
Largest international trade association for crafts. Offers teacher certification program and certification as a craft demonstrator as well.

National Quilting Association, Inc.
Box 393
Ellicott City, MD 21041-0393
http://nqa@erols.com

Professional Knitwear Designers Guild
cpolfer@juno.com

CONTRIBUTORS TO THIS CHAPTER:

Sylvia Ann Landman
Sylvia's Studio
1090 Cambridge St.
Novato, CA 94947
E-mail: Create@sylvias-studio.com
http://www.Sylvias-studio.com

Marty Donnellan
Marty Donnellan
455 Grayson Highway, Suite 111-183
Lawrenceville, GA 30045
Phone: 770-466-9405
Fax: 770-466-9405
E?mail: marty@martydoll.com
http://www.martydoll.com

Joan Schrouder
2152 Marlow Lane
Eugene, OR 97401-5107
Phone: 441-302-6367
E-mail: joan_schrouder@compuserve.com

Patricia Hammond
Hearthstone Designs
1136 Clover Valley Way
Edgewood, MD 21040-2186
Phone:-410-676-6419
E-mail:hearthst@erols.com

Markena Lanska,
Daydream Creations
4964 Eagle Ln
West Bend WI 53095-8754
Phone; 414-677-9219
E-mail: lanska@execpc.com
http://execpc.com/~lanska

Carol Heidenreich
4655 Mossbrook Circle
San Jose, CA 95130
Phone: 408-378-1552
Fax: 408-378-1552
E-mail: CHeidenrei@aol.com

Claudia Chase
1097 Bible Hill Road
Francestown, NH 03043
Phone: 603-547-6278
E-mail mirrixlooms@top.monad.net
Website: http://www.mirrixlooms.com

Appendix

CRAFT BUSINESS BOOKS

CRAFT TRADE JOURNALS

CRAFT CONSUMER MAGAZINES

CRAFT ORGANIZATIONS

CRAFT TRADE SHOW LISTINGS

CRAFT WEBSITES by TOPIC

General Crafts
Quilting
Dolls & Toys
Knitting & Crochet
Embroidery, Needlepoint, Cross-stitch, Machine
Art-to-Wear & Sewing
Woodworking
Jewelry and Beadwork
Painting
Basketry,
Ceramics & Glass
Misc Crafts
Teaching

CRAFT BUSINESS BOOKS

Brabec, Barbara, *Homemade Money, a Definitive Guide to Success*, Betterway Books, Cincinnati, OH, 1995

Brabec, Barbara, *Handmade for Profit*, M. Evans Company, New York, NY, 1996

Brabec, Barbara, *Creative Cash & How to Sell Your Arts, Crafts & Know-how*, Prima Publishing, 1999

Crawford, Tad, *Business and Legal Forms for Crafts*, Watson-Guptill
Heim, Judy, *The Needlecrafter's Computer Companion*, No Starch Press, 1995, San Francisco, CA

Landman, Sylvia, *Make Your Quilting Pay for Itself*, F&W/Betterway, Cincinnati, OH, 1997

Landman, Sylvia, *Quilting for Fun & Profit*, Prima Publishing, 1999

Landman, Sylvia, *Crafting for Dollars, Turn Your Hobby Into Serious Cash,* Prima Publishing, Rocklin, CA, 1996

Long, Steve and Cindy, *You Can Make Money From Your Arts & Crafts,* Mark Publishing, Scott's Valley, CA, 1988.

CRAFT TRADE JOURNALS

Arts 'N Crafts Showguide
Box 104628
Jefferson City, MO 65110
Craft Supply Directory Magazine
For professional crafters looking for shows, wholesalers and supplies.

Box 420
225 Gordon Corner Road
Manalapan, NJ 07726.
http://www.craftsupply.com/success.htm

Craft & Needlework Age Magazine & Directory
Comprehensive trade journal for all crafts including quilting.
PO Box 420
Englishtown, NJ 07726

*Craftrends & Sew Business (*Includes quarterly publication, *Quilt Quarterly,* in a special section*)*
Primedia Special Interest Publications
2 News Plaza, Box 1790
Peoria, IL 61656

Let's Talk About Dollmaking Magazine
Mimi Winer's Journal for Dollmakers
Box 662-LT
Point Pleasant, NJ 08742

Open Chain's, The Creative Machine (Using sewing machines for quilting)
Box 2634
Menlo Park, CA 94026-9926
Phone: 650-366-4440
Fax: 650-366-4455
E-mail*:* rfanncmn@bayarea.net
Website: http://www.getcreativeshow.com/creativemachine

Professional Quilter Magazine
Quarterly journal for professional quilters
Morna McEver Golletz, Editor
221412 Rolling Hill Lane
Laytonsville, MD 20882
http://www.professionalquilter.com

Quilter's Quarterly Journal
Publication of the National Quilting Association
Box 393 Ellicott City
MD 21041-0393
E-mail:nqa@erols.com
http://www.his.com/queenb/nqa

Crafts Report, Publishes newsletter for fine crafts
300 Water St.
Wilmington, DE19801
http://www.craftsreport.com

The Artist's Club
PO Box 8930
Vancouver, WA 98668-8930
1-800-845-6507

CRAFT CONSUMER MAGAZINES

American Quilter Magazine
Published by The American Quilting Society
Box 3290
Paducah, KY 42002-3290

Artist's Magazine
F&W Publications, Inc.
1507 Dana Ave.
Cincinnati, OH 45207 (513) 531-4744

Art Quilt Magazine
PO Box 630927
Houston, TX 77263-0927
Bead & Button Magazine
Phone: 1-800-446-5489
http://www2.beadandbutton.com/beadbutton

Crafting For Today
243 Newton-Sparta Road
Newton, NJ 07860

Crafts 'N Things
2400 Devon Ave. , Suite 375
Des Plaines, IL 60018-4618
http://www.clapper.com

Crafts Magazine
Primedia Special Interest Publications
2 News Plaza, Box 1790
Peoria, IL 61656

Decorative Artists Workbook
F&W Publications, Inc.
1507 Dana Ave.
Cincinnati, OH 45207
Phone: (513) 531-4744

Jewelry Crafts Magazine
4880 Market St.,
Ventura, CA 93003-7783

Magazine-of-the-Month Club for Consumers
Includes: Crafts, Crafts Showcase, Memory Makers, Creating Keepsakes, Decorative Artist's
Workbook, Decorative Woodcrafts, the Artist, Popular Ceramics, Cross-Stitch & Needlework,
Popular Woodworking:

Piecework Magazine
201 East Fourth St.
Loveland, CO 80537

Popular Woodworking Magazine
F&W Publications, Inc.
1507 Dana Ave.
Cincinnati, OH 45207 (513) 531-4744

Quilting Today
Chitra Publications
2 Public Ave.
Montrose, PA 18801-1220

Threads Magazine, Fine sewing, dress-making & tailoring
Phone: 1-800-888-8286
http://www.taunton.com/th
Watercolor Magic Magazine
F&W Publications, Inc.
1507 Dana Ave.
Cincinnati, OH 45207 (513) 531-4744

CRAFT ORGANIZATIONS

Arts and Crafts Archive
http://www.arts-crafts.com/__c5a09439/archive/archive.html
Commercial site of exhibitions and information on the history, artists, and products of the Arts and Crafts Movement.

American Sewing Guild, P.O. Box 8568, Medford OR 97504, 800-325-1882. Sponsors seminars, workshops, demonstrations, fashion shows, vendor malls

American Quilter's Society, P.O. Box 3290 Paducah, KY 42002-3290
Supports The Museum of the American Quilter's Society in addition to providing conventions, events, and awards for quilters. Dedicated to preserving the history of American quilt-making. Offers membership and quarterly publication, American Quilter.

Association of Crafts & Creative Industries
PO Box 2188, Zanesville, OH 43702-3388
Phone: 740-452-4541 E-mail: acci.info@creative?industries.com

Harvest Craft Festivals: http://www.harvestfestival.com

Hobby Industry Association Box 348 Elmwood, NJ 07407. Largest International Craft Trade Shows & Membership http://hobby.org/members/membersonly.html

International Quilt Market & International Quilt Festival, 7660 Woodway, Suite 550, Houston, TX 77063, Phone: (713)781-6864, extension #301, Fax 713-781-8182

National Guild of Decoupeurs, four decoupage artists, founded in 1972, 1017 Pucker Ave., Stowe, Vermont, 05672

National Quilting Association, Inc. P.O. Box 393 Ellicott city, MD 21041-0393. NQA, the oldest national quilting organization supports quilters in many ways. Includes: publication of their quarterly publication, Quilting Quarterly Journal, sponsoring annual quilt shows, exhibits and workshops, provides individual programs that include certification and special newsletters for quilting teachers and judges.

National Crafting Association, founded in 1983. Has a newsletter to help crafters succeed. Fax: 1-800-318-9410 Phone: 800-715-9594

National Craft Association, 1945 East Ridge Road, Suite #5178, Rochester, New York 14622-2467 e-mail (716) 266-5472 or Fax (716) 785-3231 800)

Offinger Management Company is an Association and Exposition Management Company in the U.S. managing several, large craft associations such as:
Assn. of Crafts & Creative Industries (ACCI)
Art Glass Suppliers Assn. Int'l (AGSA)
Ceramic Manufacturers Assn. (CerMA)
Int'l Model-Hobby Manufacturers Assn. (IMMA)
Miniatures Industry Assn. of America (MIAA)
Society of Craft Designers (SCD)
The National Needlework Assn. (TNNA)
1100-H Brandywine Blvd, PO Box 3388
Zanesville OH USA 43702-3388
Phone 740-452-4541
Fax 740-452-2552
Email omc.info@offinger.com
Website: http://www.offinger.com
Society of Paper Artists (hand-made paper, paper-mache, decoupage collage, scherenschnitte)
Susan Lowenthal Phone 203-227-3343 Fax: 203-227-3118 E-mail: susan@giftsbysusan

Society of Craft Designers
Box 3388 Zanesville,
OH 43702-3388
Phone 740-452-4541 Fax: 740-452-2552
E-mail: scd@offinger.com

TRADE & CRAFT SHOW LISTINGS

ACCI Craft Fair San Francisco San Francisco, CA Phone: 914-883-6100

American Craft Malls

Arts 'N Crafts Showguide Box 104628 Jefferson City, MO 65110

Atlanta International Gift & Home Furnishings Market, Phone: 404-220-2446

Art Glass Show, Rosemont, Il, 888-866-2472, e-mail: Website: http://www.agsa.com

Beckmans Handcrafted Gift Show Los Angeles, CA Phone: 213-962-5424

California Gift Show, Los Angeles, CA Phone: 213-747-3488

Chicago Gift & Accessories Market Chicago, IL Phone: 800-677-6278

Coomer's Malls Philip Coomer, founder of Coomer's Craft Malls in shopping malls across the U.S., offers his craft bulletin-board

The Crafts Fair OnLine Listing of craft shows and fairs

Dallas Nat'l Gift & Decorative Accessories Market, Dallas, TX 1-800-DAL-MKTS or 214-655-6100

Eureka Springs Gift Show, Eureka Springs, AR Phone: 405-799-7882

Florida International Gift Show, Orlando, FL Phone: 203-852-0500

Graphic Impressions, 1741 Masters Lane, Dept. CM, Lexington, KY 40515, (606)273-1507, fax: (606)273-0005, e-mail: e-mail: dianem@iglou.com

Kansas City Gift Market, Overland Park, KS Phone: 913-491-6688

Los Angeles Mart: Gift, Decorative Accessories & Furniture Market, Los Angeles, CA Phone: 213-763-5800

Market Square Midwest, Mid-America Gift Market, Madison, WI 717-796-2377

Neighbors & Friends, The Professional Crafter's Market Guide to National Craft Shows http://www.crafter.com/issue.html

Ozark Craft Shows, PO Box 805-CM, Branson, MO 65615, (417)3.34-3251, fax: (417)334-4739, e-mail: info@ozcrafts.com, website: www.ozcrafts.com

Philadelphia Gift Show, Ft. Washington, PA 770-952-6444

Pittsburg Gift Show, Monroeville, PA 716-254-2580

San Francisco International Gift Fair, San Francisco, CA Phone: 415-346-6666

The Crafts Fair Guide, a Review of Arts and Crafts Fairs in the U.S., Lee Spiegel Box 5062, Mill Valley, CA, 94952

Washington Gift Show, Chantilly, VA Phone: 1-800-272-SHOW

Western New York Gift Show, Rochester, NY Phone: 716-254-2580

WEBSITES BY TOPIC

Crafts, General:

American Crafters for Professional Crafters http://www.ProCrafter.com

CraftWeb. http://www.craftweb.com Opportunities & newsletter for all crafters

Be Creative Bookstore: Newest books, patterns, kits for all needle-skills" http://www.becreativebooks.com

Barbara Brabec's CraftsBiz Chat & Personal Reflections http://www.crafter.com/brabec/

Canal Surplus-hard to find art supplies, jewelry findings, interior and fashion designer's raw goods, government and private industry surplus items. http://www.canalsurplus.com/ Cottage Home Crafter's Guild! http://www.cottagehome.com/Main/crafts.htm

Craft Suppliers, Chat room for Crafters, Craft tips: http://www.crafter.com

Craft Supply Magazine-Success By Design http://www.craftsupply.com/success.html Silkee@internexus.net.

Craft Connection, general craft supplies: http://www.craftconn.com

Craftrends Live! Home Page http://www.craftrends.com

Crafts, quilting, sewing, woodworking, jewelry, beading & more: http://artsandcrafts.miningco.com/library/weekly/aa010798.htm

Crafters Gateway Home Page http://members.aol.com/SharionKC/CBE1.index.html

Crafting for Dollars-Arts and Crafts Business
http://artsandcrafts.miningco.com/library/weekly/aa010798.htm

CraftNet Village http://www.craftnet.org

CraftShows USA http://www.craftshowsusa.com/

CraftWEB http://www.craftweb.com/

Crafty Links for Crafty Folks http://www.wyomingcompanion.com/janacraft/links.htm

Dharma Trading Co. Dyestuffs, yarns, crafts, books. http://www.dharmatrading.com

Festival and Craft Show Network Online for Crafts: http://www.festivalnet.com

Handcrafted Consignments Wanted! http://www.lets_shop.com/aacbb/00000385.htm

Hobby Industry Association http://www.hobby.org/hia/members/membersonly.html
Largest international trade association for crafts

Innovation Specialities-Clock fittings/inserts/Parts for crafters.
http://www.clockparts.com/

Internet Center for Arts and Crafts Gift Shop.
http://www.xmission.com/~arts/stitch/mainstit.html

Jana's Craft Connections http://www.wyomingcompanion.com/janacraft/links.htm
Newsletter and tips for professional crafters

Masters of the Crafts The Canadian Museum of Civilization Corporation presents this exhibit of crafts by expert craftspeople.
http://www.civilization.ca/membrs/arts/bronfman/mcintro

Mega Sites for Crafters: http://artsandcrafts.about.com/msub2.htm

Nashville Wraps, Wholesale gift and store Packaging Products. Shopping Bags, Paper and Plastic Bags, Boxes, Gift Wrap, Ribbons, Bows, Tissue, Cellophane, Shrink Wraps, Shreds, Seals, Cards and Supplies. $25 minimum order http://www.nashvillewraps.com/

Net Crafts Online: Buy or sell crafts: http://www.netcrafts.com/ads/ratecard.html

Pastime Publications http://www.pastimepubs.com
List of hobby magazines featuring old time designs and patterns

Sylvia's Studio: Craft patterns, craft industry books, tapes, information: http://www.Sylvias-studio.com

The Seashell Company, shells in pints, quarts, gallons: http://www.algorithms.com/users/seashells/

The White House Collection of American Crafts: The National Museum of American Art presents this online tour of the collection, with sections on ceramic, fiber, wood, glass, and metal crafts. http://nmaa-ryder.si.edu/collections/exhibits/whc/index.html

The World Wide Web Arts & Crafts Connection: http://www.crafter.com

W.T. Lasley About.com Guide to Arts/Crafts Business http://artsandcrafts.about.com/ e-mailartsandcrafts.guide@about.com

West Mountain Gourd Farm, Gourds in all shapes and sizes. Cleaned, sterilized, ready to craft, wholesale prices. Also gourd crafting tools and gourd craft books. http://www.texas-east.com/westmountain/

Xyron, plastics, laminating, rubber stamp materials http://www.xyron.com

QUILTING

A Quilter's Legacy, 2910 Camille Dr, Dept. CM, College Station, TX 77845,
Phone: (409)693-3522, fax: (409)693-5514,
e-mail: SMichel48@aol.com, website:
http://www.brasswind.com/quiltjournal

A-1 Quilting Machines, 32232 E. Evans Rd., Springfield, MO 65804,
http://wwwlong-arm.com , 800-566-4276

AlphaMall Shopping http://alphamall.qc.ca , Bulletin board for free ads, directory of
quilt shops.

American Professional Quilting, 88033 University Blvd., Suite F, Des Moines, IA 50325,
http://www.apqs.com, 800-426-7233

American Quilt Thimbles: http://www.AmericanQuilts.com/thimbles

Appliqué Society: provides daily mailing list and patterns
http://www.theappliquesociety.org

C & T Publishing, Quilt book publisher: http://www.ctpub.com

Cindy Cimo, Sells designs and quilt patterns: http://cindycimoquiltdesigns.com

Cotton Club, Box 2263, Boise, ID 83701. Fax (208)345-1217, E-mail: cotton
@micron.net, Web Site: http://www.cottonclub.com . Mail order catalog for quality quilting
fabrics, Members may also buy books at 20% off list price.

David Walker's Quilting Website http://w3,one.net/~davidxix
Distinctive Pieces: Appliqué kits for quilting and framing:
http://www.DistinctivePieces.com

Dutchman Designs-Tesselated Quilt Puzzles: http://www.dutdes.com/op/chkcop.html

Electric Quilt Company, 419 Gould St Ste 2, Dept. CM, Bowling Green, OH 43402-3047 (800)356:219, (419)352-1134, fax: (419)352- 4332, http://www.wcnet.org/ElectricQuiltCo

Fabrications; yarn and quilting fabric: http://www.fabrications-gv.com

Fabrics On Line: http://www.quiltcom.com

Gallery of Textile Works http://www.penny-ni.com . Quilt gallery on The Web.

Gammill Quilting Machine Co. 1452 W. Gibson St., West Plains, MO 65775, http://www/gammill.net , 800-659-8224 email gammill@townsqr.com

Hearthside Designs: Quilts by Patricia Hammond: http://www.vcq.org/images/patricia_hammond.htm

High Tech Quilting http://www.infinet.com:80/~jan . Jan Cabral's collection of digital fabrics and related computer quilt drawing techniques.

Hoffman Quilting Fabrics: E-mail: lane@hoffmanis.com

Kaye Woods, TV Quilting Teacher/Designer: http://www.kayewood.com

Elsie Vredenburg: @netonecom.net, http://www.netonecom.net/~elf. Lighthouse and other quilting patterns

Kirk Collection, 1513 Military Avenue, Omaha, NE 68111, Phone: 402-551-0386, E-mail: Kirk Coll@aol.com. Specializing in antique & reproduction fabrics and quilts from 1850-1950 wool and silk battings, books and notions. http://www.kirkcollection.com

Longarm Machine Quilting, Unlimited Possibilities, a newsletter dedicated to the betterment of commercial machine quilting through the sharing of ideas. Published quarterly by Little Pine Studio, 218 N. 10th St., Brainerd, MN 56401, editor Marcia Stevens mstevens!@brainert

Make It Southwest Style Quilting Designs: 191 Big Horn Ridge NE, Albuquerque, NM 87122, 505-856-7254 fax: 505-856-7270, e-mail: MjoMc@aol.com. Request catalog by name, "Make It Southwest Style." http://www.cyspacemalls,com/quilt

Mary Ann Beattie's site with fool-proof foundation piecing for quilters:
http://www.bankswith.apollotrust.com/~larryb/PCPiecers.htm
Mumm's The Word, 1116 E Westview Ct, Dept. CM, Spokane, WA 99218-1384,(888) 819- 2923, (509) 466-3572, fax: (509) 466 6919, http://www.debbiemumm.com

Mystery Quilt Patterns QuiltsQuiltChatNews@onelist.com

National Patchwork Assoc. http://www.paston.co.uk/natpat/natpat. E-mail:trinity@paston.co.uk United Kingdom. Lists quilt shops and Quilting events in the U.K.

Needlecrafter's Computer Companion, author, Judy Heim
http://www.execpc.com/~judyheim .Tips from Judy's book and columns about craft-related computer software.
Nine Patch News http://www.members.aol.com/ninepatchn/index.htm
Have you ever deleted your issue of the newsletter, only to wish you hadn't? Everyone can access past issues of the newsletter at the website http://members.aol.com/ninepatchn

Patchwork, 6676 Amsterdam Road. Amsterdam, MT 59741, Phone: 406-282-7218, Fax: 406-282-7322, E-mail ptchwrks@alpinet.net,
http://www.alpinet.net/~ptchwrks.Specializing in reproduction fabrics for quilters

Phoenix Textiles, brand-name fabrics at 50%-75% off: http://www.phoenixtextiles.com/

PineTree Catalog: http://quilt.com/Pinetree to request the catalog. PineTree answers questions about quilting products at aardvark@ime.net

Quilt Magazine http://www.quilt.net/quiltmag . Related articles from the magazine.Quilt Bee: majordomo@quilter.com

Quilt Digest Press, c/o NTC/ Contemporary Publishing Co, 4255 W Touhy Ave, Dept. CM, Lincoinwood, IL 60646, (800)323-4900, (847)679-5500, fax: (847)679-2494, e-mail: dbwheeler@tribune.com

Quilt House, 95 Mayhill St., Saddle Brook, NJ 07663, 201-712-1234, 800-660-0415, Fax: 201-712-1199. Web Site: http://www.ezquilt.com. Specializing in tools and templates.

Quilt Tiles, Ceramic tiles based on quilt patterns. The tiles are formed from a handmade mold, and then meticulously hand painted in a wide array of colors. http://www.quilttiles.com

Quiltaholics, a fun website for quilters: http://www.quiltaholics.com

Quilt Art http://www.quilt.net E-mail: quiltart.digest@lists.his.com An Internet quilt-site and mailing list for contemporary art quilters.

QuiltBiz, Professional Quilters site: E-mail: Ozzg@nmia.com

Quilter's Corner: http://www.qcx.com. Julie Higgins website for mail-order quilting supplies.

Quilting at the Mining Co. you'll find an entire listing of all the 50 previous Feature articles at http://quilting.miningco.com/library/weekly/aa071697.htm

Quilting from the Heartland http://www.qheartland.com. TV's Quilt Star, Sharlene Jorgensen's website. Patterns and templates.

Quilters' Resource Inc, Large catalog of quilting books, supplies, fabric, notions PO Box 148850-CM, Chicago, IL 60614, (773)278-5695, fax:(773) 278-1348 http://www.quiltersresource.com/ e-mail:qripatches@aol.com

That Patchwork Place/Martingale & Co: Quilt Book Publisher, Bothell, WA 98041, (800)426-3126, (425)483-331 fax: 425)486-7596, e-mail: info@patch/vork.com,website: http://www.patchwork.com

The Quilt Shop: Your online quilting source http://www.thequiltshop.com hand-dyed, vintage, imports, domestic, appliqué patterns

Virtual Quilt: http://www.tvq.com . Excellent online newsletter plus mail order for fabrics, antique quilts and patterns and reviews of quilting software.
Water Color Quilts and Patterns: Marilyn Levy, wcquilts@lyris.quiltropolis.com

World Wide Quilt Page http://www.tvq.com. Offers patterns, guild listings, book reviews, galleries, teacher listing and block exchanges,

Yahoo's Quilting Events http://yahoo.com/Arts/Textiles/Quilting/Events .Quilting links and Websites.

Quilting Software

Electric Quilt, The Electric Quilt Co. 1039 Melrose St, Bowling Green OH 43402. 800-356-4219, orders only, 419-352-1134, technical support, mail:aquiltco@wcnet.org
Vquilt 2, Box 129 Jarrettsville, MD 21084, 410-557-6871.

PC Quilt. Designer Nina Antze designed this program first for IBM/DOS and later developed a version for Macintosh users called Baby Mac. Nina Antze, 7061 Lynch Road, Sebastopol, CA 95472 or e-mail: NinaA@aol.com.

Quilt-Pro. Windows drawing program to create quilts. Call 1-800-884-1511 for a free demo disk and ordering information.

Quilter's Design Studio, Windows & Macintosh, Box 19946, San Diego, CA 92159-0946

QuiltSoft, Windows drawing program. Box 19946, San Diego, CA 92159-0946. Call 619-583-2970, Fax: 619-583-2682

Online quilt groups:

Contact online chat-groups via e-mail. All are interactive and international quilt groups open to all quilters:

Interquilt, mbishop@needles.com

Kaffeel-Klatsch email: kaffeel-klatsch@quilt.com

Quilt Biz ozzg.@nmia.com

Quilt Art quiltart.@quilt.net

QuiltBee quiltbee@quilter.com

DOLLS & TOYS

Bear Thread Designs, Rt I Box 1640, Dept. CM, Belgrade, MO 63622, (573)766-5695, fax: (573)766-5695, e-mail; beartd@hotmail.com: http://www.bearthreaddesigns.com

ClothArt Original Dolls: http://www.martydoll.com/clothart

Doll Artist Sites http://www.xmasdolls.com/Links%20Page.htm
Grandmother http://www.idahoquilt.com/fairegrma.htm

Sierra Meadows Bears http://www.bearsandbooks.com 1-800-387-7955 toll free, USA and Canada

Spare Bear Parts, PO Box 56, Interlochen, MI 49643 (231) 276-7915 FAX: (213) 276-7921, e-mail:sales@spacebear.com http://www.sparebear.com/index.html

KNITTING & CROCHET

Allegro Yarns: Patterns, needles, yarn kits and yarn. 800-547-3808 Http://www.allegroyarns.com

Cherry Tree Yarns, Box 254, Montpelier, VT 05651, www.cherryyarn.com

Clover Needlecraft, 1007 E Dominguez St, Ste L, Dept. CM, Carson, CA 92677-2829, (800)233-1703. Crochet hooks, knitting needles, selection of symbol patterns for knitting and crochet.

Cochineal Design Studio, Box 4276, Encinatas, CA 92023, Software for knitters & other crafts: 619-259-1698. E-Mail: info@cochenille.com http://www.cochenille.com

Craft Yarn Council of America http://www.craftyarncouncil.com

Crochet Musings Links Page, also provides a daily mailing list for crocheters http://crochet.rpmdp.com/links.htm

Crochet Partners, online mailing list + free patterns http://crocheting.com/

Dove Tail Designs: Knitting, crochet, patterns, books, kits. Free catalog
http://wwwdovetaildesigns.com
Fiber Resources Page for yarns/threads: http://www.his.com/~fandl/fiber.html

Fiber Information for wool yarns: http://www.woolmark.com/techinfo.html

Frauenfelder Computer Systems, Inc. 4523 S. Pagosa Circle, Aurora, CO 80015,Phone: 888-333-4008, (303) 699-3438 e-mail: FrauComp@aol.com. Computer software for crochet only

Heartland Knitting/Crochet/Needlework: Supplies, patterns, links and referrals: http://www.geocities.com/Heartland/Garden/5625/crafts

Herrschner's Yarn Shoppe Home Page! Yarns, knitting needles, crochet hooks, books, yarn stands, bags, patterns and notions: http://www.herrschners.com/
Knitter's Magazine, magazine publishers show articles online: http://xrx–inc.com/

Knitting Basket: Yarns and only importer of German Modular Knitting Books 760 Lake Blvd. Box 5367, Tahoe City, CA 96145, 1-800-252-yarn or knitting@sierra.net, http://www.knittingbasket.com

Knitting Guild of America: e-mail: tkga@tkga.com, Website: http://www.tkga.com

Knitting & Craft pages http://www.lava.net/~parker30/knit.htm

Knitting Today, magazine publishers show designs online.
http://www.knittingtoday.com/index.html

Learn How to Knit http://www.skepsis.com/~tfarrell/textiles/knit/
Lion Brand Yarn Company, Yarns, knitting needles, crochet hooks, books, yarn stands, bags, patterns and notions: http://www.lionbrand.com

Mary Ellen Meisters's Knitting Techniques for beginners
http://www.math.unl.edu/~gmeister/papers/ Knitting/techniques.html

Sweater Knitting Machines: http://www.apocalypse.org/pub/u/liz/sweater.html
Patternworks Supplies for Knitters/Crocheters: Box 1690
Poughkeepsie, NY 12601, 1-800-438-5464, http://www.patternworks.com/
TechKnit Mailing List: http://www.bolis.com/L/listinfo/techlist #in

The DesignaKnit Software Web Ring
http://www.geocities.com/Paris/9197/dakring.htm

The Crochet Network Webring
http://www.geocities.com/Heartland/Hills/3910/

The KnitWits Knews: online newsletter
http://www.swiftsite.com/KnitWits/

The Sock Calculator WoolWorks http://www.woolworks.org/

Vintage Crochet WebRing
http://users.intercomm.com/sharonc/index.html

Woodland Woolworks, Extensive Catalog for knitting/crochet, 252 So. Maple St. Box
400, Yamhill, OR 97148, 800-547-3725, woolwrks@teleport.com

Woolworks knitting & crochet supply catalog: http://www.woolworks.org

Yarn Lady: yarnlady@deltanet.com. Http://www.yarnlady.com Broad variety of yarns,
knitting and crochet books and notions

Online yarn shops

Abbey Yarns http://www.abbey?yarns.com/

Blackberry Ridge http://blackberry?ridge.com/

Blackberry Hills http://users.aol.com/jerryped/Blackberry.htm

Cedarburg Woolen Mill http://www.exploremilwaukee.com/os9.html

Cherry Hill Yarns http://home.cherryyarn.com/cherryyarn/
Close Knit PressTM Knit Patterns: http://www.tecorp.com/ckp/iknit/main.html

Craft and Yarn Depot http://cyd.com/

Elann Fibre Company: http://www.elann.com

Elegant Stitches: http://members.aol.com/elegantst/index.html

Fingerlakes Yarns Home Page:
http://ww1.fingerlakes?yarns.com/webpages/yarn/index.html

Halcyon Yarn Home Page: http://www.halcyonyarn.com/

Harrisville Designs: http://www.harrisville.com/
Knitting Traditions: http://members.aol.com/knittradit/index.html

Mainely Mohair: http://www.a1?hummbird.com/MM?link.html

Pacific Yarn Supply: http://www.pacificyarn.com/welcome.htm

Patterns from the Past: http://www.tiac.net/users/misch/knitting.html

Peace Fleece Home Page, wool for knitting: http://www.peacefleece.com/
Ram Wools: http://www.gaspard.ca/ramwools.htm

S&C Yarn: http://www.disnet.org/SamCo/prod01.htm

Samuel Charis Knits; Fine Sweaters In Kits: http://www.knitkits.com/

Taos Valley Wool Mill: http://www.taosfiber.com/woolmill/index.html

The Mannings Handweaving School and Supply Center:
http://www.the–mannings.com/

The Yarn Forward Home Page for Knitters: http://www.yarnfwd.com/

Tradewind Knitwear Designs: http://www.interlog.com/~needles/tradwind/

Vendor List for knitting/crochet: http://www.clark.net/pub/oldsma/vendlist.htm

Webs Yarn Catalog, extensive yarn selection: http://www.yarn.com/
Wooly Brown's Yarn Company: http://www.the?tannery.com/knitting.html

Spinning

Ashford Spinning Wheels: http://www.jb.man.ac.uk/~caj/ashford.html

Drop Spindles: http://ourworld.compuserve.com/homepages/lollipops/Spininst.htm

Spindlitis for spinners!: http://www.gorge.net/business/web/terispage/spindle.html
Spinners' and Weavers' Housecleaning Page:
http://www.together.net/~kbruce/kbbspin.html

Machine Knitting

Machine Knitting Links: http://www.freenet.edmonton.ab.ca/knitting/links.html

Machine Knitting at The Knittery: http://www.home.earthlink.net/~sharyng

Tina's Knitting Machine Page: http://www.tiac.net/users/tinanh/knitting/

EMBROIDERY, NEEDLEPOINT, CROSS STITCH

American Needlepoint Art & Design. Specially painted and designed canvas for needlepoint: Http://www.americanneedlepoint.com

Artemisinc Co. Hand-dyed silk ribbon, brass button and embroidery kits: 888-233-5187 http://www.artemisinc.com

Balboa Stock Embroidery Designs: http://www.balboastitch.com

Black Work Embroidery Supplies: http://www.pacificnet.net/~pmarmor/bwarch.html Buzz Tools for Machine Embroidery Computer Programs:http://www.buzztools.com

Connie's Page for Machine Embroidery: http://members.aol.com/Prentis/Connie.html

Cross Stitching and Needlework: http://members.aol.com/togkas1/

Cyberstitch & Embroidery: http://www.geocities.com/~cyberstitcher
DMC Home Page http://www.dmc–usa.com/ International company of embroidery threads. South Hackensack Avel, Port Kearny, Building 10A, South Kearny, NJ 07032-4688. Phone: 973-589-0606,

Even-weave Fabric-stabbers WebRing for counted thread embroidery techniques: http://www.dm.net/~marg/evenweave.htm

Great Notions for Embroidery: http://home.embroideryclubs.com/samples.html

Hard-to-Find Needlework & Embroidery Books: http://www.needleworkbooks.com

Hens Nest: Links to other sites, needlework, needlepoint, cross stitch, designers in needlework, needlepoint, cross stitch, Hardanger, embroidery, crewel, books and cross-stitch notions: http://www.hensnest.com/hn_links.htm

Kreinik Metallic threads for Embroidery: http://www.kreinik.com

Lacis Threads, ribbons, tools, supplies including Lace-Making, Embroidery, Knitting, Tatting, Crochet, Costume, Millinery, Bridal, wholesale and retail: http://www.lacis.com/

Needlework Sales Supplies: http://www.discountneedlework.com
Lace and Lace-making: http://www.netcentral.co.uk/~geoffana//lacering/index.html

Oklahoma Embroidery Supplies: http://www.oesd.com/software/index.html

Ring of Stitches for Online Embroidery http://members.home.net/erieck/form.htm

Smocking Embroidery Ring: http://www.geocities.com/Athens/Oracle/2691/sewing.htm

The Embroidery Hoop & Supplies: http://www.geocities.com/~cyberstitcher/

The Crossing Stitches WebRing:
http://www.geocities.com/Heartland/Hills/5369/xstitchring.html
The Needle Arts Book Shoppe: http://www.interlog.com/~needles/home.html

Uncharted Territory: Charted designs for counted cross-stitch or needlepoint, Exquisite old masters and antique needlework: http://www.unchartedterritory.com

ART TO WEAR & SEWING, APPLIQUE

Amazing Sewing Designs, Patterns: http://www.AmazingDesigns.com

American Home Sewing & Craft Association: http://www.sewing.org/home.html
Ann Marie's Specialties, Wildly Wonderful Wearables: sam@wwwearables.com

Art To Wear, dress patterns for quilted garments:
http://www.art2wear@lyris.quiltropolis.com

Benartex, threads, fabric, notions: http://www.benartex.com

CNT Sewing Pattern Co, PO Box 4332-CM, Aspen, CO 81612, (970)925-2267, fax: (970)925-2267, e-mail: knye@rof.net . http://www.cntpattern.com

Dave Burrows, Online Custom Made Fimo Buttons to Order:10 Burkett Lane, Washington, PA, 15301. e-mail: quail@cobweb.net, http://www.cobweb.net/~quail/vbuttons.htm

Designs at Large: Company will design sewing patterns and clothing for larger women http://www.designsatlarge.com/

Digitizing Direct for Machine Embroidery: http://www.d-direct.demon.co.uk/stock.html

Elaine's Pfaff Sewing Machines: http://www.sewdesigns.com/erieck/index.html
Farthingales Co. Canadian mail-order house for dyeable silks, linens, cottons, lycra, corset, crinoline plus traditional fabrics. Http://www.farthingales.on.ca

Fashion Net. Offers news about the fashion industry, job listings, a "fashion-specific" search engine, chat rooms, and other resources. http://www.fashion.net/ firstVIEW: Collections On-line firstVIEW offers thousands of photographs of fashion collections; collections within days of actual runway shows, users must subscribe; once the collections are available in stores, free photographs available free. http://www.firstview.com/

Hint Fashion Magazine. Site offers feature articles about fashion and the fashion industry, including coverage of the latest fashion shows: http://www.hintmag.com/

General site for sewing: http://www.sewingworld.com

Glenda Black, machine sewing consultant: http://www.starflight.com/gbdesigns

Heritage Textiles: Patterns and textiles such as Blegian lace, Swedish linens, reproduction Renaissance upholstery: http://www.heritagetextiles.com International Textiles & Sewing: http://www.textiletradeshow.com

Lists of printing/viewing design software, conversion software, and where to get hundreds of free designs. Much free with price comparisons of embroidery thread and backing! http://www.geocities.com/Heartland/Plains/3959/sewfile.htm

Nancy's Sewing Notions Catalog & Sewing supplies: http://www.nancysnotions.com

McCall's Pattern Company for Sewing: (800)782-0323, http://www.mccall.com/

Pfaffer's Home Page for Sewing Machines:
http://www.quiltropolis.com/pfaffers/index.htm
Prym-Dritz, PO Box 5028-CM, Spartanburg, SC 29304. Largest notions for sewing/quilting in the U.S. http://www.dritz.com

Robin/Viking Sewing Machines: http://www.quiltropolis.com/viking2sew/swapdrop.htm

Sew Unique, 40 Gulch Rd, Dept. CM, Sheridan, WY 82801, (307)674-0778, fax: (307)-674-0778, e-mail: SewUnique@wyoming.com, http://www.sewunique.com

Suzy's Designs for Pfaff Sewing Machines http://www.yesic.com/~sdesigns/

Textile Information Management System, Canadian-based service providing interactive system for lining textile, apparel and fashion industry for members to buy, sell, display and advertise. e-mail: uni@unicate.com, http://www.unicate.com//Timsfaq.html

The History of Costume by Braun and Schneider: illustrations of clothing from various areas and historical periods, from the book The History of Costume (1861-1880). http://www.siue.edu/COSTUMES/history.html

The Museum for Textiles: images of traditional and contemporary textiles from many cultures, as well as brief descriptions; the site also provides general information about the museum and its programs: http://www.museumfortextiles.on.ca/

Threadbare Pattern Co, PO Box 1484-CM, Havelock, NC 28532, (800) 472-8837, (919) 447-4081, fax: (252) 447-7957, e-mail: patterns@coastalnet.com http://www.threadbarepatterns.com

Thread Images for Sewing: http://www.threadimages.com/

Thread Head: Sewing Threads for Machines: http://www.thread-head.com/

Viking Sewing Machines, USA http://husqvarnaviking.com

Viking Sewing Machines, Canada http://www.vikinghusqvarna.com/canada/

WOODWORKING

Argell & Thorpe School of Classical Woodcarving: http://www.agrellandthorpe.com/

Bowls and other wood spool-turning: http://www.bowlturner.demon.co.uk/

Chip Chats, The National Wood Carvers Association offers a variety of resources for wood carvers and whittlers: http://www.chipchats.org/

Electronic Neanderthal: Traditional Woodworking Resources on the Web: http://www.cs.cmu.edu/~alf/en/en.html

Walnut Hollow, wood crafting supplies:http://www.ctsi.net/ph/supplies.html

Woodworking on the World Wide Web, books, pattern, tools, supplies: http://www.kiva.net/~rjbrown/w5/wood.html

Woodworking on the Web: http://www.woodworking.co.uk/

Woodworking Bookstore: http://www.kiva.net/~rjbrown/bookstore.html

Wood and spool turning website: http://www.fholder.com/Woodturning/woodturn.htm

Wood Products: http://home.sprynet.com/~pleclair/qwpindex.htm

Wood Factory Supplies: http://www.woodfactory.com/

JEWELRY & BEADWORK

American Art Clay Co., Makers of Fimo® polymer clay. 4717 W. 16th St., Indianapolis, IN 46222, 800-374-1600, Fax (317) 248-9300, http://www.amaco.com

American Gem Society offers gem-collectors, guides, a national organization, trade information, industry news, and database of its members. http://www.ags.org/

Bead Frequently Asked Questions, online: http://www.mcs.net/~simone/fairies/faq.html

Bead & String Reference Materials:
http://members.aol.com/bdphoenix/referenceposter.htm

Beadwrangler's Allee Gems ? Free projects & collection of bead & fiber links, Tips & Techniques, Galleries Glass Beads: http://beadwrangler.com/allee?gems.htm

Crystal Growing from the University of Waterloo publication Wat on Earth, has instructions for growing crystals: http://www.science.uwaterloo.ca/earth/waton/crystal.html

Darice, craft supply distributor of beads and jewelry tools and wire:
http://www.darice.com

Diamonds Tutorial: Commercial site about diamonds, including descriptions of color, cut, clarity, and shape, as well as links to pages covering the history and geology of diamonds: http://www.diamondcutters.com/diamondtutorial.html

Enamel glass bead jewelry from PINZ: http://www.pinzart.com/shop/index.html

Fluorescent Mineral Society: international organization of professional mineralogists, gemologists, amateur collectors: http://www.uvminerals.org/

Gemology and Lapidary Pages: Offers an introduction to gemstones, including information on identification, cutting, collecting, and grading:
http://www.tradeshop.com/gems/index.html

Gems and Precious Stones: University of Wisconsin-Madison presents a tutorial on the formation of gemstones and their qualities, including photographs, and glossary:
http://www.geology.wisc.edu/~jill/306.html

Gold Institute, an international trade association of companies that mine and refine gold, manufacturers of gold product, bullion banks, and gold dealers; it offers information about the uses and production of gold in for jewelry other resources: http://www.goldinstitute.com/

International Colored Gemstone Association Gem Site: provides information about gemstone, includes a question and answer section, a featured gem each month, buying tips, and other resources for jewelers: http://www.gemstone.org/

Phoenix Experience, large manufacturers of wire-wrapped jewelry and supplies; P.O. Box P, Aiken, SC 29802, (803)-278-1002, Fax (803)-278-1002, e-mail: phoenixe@phoenixe.net, http://www.phoenixe.net

The Beader's Circle: http://www.geocities.com/Yosemite/Rapids/2216/

PAINTING

Atlantic Coast Cotton. Blank clothing for painting, embellishing at wholesale. Phone: 1-800-262-5660 E-mail: acc_help@accotton.com
http://www.atlanticcoastcotton.com/

25 links to wholesale blank apparel companies for painting:
http://www.printersworld.com click on "links", choose apparel, and wholesale.

California Rainbow Tie-dye T Shirts & Supplies: (972) 271-6254 Toll Free (877) 884-2787: http://www.catalog.com/giftshop/tiedye/td.htm

DecoArt Web Site, craft and fabric paint: http://www.decoart.com

Delta Technical Coatings & Paints, Inc., 2550 Pellissier, Whittier CA 90601, Fax: 56662-695-5805: http://www.deltacrafts.com/index_normal.asp

National Society of Tole and Decorative Painters provides an introduction to decorative painting, membership information, a guide to different society chapters, and a calendar of events: http://www.decorativepainters.com

Stenciling.Com offers a directory of resources related to painting and stenciling, including designers, teachers, vendors, and organizations: http://www.stenciling.com/

Stencil Artisans League, Inc. nonprofit organization dedicated to the promotion and preservation of stenciling and related decorative painting includes stenciling tips, event listings, discussion forums, and other resources: http://www.sali.org/
ToleNet provides information about the decorative folk arts of Europe and the Americas, including its history and photographs of the various styles: http://www.tolenet.com/

BASKETRY

Basket Cottage: Longaberger® Baskets: http://www.basketcottage.com/

Basket House: Large array of baskets and supplies, literature, links: http://www.baskethouse.com/

Basket Barn, Home of Longaberger Baskets: http://www.basketbarn.com/

Cathryn Peters' Wicker Airplane Seats
http://www.iei.net/~davide/yourpics/peters3.html

Eva Wright: Sweet Grass Basketmaker: Telephone (843) 767?6876
5330 Waterview Dr., Charleston, SC 29418, e- mail: info@chasssweetgrass,
http://www.chassweetgrassbaskets.com/

Native Basketry: Survival, Beauty: Information about Native American basketry techniques:
http://indy4.fdl.cc.mn.us/~isk/art/basket/baskmenu.html

NativeTech: The University of Connecticut Department of Anthropology information on
Native American technologies including hide tanning, flint knapping, and the making of
canoes: http://www.lib.uconn.edu/NativeTech/

New Secondary Market Club for Basket Makers: http:www.2MARKETCLUB.COM

Ruthe's Collection of Weaving Resources provides an annotated directory of weaving-relat-
ed information and resources on the Internet. http://home.netinc.ca/~rstowe/weave.html
Sharon Dugan, Basketmaker: Birch Rise Farm, 38 Oak Hill Road, Sanbornton, NH
03269 Phone: (603) 528?5120
E-mail: sdugan@cyberportal.net, http://www.sharondugan.com/

Tina Puckett's Basket Website: 918 Branch Road, Thomaston, CT 06787, Phone:
860?283?8491, Fax: 860?283?8629, http://www.litchfieldct.com/shp/tina.html

CERAMICS & GLASS

American Ceramic Society's Web Site offers technical, scientific, and educational information related to the field of ceramics, including news and press releases, access to its publications, ceramics fact sheets, and discussion forums: http://www.acers.org/

Ceramics Monthly. Online version of Ceramics Monthly provides a look at what the print version has to offer each month, selected articles on featured topics, entry information about exhibitions and sales, and book reviews:http://www.ceramicsmonthly.org/

DKK Associates, Ceramic Supplies: http://www.idahoquilt.com/dkk.htm

Le Centre international du Vitrail The International Centre for Stained-Glass Art promotes the preservation, conservation, and study of stained glass; available in English, French, and German: http://www.centre-vitrail.org/index.htm

Kutani: history of Kutani pottery, images, information about the different styles of Kutani ware, and a guide to the glazing process: http://www.njk.co.jp/kutani/ Polymer Clay Central: http://www.delphi.com/polymerclay

Sculpture Home Page: http://www.ve//_studio.com/sculpture

The Ceramics Web: information on ceramics and links to many related Internet sites; includes video: http://apple.sdsu.edu/ceramicsweb/ceramicsweb.html

The Corning Museum of Glass, information on the history and manufacture of glass, exhibits of selected objects, a glossary of glassmaking terms, and other resources: http://www.pennynet.org/glmuseum/corningm.htm

Virtual Ceramics Exhibit: Art Source, University of Kentucky online exhibition of contemporary ceramics: http://www.uky.edu/Artsource/vce/VCEhome.html

Wondrous Glass, Reflections on the World of Rome c. 50 B.C.-A.D. 650. The Kelsey Museum at the University of Michigan's online exhibition on Roman glass making and glassware: http://www.umich.edu/~kelseydb/Exhibits/WondrousGlass/MainGlass.html

World Wide Web Virtual Library Ceramics: Part of the World Wide Web Virtual Library, this site offers a directory of sites related to ceramics, including both technical and artistic resources: http://www.ikts.fhg.de/VL.ceramics.html

TEACHING

Internet Craft Teachers Association http://www.martydoll.com/ICTA.htm

MISC. CRAFTS

Dyer's List Digest: DyersList-owner@bolis.com
Dyed and Gone to Heaven: Needlework & Handicraft Resources: resources for dyeing, including expert tips and suggestions, monthly online classes, patterns, "Designer of the Month" articles, feature stories, chat room: http://www.caron-net.com/

Ikebana International, San Francisco Bay Area Chapter offers information about ikebana flower arrangement, including images. http://www.sf.ikebana.org/

Knots on the Web: links to information on knot tying, knot theory, and knot art; includes several images: http://www.earlham.edu/~peters/knotlink.htm

Lacemaker's Mailing List & pictorial guide to lace-making, including a glossary of terms and images of laces and tools: http://www.geocities.com/Heartland/Fields/1404/faq.html

Soapmaking website: http://www.rainbowmeadow.com/

The Robert C. Williams American Museum of Papermaking: offers information on the history of paper and on paper technology: http://www.ipst.edu/amp/index.html